Why I Am Not an Atheist

ALSO BY CHRISTOPHER BEHA

The Whole Five Feet

What Happened to Sophie Wilder

Arts & Entertainments

The Index of Self-Destructive Acts

Why I Am Not an Atheist

THE CONFESSIONS OF A SKEPTICAL BELIEVER

Christopher Beha

Penguin Press · New York · 2026

PENGUIN PRESS
An imprint of Penguin Random House LLC
1745 Broadway, New York, NY 10019
penguinrandomhouse.com

Designed by Nerylsa Dijol

LIBRARY OF CONGRESS CONTROL NUMBER: 2025023528
ISBN 9780593490471 (hardcover)
ISBN 9780593490488 (ebook)

Printed in the United States of America
1st Printing

The authorized representative in the EU for product safety and compliance is Penguin Random House Ireland, Morrison Chambers, 32 Nassau Street, Dublin D02 YH68, Ireland, https://eu-contact.penguin.ie.

To Ally
For Olive and Henry

He that would seriously set upon the search of truth, ought in the first place to prepare his mind with a love of it. For he that loves it not, will not take much pains to get it; nor be much concerned when he misses it.

—John Locke, *An Essay Concerning Human Understanding*

A question seems to lie heavily on our tongue and yet refuses to be uttered: whether one *could* consciously reside in untruth? or, if one were *obliged* to, whether death would not be preferable?

—Friedrich Nietzsche, trans. R. J. Hollingdale,
Human, All Too Human

You will know the truth, and the truth will set you free.

—John 8:32

Contents

PRELUDE

Looking the World Frankly in the Face

A Visitation

When I was fifteen years old, an angel of God came to me at night, pinned me to my bed, and demanded that I put my trust in the Lord.

This was no dream. I was awake—I am as certain of that as I'm certain that I'm awake while I write these words—and a terrifying presence was communicating to me. I tried to escape, but my body wouldn't move. Through great effort, I finally yelled out, and my scream chased the presence away. My heart pounded as I caught my breath. Coming back to myself, I heard my twin brother, Jim, snoring peacefully in the bunk above.

By morning, the sense of horror had passed, but I was still sure that something significant had happened. I never mentioned it—not even to Jim, whom I told everything—and I thought less and less about it over time, until it seemed possible that I'd imagined the whole thing. Then it happened again.

The visitations continued for years, varying in power and vividness, though each was terrifying and unmistakably *real.* Still I told no one. I'm not sure why. One obvious explanation is that I knew it sounded crazy, but I don't think that was it. I'd heard such experiences reported before, rarely but without embarrassment, and accepted as perfectly reasonable.

To say I was raised in a Catholic home would begin to describe my childhood, but it would get closer to say I was raised in a Catholic world. People are sometimes surprised to hear this from a product of Manhattan's Upper East Side, a well-known WASP stronghold. But New York has an enormous Catholic population—a third of the city's residents, more Romans than Rome—and it's not confined to outer-borough immigrant enclaves. My own family had been New Yorkers going back several generations and Catholics going back as far as anyone could count. One of my grandfathers was a seminarian; the other was best friends with a priest. My paternal grandmother's brother was a Franciscan monk. My own parents met while my mother was a freshman at the Catholic girls' school my sister later attended and my father was a junior at the Catholic boys' school where my brother and I were students when these visitations began.

Granted, my childhood in the eighties and nineties did not revolve around the church in quite the way of my parents' in the fifties and sixties or my grandparents' in the twenties and thirties. But it wasn't so far off. We went to Mass every Sunday and on all other days of obligation; we said grace before meals and prayers before bed. On long car rides, we passed the time with the rosary, my mother reading out the mysteries—joyful, sorrowful, or glorious, depending on the day. When people we knew were troubled or sick, we prayed for them, trusting that these prayers were more than kind gestures.

I don't mean to suggest that we lived a cloistered existence. My siblings and I watched the same bad after-school TV as all our friends. My parents were devoted fiction readers, and the latest works by Updike and Roth made their way onto our shelves each year. The whole family shared a love of lowbrow gross-out comedy, particularly spoof movies like *Airplane!* and *Spaceballs*. We didn't treat any of these habits as being in tension with religious devotion. Whoever had recorded our grainy VHS tape of *Caddyshack* had carefully excised a few moments of nudity, but this was a rare concession to propriety.

I had enough friends whose families weren't religious (or who'd already rejected their family's faith) to know that disbelief was an option, but I felt little reason to consider it for myself. Catholicism provided the furniture of my world, and I was comfortable in it. Jim and I served as altar boys even after an adolescent growth spurt left us towering over the priest. As teenagers, we regularly attended weekday-morning services at our school's chapel. Afterward we'd sneak out for a smoke before first bell with the Jesuit who'd just given us Communion.

I thought occasionally about one day joining the Jesuits myself, but this was mostly adolescent romanticism, and some part of me knew all along that I wasn't really called to it. Still, I had a strong sense—who doesn't at that age?—that I was called to *something*. And who could have been calling, if not God? This seems to me the likeliest reason I kept my nocturnal visions a secret: They marked me off from others, not in a way that shamed me but in a way that flattered me. I wanted them for myself.

I WAS EIGHTEEN when my doubts began. That's a common age to start questioning the values with which you were raised, but in my case the cause of these questions was more concrete. After high school, Jim and I went to Princeton, where our older sister, Alice, had just finished her freshman year. A month into our first semester, a speeding car hit Jim on a street near campus.

In those pre–cell phone days, I was lucky to be in my dorm room when a call came from a friend on the scene, and I got there in time to ride in the ambulance. Jim was in good spirits, despite a broken leg and some bruises. Things could have been much worse, he said. Then they did get worse. By the time we got to the hospital, he was disoriented. An emergency room doctor asked where he went to school, and he named the high school from which we'd graduated six months earlier. The doctor asked him to name the president. When Jim looked at me for help, my worried face made clear how much was riding on the answer. If only I would tell him, his eyes said, everything would be all right. So why did I refuse? The doctors hooked up a monitor, which showed his oxygen levels dropping rapidly. They wheeled him away to a ventilator.

Alice had arrived by then at the hospital, and we waited together for our parents to get down from New York. In the meantime, an intensive care doctor explained to us that Jim was suffering acute respiratory failure. A bit of bone from his shattered leg had likely made its way into his bloodstream and from there to his lung. Almost as an afterthought, this man we'd never seen before added that our brother was unlikely to make it to morning. Then he continued on his rounds. The first thing we did, after he left us, was to pray.

As it happens, Jim did survive the night. He spent several more weeks in the hospital, sedated and intubated, during which time no one could tell when or whether he'd come through, or what condition he'd be in if he did. After regaining consciousness, he was slow and confused, which we were told might be a temporary effect of sedation or a sign of permanent damage. His impairment took the form of drunken dopiness: He told jokes that made no sense, and he didn't understand why we responded with worry rather than amusement. This too passed, and it gradually became clear that the sudden drop in oxygen on the night of the accident had done no lasting harm. After a few more days he returned home, wheelchair bound, to begin a physical recovery that lasted more than a year.

I understood how lucky we were. Our prayers had been answered: Jim was all right. And I thanked God for that. Alice and I were lucky to have each other on campus, and Jim was lucky to have our parents in New York. We were lucky to live in a time and a part of the world with the care he'd needed, lucky to be able to afford that care. Lucky, really, in too many ways to count.

But the memory of that first night, when I didn't think he'd survive, stayed with me. To appreciate myself as lucky meant appreciating how easily things could have gone otherwise, how many people lost their lives in capricious ways or had the ones they loved most taken from them, how many had no family to depend on. It would have been obscene to think that our devotion had spared us the full depths of suffering—not least because so many people far more devoted than we were did not get spared.

Of course, I'd known that already, but the problem of suffering had always had an abstract quality for me. I hadn't thought much about the challenge that it posed to religious believers, even when we'd discussed the issue in high school theology classes. Like many self-dramatizing teenagers with charmed lives, I had played at suffering—over social setbacks, relationship dramas, minor family discord—and so I'd thought I had some sense of it. What struck me about the real thing was precisely the understanding that I'd been saved from the worst of it.

Putting it this way may make that understanding sound more high-minded (or less self-centered) than it was. I did understand that other people out there were suffering more than I, but I also understood that I had untapped potential for more suffering myself. I still had so much to lose, and I would eventually lose all of it. Everyone I loved would be taken from me, unless I was taken from them first.

I thought back on various family tragedies that had happened either before I was born or before I was old enough to register them—two uncles dead young, leaving behind small children and, in one case, a pregnant widow; one of my grandmother's brothers dead at twenty in World War II, another (the Franciscan monk) dead in his thirties of cancer; my grandfather's mother, aunt, and grandmother dead within days of each other during the influenza epidemic, when my grandfather was just two years old. This did not represent a cursed lot, just the normal course of life and death. Every family had such stories—or worse.

The recognition of our finitude and mortality pushes some people toward belief, but it had the opposite effect on me. On campus that spring, I started skipping Mass. Most weeks the decision was made passively: I intended to go, but when the time came, I simply kept doing whatever I was doing. I would inevitably feel some guilt over this, and it was mainly in response to that guilt that I would tell myself I was actually acting on principle. The questions I'd been struggling with made the choice feel more significant. It wasn't so much that I didn't believe in God but that I didn't believe that the God of all this suffering was worthy of my weekly devotion.

Eventually I gave up even the intention to attend church on my own, but I continued going with my family at home. I would still have described myself as Catholic, if anyone had asked. Plenty of people I knew described themselves as such, even participated more or less fully in the faith (especially when family was involved), while admitting when pressed that they didn't really buy into all of it. I thought of myself as belonging to this ambivalent camp.

Fear Is the Basis of the Whole Thing

I might have remained there—as many do all their lives—had it not been for a chance encounter with a book.

We spent summers at a house on Long Island that had belonged to my maternal grandmother before her death. Signs of faith filled that home: a ceramic holy water fount by the door; a crucified Jesus looking down from the wall. But for me its most notable feature was its books: biographies of saints, layperson's guides to theology, the complete works of John Henry Newman, novels by the likes of Graham Greene, Flannery O'Connor, and Evelyn Waugh, in hardcover copies dating from their original mid-century publication.

Having already decided that I wanted to write novels myself, I passed many days pulling titles down and reading them. On one of these summer days, I decided on a book called *Why I Am Not a Christian*. I'd noticed the somewhat scandalous title many times before, but I didn't reach for it now out of my growing sense of apostasy. What had struck me for the first time was the name of its author—Bertrand Russell, whom I'd read in an introductory philosophy course that year.

Throughout most of the twentieth century, Russell was among the world's most widely read philosophers. His abstruse works in mathematical logic were highly respected by his academic peers, but he also explained the discipline to general readers in popular books like *The Problems of Philosophy* (which I'd read in class) and *History of Western Philosophy.* This work made him famous and earned him a Nobel Prize for Literature, making him one of the very few winners who was not primarily a novelist, playwright, or poet.

As a young man, Russell had abandoned at considerable psychological cost the Christian faith in which he'd been raised, and he was a lifelong critic of organized religion. In 1940, the City College of New York invited him to take up a visiting professorship in philosophy. After the appointment was announced, local religious leaders (many Catholic) and right-wing journalists (ditto) lobbied the city to retract the invitation on the grounds that Russell's views on God and morality made him unfit to teach. (He decided to spend the semester at Harvard instead.)

There was plenty in Russell's actual beliefs to outrage conservatives, but the campaign against him shamelessly distorted his work, as such campaigns tend to do. He was made out to be a Stalinist, although he'd spoken out against Soviet-style socialism almost as soon as the Bolsheviks came into power. He was said to approve of homosexuality, although this was one issue on which his views were entirely consistent with the prejudices of his day. His work was described as "salacious" and "obscene," although it is almost comically prim and Victorian in tone, even when discussing contraception and "free love." In part to correct this misinformation, an NYU philosophy professor named Paul Edwards put together a collection of Russell's essays on "religion and related subjects," which he published in 1957, borrowing its title from a talk that Russell had delivered thirty years before.

Why I Am Not a Christian is a hodgepodge, collecting fifty years' worth of talks and occasional writings of varying length and quality, some with only a tenuous connection to religious belief. Nonetheless, the sum total changed my life. It was one of those books that wind up in the hands of just the right reader at just the right moment, so that it seems to be speaking directly to some secret need.

Throughout the book, Russell makes two fundamental critiques of religion. The first is "intellectual": The teachings of the major religions about God are almost certainly false. The second is "moral": Religion is a great cause of suffering in the world. He spends comparatively little time on the first point. Russell takes for granted that the Enlightenment and the Scientific Revolution had effectively demolished monotheism's metaphysical claims. He makes short work of the medieval proofs of God's existence, but he is quick to acknowledge that these "intellectual arguments" are not the reason that faith persists. "Most people believe in God," he notes, "because they have been taught from early infancy to do it."

I could relate. The first-mover argument and the argument from design had not been important parts of my childhood religious education, so watching a master logician carve them up was hardly world-shattering. Far more significant was being faced with the fact that for most of my life I had believed something incredible without any evidence, merely because I'd been told to believe it.

Most of Russell's case against religion rested on the second, "moral" critique. It was common in Russell's time—as it is today—for people who can't defend religion's truths to defend its social value. Russell considered it reprehensible to accept a falsehood on these grounds, but he believed in any case that this value was vastly overstated. Religion generally impedes social progress, Russell said. It has been "a source of untold misery to the human race," primarily because it "teaches ethical codes which are not conducive to human happiness." Religion conflicts with human happiness especially through morbid sexual ethics, which turn natural urges that ought to be a source of pleasure and joy into causes of shame and disgust, emotions that can have a catastrophic effect on people's lives.

Beyond anything that religion asks us to believe, there is the problem of the *way* religion asks us to believe things—"on faith," independently of the evidence for or against them, which "produces hostility to evidence and causes us to close our minds to every fact that does not suit our prejudices." This in turn becomes a source of more suffering, because it keeps humanity from dealing rationally with the real problems that we face.

So why does religion persist, if there are no rational justifications for it and it doesn't make people happy? Russell's answer is simple: "Fear is the basis of the whole thing—fear of the mysterious, fear of defeat, fear of death." I might not have been so struck by the idea, had I not been spending so much time of late in the grip of just this fear. While reading Russell, I thought of my family praying together on the night of Jim's accident, begging our all-powerful God to spare his life, and the image looked very different to me now.

The lasting impact of Russell's book on me came from his insistence that we must respond to our fear not by dogmatically accepting the creeds handed down to us by tradition and authority but by "look[ing] the world frankly in the face" with a "fearless outlook and a free intellect." Russell's words suggested less a particular set of beliefs than an approach to knowledge about the world. He very rarely uses the word *atheist*, preferring such terms as *freethinker*, *skeptic*, and *rationalist*. By the time I'd finished reading *Why I Am Not a Christian*, these were the terms I hoped to apply to myself.

The next Sunday, I stayed in the pew while the rest of my family went up for Communion. That doesn't sound like much, but the act felt monumental to me. Up until the last moment, I wasn't sure I would go through with it. My mother cried in the parking lot after Mass. (She thought I'd forgone the Eucharist because I'd committed a mortal sin.) I was sorry to cause her pain, but I felt it couldn't be helped. I had faced up to the question of whether I would live my life on the basis of reason or faith, and I'd thrown in my lot with reason.

Later that summer, I was helping my mother make lunch, listening to NPR on the kitchen radio, when a segment came on about sleep paralysis, a condition that leaves people awake but unable to move. The experience is often accompanied by a feeling of terror, the host explained, as well as hallucinations. Sufferers report strongly sensing a presence in the room with them, and researchers have connected the condition to historical accounts of nighttime demons—incubi and succubi—as well as modern reports of alien abductions. The segment featured interviews with chronic cases, who make up around 5 percent of the population.

"That happens to me," I said.

"You've never mentioned it," my mother responded doubtfully.

I shrugged this off. Explaining that silence meant explaining my private interpretation of these events, which for obvious reasons I wasn't eager to do. That interpretation seemed now to exemplify everything that was wrong with my old beliefs: I had experienced a reasonably common physiological affliction and, rather than trying to find a rational cause for it, I had retreated into superstition. I'd actually convinced myself that God was sending me a message. It seemed highly significant that the most striking feature of the experience was precisely *fear.* All at once my last remaining justification for belief became a powerful argument against it.

My parents and I worked out an uneasy compromise by which I continued to attend Mass when I was home but never took Communion. Every

Sunday, my father put a hand on my shoulder as he passed me coming in or out of the pew, as though acknowledging my choice while also expressing appreciation that I was there. Toward the end of the summer, I went to see a priest at our local parish, to speak with him about my doubts. Perhaps part of me was still ready to be talked out of them. Instead, the priest—another Jesuit—told me that he had also stopped going to Mass at my age. We all have to work these questions out for ourselves, he said.

It was a relief to have made this break, to feel that I was now living honestly, rather than displaying the outward form of a truth I could not accept, but this relief went only so far. Giving up God did not mean giving up my anxiety about death and suffering. I suffered from depression throughout the rest of my college years. I drank too much and took more than my share of recreational drugs. I still had frequent bouts of sleep paralysis, made worse by these habits and by the irregular hours of college life, but I no longer experienced them as spiritual visitations. Some part of me now knew their real cause even as they were happening. Strangely enough, this half knowledge did not lessen the frightful feeling. It simply stripped my terror of content—I was not afraid *of* anything, but I was still afraid.

Sometimes I missed my faith and even envied those who could believe, but the fact that disbelief could be difficult ultimately seemed like a point in its favor. I hadn't entirely given up the feeling that I was called to something great, even as I had given up the context within which this calling was explicable. The feeling now was absorbed entirely into my sense of literary vocation. I wrote very little during this time but thought constantly about becoming a great writer. Anxiety and depression had fueled many great writers, and I hoped it might do the same for me. Perhaps, I sometimes thought, my calling was not just a secular one but even an antireligious one. Perhaps I would make lasting art from the discomfort of living in a godless universe. In these moments, there seemed to be something dignified in the fear that I felt, and I was almost glad to have it.

At other times, it overpowered me. I spent long days in bed, unable to drag myself to class. I felt tired and slow, and I suffered a growing number of minor physical ailments that I was too indifferent to address. My appetite disappeared entirely. When forced to eat, I quickly threw up my meal. My family eventually intervened, worried that I had an eating disorder. I insisted that I didn't care about my weight. (I didn't add: *any more than I do about anything else.*)

One day I woke with my ankles so swollen that I couldn't walk on them, and I agreed to go to the campus infirmary. The doctor prescribed an X-ray of my chest. This seemed a strange response to a problem with my feet, but he speculated that I might have tuberculosis. In retrospect, I imagine he had other concerns in mind. Rather than talking me through the results, he sent me to the local hospital, where I came to be diagnosed with stage 3 lymphatic cancer. My body, the oncologist later told me, was "caked with tumors." It was the winter of my senior year, and I was faced with the very real possibility that I would not live to graduation, yet I felt an odd sense of relief. I had known that I could not go on as I'd been going, and now the real problem had been named.

Who knows what this experience would have done to my faith if I'd still had it. Perhaps I would have found solace in belief. Instead my skepticism hardened into something more severe. I saw my illness as a test of my newfound commitment to looking life frankly in the face. (Who might be doing the testing I did not ask myself.)

After several weeks of uncertainty, a biopsy revealed my lymphoma to be the more treatable Hodgkin's variety. I began a six-month course of chemotherapy, and the cancer responded quickly. As with Jim's accident, a catastrophic threat had been followed by what could be seen under the circumstances only as a run of luck. But this time, I hadn't prayed for that outcome, and I didn't thank God when it arrived. Quite the opposite: Having faced mortality without recourse to faith, I thought, I would never be going back. I went from being merely a disbeliever to being a committed, almost evangelical atheist, the kind who takes every conversational opportunity to sound off on the subject, who revels in offending believers with the cold facts of life. Just as Catholicism had been something more than a family tradition, something central to my identity, so atheism represented not just a rejection of that tradition but the embrace of a new me.

What Has the Universe Got to Do with It?

In many ways my postcollegiate years—the early years of the twenty-first century—were an ideal time to be a budding unbeliever. It was the heyday of the "New Atheists," a collection of popular writers whose aggressive attacks on religion made forthright disbelief suddenly fashionable. (Particularly fashionable, it seemed, among young men with college degrees.) Many books have already been written about the movement, and this won't be one of them. Its moment of influence already feels like a distant memory. But these writers played an important part in the personal story I'm telling, so it's worth saying a bit more about them.

The New Atheism was kicked off by Sam Harris, who was an unknown writer recently minted with an undergraduate philosophy degree when he published *The End of Faith* (2004), a short polemic on the existential threat that religion—particularly Islam but also the fundamentalist Christianity in ascendence during the George W. Bush years—posed to Western civilization. The book was a surprise bestseller, and in the wake of its success, several more established writers who'd been circling the "God question" for years made their own direct strikes.

Richard Dawkins was a highly respected evolutionary biologist with a talent for popularizing scientific ideas, Daniel Dennett a major academic philosopher whose primary areas of study were consciousness and the question of free will, Christopher Hitchens a charismatic gadfly and literary journalist. The work of all three made them longtime antagonists of organized religion, but they each now took on the topic more directly. In quick succession, Dawkins's *The God Delusion* (2006), Dennett's *Breaking the Spell* (2006), and Hitchens's *God Is Not Great* (2007) followed *The End of Faith* onto bestseller lists. The group styled itself a coterie—the Four Horsemen—blurbing each other's work, participating in recorded conversations, debating prominent theists onstage. Together they became the public face of a resurgent atheism.

Like Russell before them, the New Atheists advanced both an intellectual and a moral case. On the first point, they had little truly new to say, which they readily admitted. The factual case against religion had long been obvious to those who judged the question rationally, they insisted; it needed repeating and elaborating only because believers had so effectively suppressed rational judgment on the matter. For example, Darwin long ago dealt a fatal blow to the so-called argument from design by showing how an undirected process of random variation and natural selection could give rise to the complexity and appearance of order that the natural world displays. A century ago, Russell could mention this truth in passing, as something that almost went without saying, but religious fanatics had since succeeded in confusing this point with talk about "intelligent design" or evolution's status as a theory rather than a fact. So Dawkins and Dennett had each written multiple books explaining exactly what evolutionary theory entailed, why it was almost certainly true, and how incompatible it was with the existence of a creative God.

As for the malignant influence of religion on society, the New Atheists had another century of material at their disposal, and one of their greatest concerns—religious-fundamentalist terrorism—had not been on Russell's radar. But their sharpest criticisms echoed Russell: Precisely because the claims of religion are so obviously false, religions demand that their adherents accept them "on faith," and so discourage free inquiry and the objective examination of evidence. Every important advance in human culture has come through a greater understanding of the natural world, and religion actively works against this trend, teaching instead (per Dawkins) "that it is a virtue to be satisfied with not understanding." Religion makes a fetish of mystery, because it is only in a world that appears mysterious to us that religion can survive. Human progress is the story of apparently mysterious phenomena being conquered by reason, and so religion necessarily sets itself against rationality and progress alike.

This would all be familiar to a "freethinker" of Russell's day, or even one from the eighteenth century. What really distinguished the New Atheists was their tone. They insisted that people were too polite about religion, that religious claims had been systematically protected from the kind of rational scrutiny that other claims needed to survive in order to be taken seriously. In the light of this scrutiny, they said, religion appeared absurd. So it was, and so it ought to be treated. And now that religious fanatics had the power to destroy cities, to take thousands—perhaps millions—of lives in one go, there was no time left to be polite.

It would be difficult to overstate the importance of 9/11 to the New Atheist project. Harris begins *The End of Faith*—a book that he claims to have started writing on September 12, 2001—with the image of a suicide bomber blowing himself up along with twenty other people on a public bus. On the first page of *The God Delusion*, Dawkins describes a billboard advertisement showing the New York skyline with the Twin Towers standing intact alongside the caption: "Imagine a world without religion." Hitchens gets all the way to chapter 2 of *God Is Not Great* before invoking the attacks, but in the last years of his life he was as well known for his support of the wars in Afghanistan and Iraq as for his stance on religion. Even Dennett, whose objections to religion were generally more philosophical than political, states clearly that the timing of his book was motivated by the fact that "a toxic religious mania could end human civilization overnight."

The New Atheists pointedly refused to distinguish between the extremists who posed this threat and more tolerant believers. Dennett likened moderate religions to "attractive nuisances" such as unenclosed swimming pools: "Those who maintain religions, and take steps to make them more attractive, must be held similarly responsible for the harms produced by some of those whom they attract and provide with a cloak of respectability." Harris went a good deal further than this. "Religious moderates are themselves the bearer of a terrible dogma," he wrote. "[T]he very ideal of religious tolerance—born of the notion that every human being should be free to believe whatever he wants about God—is one of the principal forces driving us toward the abyss." The overall message, put into the terms of that moment, was this: You're either with us, or you're with the terrorists.

The take-no-prisoners approach was controversial, even among fellow atheists, and perhaps it should have bothered me. After all, the tolerant, liberal-minded believers the New Atheists attacked were the ones I'd known and loved. They were my parents, my aunts, my teachers, and my friends. As far as I could tell, these were all good people. I had long been one of them myself. But I had already rejected their kind of belief, and I didn't mind seeing it roughed up a bit.

And yet I realized very quickly that I was not the audience for these books. I wasn't looking to talk my way out of belief—I was already out—and I didn't need knockdown arguments against God's existence that I could use in my defense against religious family and friends. I had done the hard work of making my break. My family was saddened by the choice, but they were not confused by it. They did not attempt to talk me down from my position, and they did not expect me to justify it. As for friends:

After college I entered a graduate writing program at the New School in Greenwich Village, not a milieu especially known for being hostile to heresy. There were still plenty of places where it was difficult to be an atheist, but I didn't live in one, and I didn't need the assurance that other people shared my skepticism, which seemed a big part of what these books existed to provide.

Nor did I need a primer on the moral evils of organized religion. Not that I disagreed on this front; it just wasn't the point. I was a lifelong New Yorker, and I knew several people who'd died on September 11. The attacks devastated me, but my atheism had nothing to do with them. I simply didn't believe.

So why did I eagerly read all these books? What did I hope to find in them, if not a definitive dismantling of the case for belief in God? I wanted to know what to believe instead.

Many atheists would say that this desire rested on a fundamental misunderstanding. If I was still in search of *beliefs*, they would insist, I hadn't really gotten over my religious upbringing. A good atheist does not deal in beliefs but in knowledge, not in faith but in facts. Atheism is not another creed but precisely the rejection of creeds of any kind.

I was prepared to accept all this. I wanted to look the world frankly in the face, to see things clearly in the light of reason. The trouble was that when I took this approach, I could find no obvious factual or scientific answer to the question that seemed most pressing to me: *How am I to live?*

It wasn't that my fellow atheists weren't ethically minded. Quite the opposite. The New Atheists in particular were largely fueled by a sense of moral outrage. One could obviously not make a moral case against religious belief without a strong moral sense. But they tended to take this underlying morality for granted. It was just self-evident that we ought to treat others as we wished to be treated. Anyone who felt otherwise was obviously a sociopath—or else a religious fanatic. When it came to justifying this moral sense, they fell back on intuition, tradition, and cultural consensus—just the criteria that they roundly rejected in other areas.

Of the Four Horsemen, only Harris aspired to a "science of good and evil" that could subject moral claims to the same rational scrutiny as all other claims. But the chapter he dedicates to the topic in *The End of Faith* quickly devolves into an argument about the indefensibility of pacifism and the moral necessity of government torture. (It was a strange time.)

Besides which, I wasn't just looking for practical guidance. The question *How am I to live?* is not only ethical in the narrow sense. To ask it is to inquire not just after what is right but after what is *good*. It is to ask not just *What should I do?* but *How should I be?* And to ask that question suggests that the answer matters, that how we are counts for something—or at least that it ought to count for something. In other words, I was after more than rules of conduct. I wanted a meaningful life.

In a famous scene from *Annie Hall*, the young Alvie Singer refuses to do his homework after learning that the universe is expanding and will eventually break apart. "What has the universe got to do with it?" his exasperated mother asks. "You're here in Brooklyn!" Over the years I have come to realize that some people naturally worry over the expanding universe, while others are here in Brooklyn, living the lives they've been given the best that they know how.

The difference is not one of intellect or even thoughtfulness but of temperament. As far as I can tell, the two sorts are dispersed evenly among believers and unbelievers. It may be that this questioning tendency exists on a spectrum. Even the most existentially minded people spend much of their lives unselfconsciously attending to everyday concerns, while even the most grounded occasionally stop to ask, *What am I doing here? What is the point of all this?* If this is so, I have come to understand, I exist near one end of the spectrum. I ask myself these questions all the time, and I have a strong intuitive sense that their answers have a deep relevance to how I shape my own life.

The most generous interpretation of the New Atheist view on what makes life worth living is that people ought to have the freedom to figure such things out for themselves. This seems fair so far as it goes, but it left me right where I'd started. I still needed to do the figuring. For it is one thing to look the world frankly in the face, and it is another to make your peace with what you see. That's what I set out to do.

Take Up and Read

Tolle lege—take up and read. So a voice counseled Saint Augustine at a time when "a deep consideration had . . . drawn together and heaped up all [his] misery." As he recounts in his *Confessions*, Augustine took this as a call to read the Bible, and this call ultimately played a decisive role in his final conversion. I too decided that the answer to my questions was to take up and read. I had long been a devoted, even obsessive, reader of fiction, but in my early twenties I began seriously reading philosophy, which seemed the primary rational means by which humans have sought secular answers to the question of meaning.

I'd completed a handful of undergraduate courses on the subject, enough to have a general sense of where to start, but in the years after college I committed myself to a proper education. I read the philosophers most frequently cited by modern-day atheists—John Locke, David Hume, John Stuart Mill. And I read those whom meaning-hungry young people habitually embrace as secular gurus—Friedrich Nietzsche, Ludwig Wittgenstein, Albert Camus. But I also read ones who are mostly just read by other philosophers or their students. With the help of guidebooks and online lectures, I worked my way slowly through Immanuel Kant's *Critique of Pure Reason*, Baruch Spinoza's *Ethics*, and Martin Heidegger's *Being and Time.*

Even when I was struggling with the most challenging of these works, the reading felt urgent to me. I wasn't submitting papers or getting grades; I wasn't looking to earn a degree or pursue a career. I wasn't even trying to impress people at literary parties. (For that I had thousand-page postmodern novels.) I certainly didn't envision one day writing a book like this one. I was doing it entirely for myself. I was trying to figure things out, and I concerned myself only with those books that seemed like they might be a help in that project. Kant's three "critiques" are often cited as the moment when philosophy stopped being accessible to nonspecialists, but in Kant's own view he was addressing very simple questions—*What can I know? What must I do?* and *What may I hope?* I was decidedly a nonspecialist, and these were the kinds of questions I was looking to answer. Slowly I came to understand that for me, giving up God would be not the end but the beginning of the journey.

Among other things, this reading taught me that atheists *do* hold beliefs, not just about morals and ethics but about how the world actually is, how humans fit into that world, and how we come to have knowledge about it. Another way of putting this is that the majority of modern Western atheists share a *worldview*.

I mean by this somewhat portentous word simply the picture of reality and our place within it that we carry through our day-to-day lives, what the American philosopher William James calls "our more or less dumb sense of what life honestly and deeply means." As James emphasized, we can't all explicitly articulate our worldviews, but we implicitly embrace them to the extent that we have reasons for acting how we act, valuing what we value, believing what we believe.

The most prevalent modern atheist worldview has many variations that go under many names—*empiricism*, *positivism*, *physicalism*, *naturalism*—but the term that I believe best captures the fullness of its present-day iteration is *scientific materialism*.* Roughly speaking, this view holds that the material world is all that exists, that humans come to know this world through sense perceptions, and that the methods of science allow us to convert the raw data of these perceptions into objective facts about the world. It further holds—as a matter of fact, shown by sense perception, not a founding theoretical truth—that our world is governed by a set of immutable physical laws and that our knowledge of these laws can be both tested and put to practical use by making predictions about future events in this world.

Not only do most atheists hold this worldview, but most of them take the view to be so obviously and self-evidently correct that only a person who does not understand it (perhaps because he has been deluded by religious faith) could possibly deny it. This understanding of scientific materialism is one species of what the Catholic philosopher Charles Taylor calls "subtraction stories." Such stories assume that there is a natural, default view of reality that is inevitably left behind after the supernatural beliefs of religion have been swept away. Generally speaking, the natural view is taken to be the one provided by the empirical sciences. As a historical matter, subtraction stories tell us, the process of secularization has stripped away religious superstition, revealing more and more of the world as it really was all along. On the personal level, subtraction stories tell us that an individual who leaves faith should not go in search of some other

* I first encountered the term in the work of the philosopher Thomas Nagel, who is both an atheist and a critic of this worldview, but it was used approvingly by Daniel Dennett among others, and I mean it to be neutrally descriptive rather than adversarial.

belief system with which to replace it but instead accept the reality of this natural world, for better or worse.

My reading led me to question this subtraction narrative. More than this, it led me to recognize scientific materialism's fundamental limitations, ones that the giants of secular empiricist philosophy recognized from the start, despite their frank hostility to the claims of religious faith. Throughout my journey, I repeatedly found the great modern thinkers to be very different from the pictures of them given in popular accounts, which are often written by atheist journalists or practicing scientists rather than philosophers or intellectual historians. Above all, these thinkers were far more alive to the challenges involved in constructing a compelling secular worldview, and to materialism's failings when it comes to meeting those challenges.

THE MOST FUNDAMENTAL of these failings—though far from the only one—is materialism's inability to account for our subjective experience as freely acting, conscious agents. A law-governed physical world in which human beings exist as material objects like any others does not seem to have space for free action. Consciousness itself does not seem to be material. It is not publicly available through sense perception, not subject to the kind of observation that scientific materialism takes as the hallmark of knowledge. By the standards of the materialist worldview, it doesn't seem to exist at all. For me, this limitation proved fatal. I was far too introspective a person, spent far too much time within the confines of my own head, to accept a worldview that told me that whatever was going on in here wasn't real.

Luckily, I soon came into contact with another family of atheist belief, one less prevalent than scientific materialism but nonetheless still widespread. This is the atheism of Nietzsche and Heidegger and all of their existentialist epigones. I eventually came to understand this tradition as *romantic idealism*.*

Romantic idealism generally begins in precisely the place where scientific materialism leaves off, with the will of the subjective, conscious agent. It takes this subjective will, rather than objective physical matter, as the bedrock feature of reality. At its most extreme, romantic idealism treats each one of us as willing our own world into being, creating the reality in which we live. Even when it does not go this far, it tends to treat our subjective experience of reality as the proper grounds of knowledge, in fact the only thing we can ever be said to know, rather than a starting point to be transcended through science to arrive at an objective picture of the external world. This is what makes the movement "idealist."

The ethics of romantic idealism are an ethics of authenticity: The greatest good is living in a way that is true to our personal experience. This ethic is what makes the movement "romantic." The movement does not reject religious belief because it is untrue, for it does not accept the materialist account of what it means for a thing to be "true." Instead it rejects conventional theism for being inauthentic, a ready-made and inherited response to a problem that we ought to work out for ourselves.

While atheism is closely associated with rationality, romantic idealism is unapologetically irrational. In place of reason, observation, and scientific study, it valorizes emotion, imagination, and artistic creativity. Romantic idealism arose in the post-Enlightenment era, and it grew in opposition as much to the principles of Enlightenment rationality as to religious authority. The two atheist traditions have been hostile to each other ever since, often more hostile than they are to their common foe.

From the standpoint of romantic idealists, scientific materialism is

* This term is not as common as *scientific materialism*, and is sometimes applied in a different way than I am using it, but it neatly captures the most important elements of the movement I'm describing with it.

another expression of theism's universalizing impulse: It wants to tell us that there is just one truth, one reality to which we must accommodate ourselves. From the standpoint of scientific materialism, romantic idealism is just the latest form of religious superstition teaching people that how they "feel" about reality is more important than the cold, hard facts of the matter. And the antagonism persists to this day. Twenty years after the rise of New Atheism, the two surviving "horsemen"—Sam Harris and Richard Dawkins—reserve much of their vitriol for postmodern relativism, critical race and gender theory, New Age spiritualism, and other forms of secular thought that have strong roots in romantic idealism,* while these movements still treat scientific materialism as a kind of coercive power seeking to oppress difference.

From my own perspective, romantic idealism held enormous and immediate appeal, in large part because of its emphasis on creativity. My own life had one unquestionable source of meaning during this time: my writing, which still felt like a calling. When I asked myself the question *How am I to live?*, the one firm answer I could give was that I was meant to write something great. I knew that these ideas—that there was anything at all that I or anyone else was "meant" to do, that there was even such a thing as artistic "greatness"—were inconsistent with the view of reality that I'd adopted, but the feeling was simply too strong to be conquered. While I was writing or reading, I often felt connected to some larger truth that seemed to have answers to the questions troubling me.

But when those moments passed, I felt very differently about these things. Living often seemed to me not worth the trouble. Our individual lives are a blip of time, and we're all destined for oblivion soon enough. What is the point of delaying things—especially when life itself is often painful or just tedious? There is a strong streak of pessimism in the ro-

* Dawkins has called identity politics "one of the great evils of our age."

mantic idealist tradition, and many of the tradition's thinkers have dedicated thought to the problem of suicide. Quite a number of them concluded that life is not, after all, worth living. The only good argument against suicide, they insist, is that taking your own life is just another act of will, no more defensible than any other.

I spent much time during my twenties and early thirties contemplating suicide. I was never at serious risk of committing the act, but it was a matter of abiding fascination. Having come somewhat near to death already, I could see that there was actually something inviting about it. I came to think that my great fear of mortality had a bit of longing mixed in.

At the same time, a part of me recoiled from this longing, and recoiled from any worldview that could not justify going on with life. A part of me also rejected romantic idealism on other grounds. I still had enough of the scientific materialist in me to respect the reality of a world outside my head that wasn't wholly under my own control. I came to understand my failure to engage with that world on its own terms as a chief source of my unhappiness.

So I did what many, many people do: I muddled along. (In Brooklyn, no less.) I tried to focus on the tasks in front of me—doing my work, paying my rent, being a reasonably attentive friend and family member—while using all the means our modern world affords us to quiet the persistent worry that these tasks did not ultimately amount to a worthwhile life.

I WAS IN my mid-thirties when the doubts returned.

After nearly twenty years of searching unsuccessfully for a livable atheist worldview, I began to suspect that atheism itself might be part of the problem. This might seem another natural stopping place. First I rejected traditional belief, then I rejected the more strident forms of unbelief, and finally I arrived at a moderate compromise position. The common name for this position is *agnosticism*. Depending on how you understand that term, it describes either a very old or a fairly recent response to the problem of belief. If you take agnosticism to be simply the view that human beings can never *really* answer the question of God's existence, then it is likely as old as belief itself. That position has historically been called "skepticism." To this day, I consider myself a skeptic, and in this sense I can claim to have accepted agnosticism.

But a healthy respect for the limits of human knowledge can take you only so far. Being a skeptic means recognizing that we must inevitably act on beliefs we can't wholly justify. The most extreme skeptics will tell you that we have no rational certainty that the future will be anything like the past. That I can step outside in the morning and see a world largely unchanged from the one I left last night is a belief, not a piece of knowledge, but I must decide whether to get out each day. By my actions I affirm my belief in what I will find.

Is the question of God's existence one of those matters about which life obliges us to act one way or the other? Agnosticism could also be defined as the view that we need not hold any opinion on God at all. We can easily go about our lives without even a provisional answer to the question, and so we ought to set it aside entirely. On the individual, practical level, even this position is very old. It is roughly the "Brooklynite" position I referenced above, the view that asks, "What does all this business have to do with me?" To many people, spiritual matters just don't feel urgent. Without a social structure that forces them to hold some view on religious questions, they are simply not moved to ask them.

In just the past hundred and fifty years, however, this view has become increasingly prevalent in philosophy, a discipline that has historically been concerned with precisely "all this business." The term *agnostic* was coined in the late nineteenth century to describe the philosophical position that the question of God's existence is not just unanswerable but irrelevant to any possible human concerns. Many—perhaps most—contemporary philosophers count themselves agnostic in this sense. They suspect that attempts to answer "ultimate questions" are a thorough waste of time. At best, philosophy might be a form of therapy that can help us stop asking the questions and just go about our lives here in Brooklyn.

For these philosophers the problem is not—as many scientific materialists would have it—that the questions have in fact been answered and that certain people simply can't face up to that reality. The problem is that after thousands of years of trying, we are no closer to answering them. Perhaps the questions do have answers, but these answers are beyond human understanding. Perhaps they are reasonable questions for which no answers happen to exist, even in principle. Or perhaps the questions are unanswerable because they don't really make sense. Perhaps they don't have any possible answers because they aren't even real questions.

But for me, at least, these questions—*How am I to live? What do I owe to other people (or even to myself)? What is the meaning of life?*—felt real enough, and they continued to call out for answers. A life in which one has learned by way of therapeutic philosophy to stop asking these questions seemed little better than a life in which one has silenced the questions by way of drugs or alcohol or shopping or endless social media scrolling. I didn't want such a life. So the journey went on.

A History of My Opinions

That journey is now nearly three decades old. Given this book's title, it would be pointless to withhold the fact that it has led me to an outright rejection of atheism. And I might as well get out of the way the fact that it eventually led me back to the Catholic Church, albeit in a very different relationship from the one I had as an adolescent altar boy. This development did not end my journey any more than my earlier departure from the church had. I have come to believe that the journey will never end while I am still alive, that continuing on the journey is in some sense the work I am on this earth to do. But I also think I have made real progress along the way, and for reasons that I hope become clear by the end of these pages, now seems a fitting time to give some account of where I've gotten so far. This is what I intend this book to do.

I want to tell the story of my own passage into and out of atheist belief by telling the story of the books I read along the way and the worldviews that I worked my way through. What follows is not a simple chronological account of my reading and thinking over these years. I've imposed a certain retrospective order on a chaotic process that included various wrong turns and dead ends. Nor is it a straightforward intellectual history. First I offer an account of the worldview I'm calling scientific materialism—what it is, how it came to be, and where it seems to be leading us from here—before attempting to explain why I came to find it unsatisfactory. Then I attempt to do the same with the worldview I'm calling romantic idealism.

In reality, these traditions can't be entirely separated in this way. Nor are they the only forms that atheism takes in the modern world. Among other things, my account is entirely concerned with Western thought. I have no intellectual justification for this limitation. I can defend it only by saying that I was raised in a Western theistic tradition, and when I left that tradition, Western forms of atheism seemed the most obvious available alternatives. Many Eastern spiritual traditions have very different understandings of theism and atheism both, and many Westerners who have found themselves in my position—alienated from Western theism and atheism alike—have made a home in these worldviews. Perhaps in another life, I would have done so too. As it was, I did not. I have no excuse for my relative ignorance of these traditions, but at least I won't compound that ignorance by pretending to speak knowledgably about them.

With that said, I do think scientific materialism and romantic idealism between them account for the vast majority of present-day Western atheists. And I think that a close examination of these two families of belief clearly shows the challenges faced by any worldview that does away with a sense of the transcendent. But I also recognize that there are other possibilities out there, and I don't pretend that if these worldviews are shown to be insufficient, some version of theism must be true by process of elimination.

Finally, it's not my intention to talk anyone else out of disbelief; it is my intention only to provide a record of one person's struggle with a set of questions that we all must answer for ourselves. This sense that we are all obliged to work things out in this way comes directly from my experience of romantic idealism, and I continue to hold dear many other beliefs acquired in my years of reading secular philosophy. So the fact that I ultimately rejected these atheist worldviews is only part of the story. I still find them valuable, and for this reason alone I want to give a fair account of them.

In many ways my experience of the tensions within these worldviews—their promise and their disappointments—made belief possible for me again. I eventually came to understand theism as a means of reconciling what is most valuable about these mutually antagonistic views, making of their fragments a surprisingly coherent whole. I would not be the theistic believer I am today without my experience of atheist belief.

Above all, I want to show you that atheists do indeed have beliefs, that they must, because we all must. In doing so, I want to shift the conversation to the atheists' own ground, subjecting atheistic beliefs to some of the scrutiny that atheists apply to religious beliefs. If you are an atheist yourself, perhaps you will find that your beliefs survive this scrutiny and are even strengthened by it. All the better. My own beliefs have been strengthened by atheist scrutiny, even harsh and sometimes impolite scrutiny. If you are a religious believer, perhaps you will come from reading this book to understand a bit better the sorts of things atheists believe and why it might be reasonable to believe them. Perhaps, paradoxically, my skeptical defense of belief will stir some doubts about your own certainties. This too will be all to the good. As a skeptic, I believe that our doubts are among the most precious things that we have.

EVERY CATHOLIC CONVERSION narrative inevitably draws comparisons (seldom flattering) to the classics of the genre, from Augustine's *Confessions* to Merton's *Seven Storey Mountain*. While writing this book, I have thought often of a slightly less famous example, another book taken down from my grandmother's shelf.

John Henry Newman was a prominent Anglican clergyman who converted to Catholicism in 1845. He was one of Victorian England's great intellectual figures, and his conversion shocked a culture that viewed the Catholic Church as irremediably anti-intellectual. Some suspected that Newman had served for years before his conversion as a secret agent of Rome, fomenting dissent within the English Church.

In response to this accusation, Newman wrote his *Apologia Pro Vita Sua*, an account of what he had believed as an Anglican, what he now believed as a Catholic, and how his beliefs had come to change. He made clear that he didn't write the book in order to proselytize on behalf of his new faith. "I am not setting myself up as a pattern of good sense or of anything else," he wrote. "I am but giving a history of my opinions, and that, with the view of showing that I have come by them through intelligible processes of thought and honest external means."

My own return to belief is not a matter of any public interest, but I recount it in the spirit of Newman's book. I have come to embrace the romantic idealist notion that we all must work through the meaning of the life into which we've been thrust, and my own working through has led me to the conclusion that this life is the product of a creative power far greater than myself, that I owe everything to the love of this creator, and that this creator calls me to discharge that debt by lavishing on the rest of his creation the same love he lavishes on me. I hope to make that answer to the question *How am I to live?* comprehensible in these pages, but I don't aim to convince anyone that it is the only possible answer. Since my journey is not over, I could hardly recommend where I am now as a final resting place for anybody else.

If there is one point I do mean to argue, it is merely that "looking the world frankly in the face" does not *require* us to abandon God, that it is possible to be at once a skeptic and a believer both.

PART I

A Universal Science

One

STRANGE PRISONERS

Before offering a picture of these atheist worldviews, I need to say a bit more about what I mean by this word. There is no perfectly settled philosophical definition of the term, and the very idea that we all must inevitably occupy some worldview or another is itself controversial. In that sense, I am begging the question a bit by starting from this assumption. But I hope before I'm done to have gone some way in justifying that approach.

As I came to understand it, a proper worldview consists of three related elements: (1) a theory of the underlying nature of reality, (2) a theory of how we ought to act, and (3) a theory of knowledge. I suspect that nearly everyone alive has given some thought to the first two, the subjects of metaphysics and ethics, respectively. Fewer people spend time on the nature of knowledge. Even those familiar with the intellectual subdiscipline that deals with the subject—epistemology—may consider it one of those areas where philosophy drifts from real human concerns into academic navel-gazing.

One of the first things I learned when I started seriously reading modern philosophy, however, was the central position epistemology holds within it. This makes sense when you think about it. Before we can tackle even the most urgent subjects, we need a sound method for separating the true from the false from the senseless. We need to know what form genuine knowledge takes. This becomes clearer if we define metaphysics as *knowledge* about the nature of reality and ethics as *knowledge* about proper human action.

When we put things this way, however, a problem emerges. Surely the underlying nature of reality ought to determine what form our knowledge about reality takes? There's an inevitable circularity here: The soundness of an epistemological approach depends on the object under study, but our understanding of the object depends on our approach.

The matter gets only more complex when we turn to ethics. There's great disagreement on the epistemological issue of whether questions of value can be treated in the same terms as questions of fact. Is knowledge in this area even possible? Is there such a thing as ethical "truth"? Your answers will depend quite a bit on the metaphysical status you accord to ethical values (and to truth itself). The question of value would seem to depend on metaphysics and epistemology both.

But there's also a very real sense in which ethics must take precedence. The decision to pursue certain kinds of knowledge is a decision to act in a particular way, which is to say that it is an ethical decision. Modern sensibilities find something atavistic in the idea that some truths are just too dangerous or destructive to be pursued, but we all take for granted that knowledge of how to make a nuclear bomb, for example, should be kept out of certain hands, and many of us would have no hesitation in stating that humanity as a whole should never have acquired this knowledge in the first place. (It's insufficient to separate possession of the knowledge from use of that knowledge; the knowledge was sought out—one might say, the knowledge was created—for the purpose of using it.)

Ethics can also claim a different sort of precedence. On a very basic level, it's the one component of a worldview that we can't do without. Even the least reflective among us make countless choices every day. We may be entirely unsystematic about them, but our choices inevitably reflect a set of values. As William James notes, our sense of these values might be rather vague, but the choices themselves are necessarily concrete.

Certain worldviews make ethical demands of us that are not just impossible to achieve in practice but impossible for us to aspire to achieve. If we can't recognize a worldview's "good," we are going to reject that worldview, no matter how theoretically convincing it might be. Conversely, people will believe all sorts of things they can't otherwise justify, so long as those beliefs make life livable.

So it's difficult to identify one of these elements as the obvious foundation on which the others must rest. In a compelling worldview, the elements instead reinforce each other. When this happens, we generally don't think of ourselves as occupying a worldview at all; we are simply living in the world. From inside a coherent and livable worldview, other worldviews seem not just wrong but absurd, while criticisms of a worldview that seem devastating from the outside are viewed from within as utterly missing the point.

Yet people do sometimes consciously abandon worldviews, even compelling ones. This is precisely what I did when I gave up on God. I did not feel called from my theistic worldview to some other, better option. The walls of the house where I'd spent all my life had suddenly collapsed, and I needed a new place to live. But it's incredibly difficult to build a worldview from scratch. Whenever one attempts to lay foundations, the circularity I've been discussing shows itself. At the same time, already existing worldviews can be sometimes unwelcoming. Accepting any one of their elements seems to depend on having already accepted the others.

How does one overcome these barriers?

THIS PROCESS IS the subject of perhaps the most famous metaphor in the history of Western philosophy. In Plato's *Republic*, Socrates asks one of his interlocutors (Plato's older brother, Glaucon) to imagine a group of people trapped all their lives in an underground cave. Far above and behind them, the cave opens out into sunlight, but the light does not reach to where they're sitting, and they can't turn to see it, because they are shackled in place, facing the cave's back wall. Yet they are not in utter darkness. Between them and the opening a fire burns, and between them and the fire is a low wall, "like the screen in front of puppeteers above which they show their puppets." People walk back and forth along the wall, carrying statues of humans, animals, and various other objects that project their shadows on the back of the cave.

"It's a strange image you're describing," Glaucon quite reasonably notes, "and strange prisoners."

To which Socrates responds: "They're like us."

In the Platonic view, those of us mired in the ever-flickering, ever-changing world of sense perception are the prisoners in the cave. What we take as reality is only a shadow show. Because our heads are locked in place, we can't even see our own true selves—enduring souls temporarily passing through these physical bodies—let alone see the real objects whose shadows appear on the wall. Philosophy exists to free people from their bonds so that they might turn away from the shadows, recognize the reality of their situation in the cave, and ultimately leave the cave entirely to stand in the sun of the eternal and unchanging Good.

You don't have to share Plato's metaphysical rejection of sense perception to recognize the power of his metaphor. The trope of the cave has had such enormous influence because it can be applied to any movement from the darkness of a mistaken view to the sunlight of the truth. A few points about its picture of conversion have resonated throughout the ages. The first and most basic is that a change in worldview *is* a conversion—a turning. So long as the prisoners face in this particular way, someone who describes their situation accurately will sound insane. As Socrates has it, language fitted to the shadow world can't even describe the sunlit aboveground reality. A person who wants to share the experience can only get you facing in the right direction. What's needed is not the acceptance of some expository theory but the dramatic reorientation of one's entire life.

This turning is not an especially pleasant experience. Socrates asks Glaucon to imagine someone suddenly freed of these lifelong bonds, able to stand up and face the light. Such a person, Socrates says, would be "pained and dazzled and unable to see the things whose shadows he'd seen before." He might think that he'd been torn away from reality, rather than delivered over to it.

Once his eyes adjusted, he would see the fire within the cave and the statues being carried along the wall, and he would recognize that he'd been mistaken about reality. To be truly free, however, he would still need to get out of the cave entirely, to stand in the light of the sun. Leading people to that point is a kind of violence: "If someone dragged him away from there by force, up the rough, steep path, and didn't let him go until he had dragged him into the sunlight, wouldn't he be pained and irritated at being treated that way?"

Initially, the person dragged into the glare of the sun would be unable to make out anything. He would not see the truth he'd been told to expect, and he might want to return to his old life. But this wouldn't be possible: His eyes would have adjusted enough to make them useless in the dark cave, even if they couldn't yet see in the light. For a time, at least, such a person would be dissociated from any reality at all.

Someone who returned to the cave and stumbled around in the darkness would naturally "invite ridicule" among the prisoners. It would be said that he had "returned from his upward journey with his eyesight ruined," and this would be proof that such a journey had not been worthwhile. If this person tried to lead others up where he'd been, the prisoners would "somehow get their hands on him," and they would kill him.

The *Republic* was written about twenty-five years after the death of Socrates, and Plato is clearly putting some retrospective prophecy into his teacher's mouth. For it did appear to most Athenians that the young men who fell under Socrates's sway came to believe strange and improbable things that ruined them for productive society, and they naturally blamed Socrates for this. He was eventually tried for corrupting the Athenian youth, found guilty, and put to death.

One of the reasons that Socrates has come to be emblematic for so many people, including many who disagree with each other about almost everything else, is that most of us feel that our lives ought to be oriented toward the truth, even if we can't agree on what that truth is. Socrates teaches us that the first step in living the truth is being freed from the falsehoods we too easily accept. So long as we are imprisoned by the false, we can't possibly turn ourselves toward the true.

When I began seriously reading philosophy, I didn't imagine that I needed help breaking my chains, turning from the shadow show. As I saw it, certain events in my life—my brother's accident, my own cancer diagnosis—had shaken me free. I'd already made the turn, and I recognized the reality of my situation. Now I wanted to escape the cave, to see things as they really were, to stand in the sun.

THE NEXT FEW CHAPTERS will offer an account of the rise of the primary modern-atheist answer to the question of how things really are once you've broken free from theism's chains. But first I want to fill out the description of what I call "scientific materialism" with the three-part structure I've just introduced.

The "materialism" part entails the claim that physical matter is all that exists. I want to call this the worldview's metaphysics. As we'll see, most materialists describe their view instead as a *rejection* of metaphysics. In place of metaphysics, they would say, they simply have physics. But the claim that reality is entirely composed of physical matter is not itself a claim that physics can address. It's not a claim about any entity within the physical world, or even a claim about the physical world in its entirety. It is, inevitably, a metaphysical claim.

The "scientific" part describes the worldview's epistemology. Scientific materialism is empirical; it claims that knowledge about reality comes to us exclusively through sense experience. But it claims more than this. Because reality is composed of physical objects, scientific materialism tells us, our subjective sense experiences must be objectified in order to serve as a proper basis for real knowledge. This objectification occurs on the model of the physical sciences, which convert sense experiences into quantifiable data points and subject them to prediction and experimentation.

And what about the worldview's ethics? To the extent that we can have real ethical knowledge, scientific materialists insist, it must concern material reality, and it must be subject to the same process of objectification, quantification, and experimentation. The dominant scientific materialist ethic is utilitarianism, which judges acts on their objective consequences in the physical world rather than their subjective motivation, attempts to quantify these consequences, and subjects the problem of maximizing positive consequences to experiment.

The rise of scientific materialism is part of the much larger shift from the medieval Christian worldview to what we now understand as modernity. That shift—the secularization of the West, the disenchantment of the world—is among the most significant developments in human history, and entire libraries are filled with accounts of it. I'm not really equipped to tell that story, even in a radically abridged form. Instead, I am going to pull out certain threads that relate directly to the assumptions of contemporary atheism.

Even given these parameters, what follows will be radically incomplete. I want to tell the story of how I came to understand scientific materialism, what books and thinkers led me to this understanding. My primary aim is to arrive at a working picture of this worldview that one of its adherents would accept as an accurate self-description. I also hope to show that scientific materialism is, indeed, a historically conditioned worldview, rather than simply a neutral picture of "the world" to which we moderns are lucky enough to have privileged access. Having done that, I want to invite readers convinced by scientific materialism's account of reality to consider the possibility that *they* are the strange prisoners, turned away from the real action.

For reasons I've already explained, it doesn't seem to me productive to attack scientific materialism from the standpoint of some other worldview; instead I want to challenge it from within. I'm going to argue that scientific materialism is internally contradictory and even incoherent, that despite taking experience as the bedrock of knowledge, it fails to account for fundamental and unmistakable features of human experience. Finally, I'm going to argue that it is—not just for some but for most of us—simply unlivable.

Two

FROM GENERALITIES TO PARTICULARS

Most of the larger secularization accounts include a healthy dose of subtraction story. In these renditions, a long-standing spiritual superstructure is gradually dismantled, revealing the mundane, commonsense reality waiting underneath.

One especially popular version of this story takes a slightly longer historical view. It holds that a spirit of free inquiry and experimentation distinguished the ancient pagan world before the conversion of Rome. The rise of Christianity turned our attention toward an imaginary celestial realm and denigrated flesh-and-blood reality. Christianity taught that the Bible held the answer to any question worth asking, imposed uniformity of thought by punishing heresy with death, and effectively eliminated the systematic study of the natural world. For more than a millennium, scientific practice as such ceased to exist. All of the learning of Greece and Rome—our precious intellectual heritage—was nearly lost forever.

Largely by chance, this version continues, late medieval scholars recovered the great works of antiquity, leading to the emergence of Renaissance humanism,* which returned to us the spirit of rational, scientific

* Much of the story is contained right there in the name.

investigation. The church resisted this change violently, but the force of science, once unleashed, was far too powerful to stop.

This power's greatest source lay in reason's ability to improve our material condition. Under the reign of science, the average human life simply got better—longer, healthier, less painful, less subject to the whims of nature, less likely to be dominated by the drudgery of physical labor, and for all these reasons less susceptible to the claims of religious superstition and less inclined to forgo the pleasures of this world for some hypothetical reward in the next. The gradual rejection of religious belief was at once an inevitable result of scientific progress and the driver of further progress, creating a virtuous cycle that could end only with a complete victory for secular rationality.

This story is told not just about science but about intellectual life as such. Standard histories of Western philosophy run from the pre-Socratics to early Roman stoics like Seneca and Marcus Aurelius before jumping to the sixteenth century and the appearance of Francis Bacon and René Descartes. Whatever thinking went on in between was not really philosophy, the story goes, even if it understood itself as such. Since modern philosophy represented a definitive break from the so-called philosophy of the earlier era, we don't even need to study this benighted practice for historical reasons.*

This is all nicely summarized by the term *Dark Ages*—somewhat out of favor these days but still commonly used even in academic settings when I was growing up—to describe late antiquity, along with the use of *Enlightenment* to describe the intellectual flowering that followed the Renaissance. Nothing really new was created; we just turned the lights on. This

* A recent two-volume survey by the journalist Anthony Gottlieb is typical: It spends four hundred pages on the Greeks and early Romans and another three hundred on the period from Descartes to Kant; the thousand years in between gets a single short chapter: "The Haven of Piety."

isn't just a retrospective gloss on things. Early modern thinkers explicitly described themselves as rejecting received tradition in favor of the abiding features of individual human experience. The term *humanist* dates to the Renaissance, as does *Dark Ages*—and, for that matter, *Renaissance* itself. By the middle of the eighteenth century, the French spoke of a *siècle des Lumières*, while Germans traced the contours of the *Aufklärung*.

THE STORY I'm telling begins with these early moderns, and it can't help implicitly recapitulating this version of events, but I want to complicate it slightly first. One complication is that the Christian view of a transcendent reality more worthy of our attention than the flux of the natural world owes more to Greek philosophy than it does to biblical theism. As the famous formulation goes, Christianity united Athens and Jerusalem, but its metaphysical elements came mostly from the first. In particular, Plato's description of a mental or spiritual plane to which we might ascend through contemplation, achieving unity with an unchanging and eternal Good, became central to Christian metaphysics.

Another complication is that medieval Europe had a robust tradition of empirical science. Unlike Platonism, Christianity does not treat the material world as a degraded representation of transcendent reality and thus unworthy of serious attention. The Judaism from which Christianity emerged holds that the material world is fundamentally good, the creation of a loving God, and that knowledge of this creation is a species of knowledge of God.

It's certainly true that the guiding principles of medieval science differed radically from our modern practice, but this difference too comes down from the Greeks. Following the split between the Western Latin and Eastern Greek Roman Empires, much Greek philosophy was indeed lost to the West for most of a millennium. When it returned in the thirteenth century by way of Jewish and Islamic scholars from the East, the major rediscovery was Plato's student Aristotle, who was the greatest philosophical influence on Catholic intellectual life for the remainder of the medieval period, and this influence was most profound in the study of the natural world.

Unlike Plato, Aristotle took an acute interest in the subject. He left behind treatises on cosmology, animal biology, and many other topics we would now categorize as natural science, and his study of physics was perhaps the centerpiece of his thought. His method was in its way highly empirical: He collected detailed observations from nature, and even his political writings involve catalogs of actually existing regimes rather than abstract speculation about the ideal state.

But Aristotle did not at all reject metaphysics. The word itself derives from the title given to his lectures on the subject. (*Meta* means "after" or "beside," and his *Metaphysics* were either delivered or filed next to his *Physics*.)* Though he broke with Plato on the details, he fundamentally agreed that knowledge could not simply be awareness of the ongoing stream of experience. As he writes at the beginning of his *Physics*, nature presents to us "rather confused masses," until we have the metaphysical categories by which we organize it. This leads to the most distinctive feature of Aristotle's scientific work. He insists that the study of nature must "advance from generalities to particulars," which is to say through deduction. This approach is reflected in his famous and enormously influential syllogistic logic, which likewise begins with generalities and applies them to particular cases, as exemplified in the most famous syllogism: (1) All men are mortal; (2) Socrates is a man; (3) Socrates is mortal.

By showing us the formal structure of reality, the generalities of metaphysics make sense of nature. They separate its necessary and essential

* This doesn't make the name merely arbitrary: As the philosopher Jonathan Lear notes, Aristotle knew what he was after in putting the subjects next to each other.

features from its merely accidental and contingent ones. Metaphysical truth is instantiated in the physical world; the point of metaphysics is not to transcend empirical reality but to understand it.

For nearly every ancient philosopher, the most notable feature of the world of experience was change. Many took this fact to indicate that experience could never provide enduring knowledge. What would it be knowledge *of,* if the source from which we drew it was immediately altered beyond recognition? Aristotle instead concludes that we must come to know the causes of change itself.

For Aristotle, these causes aren't limited to the kind of causes with which modern physics concerns itself. A cause is an answer to the question of why a thing exists as it does. There are plenty of areas where we still view causality in this way. If I see a friend going out for a run and I ask him why he's doing it, he's unlikely to explain to me the physical mechanics that allow for human locomotion. Instead he might tell me that he's training for a marathon in the fall. Because humans have agency, it makes perfect sense to think of that goal—that "telos," from the Greek—as the "cause" of this run, though this means that the cause follows the effect in time.

Similarly, it sometimes makes sense to think about inanimate objects in terms of the ends to which they are put. If you want to know the "why" of a hammer, one answer is that it is made out of metal and wood (its "material cause," in Aristotle's terms). Another answer is that it occurs whenever a heavy metal face that has been shaped in a particular way is joined to a lighter wooden handle (its "formal cause"). We might go further and say that what really *makes* hammers, the real "why" of them, is the physical process by which the metal is shaped and joined to the handle (its "efficient cause"). This kind of cause answers the "why" question by answering the "how" question. All of these causes relate to the hammer as a physical object, apart from its purpose. But if you really want to know what makes something a hammer—rather than, say, a piece of postmodernist found-object sculpture—the most fundamental answer is its telos, which is putting nails into things (its "final cause").

We know this answer because a hammer is a human artifact, made with intention and for a known purpose. But Aristotle applied teleology to his study of the natural world, despite not believing in a conscious creator God who made this world with ends in mind. He didn't argue that natural objects were brought into existence by their final causes, but he insisted that we could not really understand their workings without asking "why" questions that were not simply "how" questions.

Final causes can't be derived empirically, simply by study of the object in question, but in Aristotle's view they give sense to this empirical study. For Aristotle, everything has a telos, and understanding teleology is a key part of understanding the natural world. Why does an acorn fall from a branch? Well, for many reasons, but certainly one of them is that it falls in order to plant itself in the earth and grow into a tree. Acorns exist to become trees—that is their "why." Put differently, acorns are themselves potential trees, and their purpose is to realize this potential.

Reliance on final causation is one of the great differences between Aristotelian science and the modern version. The other is this: Everything I've described above is true only for the endlessly changing terrestrial world. When we look up at the sky, Aristotle noted, what we see there seems relatively fixed, especially compared to the endless churning down here on earth. The heavens move, but they do so in regular and predictable cycles, unlike so much of nature around us.

On the grand scale, Aristotle's picture of the world places the earth at the center of a series of celestial spheres, the first containing the sun, moon, and planets, the subsequent ones containing layers of stars. The spheres rotate around us, but the bodies within them are perfect and unchanging. Change occurs only in the "sublunar" realm. This view of the heavens fits neatly with both Ptolemaic astronomy and the cosmological picture implied by the biblical creation story, and it was central to the medieval worldview.

For hundreds of years, the practice of natural science was dictated by Aristotle's deductive approach. The greatest Catholic philosopher, Saint Thomas Aquinas, dedicated his life to reconciling Aristotle with Christian doctrine, and he felt driven to this goal because he took it as an item of faith that reason and revelation were ultimately consistent with each other. Following Aquinas's example, a robust tradition of "Scholastic" philosophy within medieval universities and monasteries put Aristotle to work in understanding experience through the light of revelation.

Here is another complication in the story, then: All sorts of things about the late medieval worldview might strike us now as irrational, but those who lived within it didn't experience it that way. Medieval elites prized rationality every bit as much as their philosophical descendants do; many features of medieval intellectual life that seem strange to us now—the elaborate moral casuistry and "angels on the head of a pin" speculation—are precisely signs of the era's hyperrationality.

I'm noting this not in defense of medieval Catholic scientific methods but because the features of medieval intellectual life that were most repugnant to early modern thinkers have their roots in Thomistic readings of Aristotle. The great targets of early modern thinkers were "the schoolmen." Often enough modern thinkers rejected the very idea that reason could answer metaphysical questions. Meanwhile, those defending the status quo had on their side a method devised by perhaps the greatest philosopher who ever lived. They did not see themselves as resistant to intellectual inquiry, defending a fundamentally irrational religious view against the encroachment of "science."

A NUMBER OF FACTORS converged to crack open the medieval worldview, making it possible not just for a few eccentrics but for large portions of society to step outside of it. The Protestant Reformation set in motion by Martin Luther in 1517 put the Catholic Church's terrestrial authority into question, initiating a period of horrific religious conflict in which tens of thousands died over minute metaphysical distinctions. This naturally called into doubt both the church's power to settle such disputes and whether it was necessary (or possible) for humans to settle them at all. Technological advancement brought a series of scientific discoveries that dealt fatal blows to Aristotelian physics and cosmology. Finally, global exploration delivered news of cultures in the Americas and eastern Asia that were radically different from Christian Europe, suggesting that what had long been taken as the permanent human order might be better understood as simple custom. Movable-type printing presses—which by 1500 could be found in every major European city—amplified these developments.

One of the earliest and clearest expressions of this convergence comes in the work of Michel de Montaigne. Born into a family of the minor French nobility in 1533, Montaigne spent his early adulthood as a member of the local *parlement.* Upon inheriting his family estate at his father's death in 1568, he resigned this position and retired from public life, spending the next decade reading, thinking, and writing a series of short literary reflections that together stretched to nearly a thousand pages.

Montaigne was fluent in Latin as well as French, and he had a comprehensive knowledge of Roman literature. His study of classical Stoicism and Epicureanism, his knowledge of the most recent discoveries about the human and the natural world, and his frustrating experience with politics during a period of extreme religious conflict all gave him an unusually detached perspective on his own time and place.

In a famous essay, "Of Cannibals," he writes of a friend who lived for a decade in Antarctic France (a colony in present-day Brazil), bringing back stories of tribes who went to war naked, their whole bodies shaved, and, after winning a battle, roasted and ate the vanquished. Reports of Indigenous American life naturally fascinated sixteenth-century Europeans, who tended to be struck by the barbarity of these people whom the news of Christ and the goods of Christian civilization had not yet reached. Montaigne comes to a rather different conclusion: "Each man calls barbarism whatever is not his own practice." He doesn't condone cannibalism, but he wants his peers to look with a similar eye at the cruelty of their own society, particularly the kind unleashed by religious persecution. "There is more barbarity," he writes, "in tearing by tortures and the rack a body still full of feeling . . . than in roasting and eating him after he is dead."

The great cause of religious conflict, in Montaigne's view, was the idea that we could argue rationally about spiritual matters. One might think that the *inability* to argue rationally about such important questions drove people to violence, but Montaigne blames instead the notion that religious questions have a knowable answer to which all people could be expected to consent.

In his longest and most famous essay, "Apology for Raymond Sebond," he expresses his allegiance to Pyrrhonism, a school of ancient skepticism that advocated suspending judgment on any point about which you could not be completely certain. Montaigne's doubt was so profound that he would not even say, as Socrates did, that he knew only that he knew nothing. He preferred to put the matter into the form of a question: "*What do I know?*—the words I bear as a motto, inscribed over a pair of scales."

MONTAIGNE'S TOLERANCE and moderation have made him an intellectual model ever since he first published his *Essais* in 1580. I read some of them in college, not in philosophy courses but in the literature department, where he is (justly) revered as the creator of an enduring literary form, and I came to know him as an exemplary modern figure, a man who threw off the yoke of tradition in favor of a close examination of the self.

I also understood his constant reference to ancient thinkers to be—paradoxically—something new to European intellectual life. Montaigne was the model of the Renaissance humanist who has recovered the wisdom of the past and thus can see beyond the confining strictures of the Christian era. As I understood it, Montaigne's skepticism had been an influence on his followers ever since.

Reading his work in its entirety a few years later, I found something slightly different. First of all, Montaigne's essays contain countless expressions of Christian piety. Present-day readers often take such professions of faith among early modern thinkers as self-protective fig leaves, and this is clearly correct in some cases, but Montaigne seems sincere in his belief, and he actually anticipates the charge, writing of "those who in recent years had the habit of reproaching each and every man in whom there gleamed some light of intelligence and who professed the Catholic religion, with dissimulation; and who even maintained, thinking to do him honor, that whatever he said for appearance, he could not help having his belief within reformed according to their measure."

All evidence suggests that Montaigne was a sincere believer. Does this suggest hypocrisy? Was he not, after all, the skeptic he claimed to be? Quite the opposite. Skepticism about human knowledge motivated his belief. What struck him most about the doctrinal disputes between Catholics and Protestants was that they attempted to argue rationally about details without recognizing that the entire system rested on faith: "We do not probe the base, where the fault and weakness lies; we dispute only about the branches."

When you did probe the base, you found that nothing was grounded in reason. And if the foundation wasn't grounded, what use was reason for building upon it? "Now there cannot be first principles for men, unless the Divinity has revealed them; all the rest—beginning, middle, and end—is nothing but dreams and smoke." Montaigne did not at all oppose taking things on faith. Given the limits of reason, he thought, we had no choice but to do so. We don't need to stop taking things on faith; we need to stop imagining that the principles we've taken on faith were arrived at through reason and that we can reason other people into sharing them.

I had not been wrong, then, to see Montaigne's skepticism as a major influence on the thinkers who followed. But I eventually came to understand this influence very differently. Those who followed Montaigne treated his extreme skepticism less as inspiration than as challenge. Montaigne did not seek to replace the prevailing Scholastic rationalism with a new, secular rationalism. He replaced it instead with pure faith, because his skepticism told him that this was the only available option. For those who wanted to move beyond faith, skepticism would become not a rallying cry but a problem to be solved.

If we can't rely on religious tradition or scriptural revelation or ecclesiastic authority to deliver the truth, what can we possibly know? Reading Montaigne gave me my first suggestion of the challenge this question actually presents.

Three

THE BOUNDS OF HUMAN EMPIRE

Not long after Montaigne's *Essais* appeared, the statesman and philosopher Francis Bacon brought the word into English for his own collection of short meditations. The first of Bacon's essays, "Of Truth," explicitly invokes skeptics in Montaigne's mode, who "count it a bondage to fix a belief." Bacon admired Montaigne—he quotes him approvingly in this same essay—but he insisted that it was possible to establish a foundation on which real knowledge could be built. For Bacon, that foundation was practical use.

Ancient philosophers had long distinguished between the *vita contemplativa* and the *vita activa*, arguing over which was the higher calling. Bacon aimed to join contemplation and action—both in theory and in the conduct of his own life. Like Montaigne, he had a political career that influenced his philosophical work, though his unfolded far closer to centers of power, including stints as England's attorney general, solicitor general, and lord chancellor. Retiring voluntarily from public life and dedicating himself to study would have been inimical to Bacon.* He was constantly considering how his philosophical thought could be put to practical use.

* Instead his career ended ignominiously and involuntarily, by way of a bribery conviction.

When James I ascended to the throne in 1603, Bacon published a treatise in which he called on the new king to be a patron of intellectual life. *The Advancement of Learning*'s first volume considers the factors that had impeded the accumulation of knowledge up to that point. In Bacon's view, the greatest impediment of all was "the mistaking or misplacing of the last or furthest end of knowledge." That end, Bacon insists, is "the benefit and use of men." A true flowering of knowledge would occur only when "contemplation and actions [were] more nearly and straitly conjoined."

Bacon did not just believe as an ethical or political matter that learning ought to have the aim of human betterment; he believed as an epistemological matter that usefulness was our best test of knowledge. The way out of Montaigne's skeptical morass was "to separate and reject vain speculations and whatsoever is empty and void, and to preserve and augment whatsoever is solid and fruitful."

The key to Bacon's rejection of "vain speculation" was his distinction between physics and metaphysics. In Bacon's view, both disciplines concern the natural world, but metaphysics studies final causes, while physics studies efficient ones. In theory, separating the two need not mean rejecting the reality of final causes, "both causes being true and compatible, the one declaring an intention, the other a consequence only." In practice, however, the matter is somewhat different. If the test of knowledge is the ends to which it can be put, then all real knowledge must be knowledge of consequence, not intention.

IN HIS MAGNUM OPUS, *Novum Organum*, Bacon outlines a method for doing science without consideration of final cause, which turns Aristotle on his head. Rather than moving from generalities to particulars, the aim is to start with "the senses and particulars" and end with "the greatest generalities."

In place of Aristotelian deduction we have Baconian induction: One proceeds by gathering empirical data about the natural world without any preexisting metaphysical framework. This data must then be collected and organized so it can be objectively studied to allow for the gradual movement from particulars to generalized axioms, which can then be used as guides to structure further empirical study. That is a vital point: Aristotle is correct that we can't have any real knowledge of the natural world without general principles; his mistake is to think we can derive these principles abstractly. We must always start with the particulars, and the general truths we derive from them are always provisional, subject to change on the basis of new evidence.

A key feature of the inducive method in Bacon's view is that it builds on itself, producing new technologies that can be used for the "betterment of mankind" and also allow for more sophisticated experiments and thus more sophisticated technologies, creating a kind of feedback loop, forever accelerating the rate of progress. Bacon's most popular work offers a picture of what this will mean for humanity.

The New Atlantis is a speculative fiction about the discovery of an island culture that has attained a utopian level of material comfort through the creation of a kind of research institute called Salomon's House. "The End of our Foundation is the knowledge of Causes, and secret motions of things," the house's director tells the narrator, "and the enlarging of the bounds of Human Empire, to the effecting of all things possible." Through a program of "new experiments, or a higher light, more penetrating into nature than the former," the researchers at Salomon's House have produced effects that would have seemed fanciful to Bacon's contemporaries but are strikingly similar to refrigeration, air-conditioning, photography, sound recording, and other modern-day technologies.

For Bacon, these technologies and the improvement of human life that they allow are a definitive refutation of skepticism. It would be absurd to wonder, for example, whether the kind of data gathered from controlled experiments is telling us something "true" about life outside the conditions of the laboratory. It has passed the one test of truth that matters: It can be put to use.

BACON IS OFTEN CITED as the first philosopher of the modern era. His chief competitor for this title was also influenced heavily by Montaigne's skepticism, and he also sought a way out of it. Born into a Catholic family in 1596, René Descartes was sent at a young age to be educated by the Jesuits. He excelled at mathematics, which he loved "on account of the certitude and evidence of their reasonings," and this certitude became his standard for all human knowledge.

He rejected philosophy on grounds similar to Montaigne's—that "it had been cultivated for many ages by the most distinguished men, and that yet there is not a single matter within its sphere which is not still in dispute, and nothing, therefore, which is above doubt." The natural sciences as practiced at the time he also rejected, because they "borrow their principles from philosophy," that is, they relied on Aristotelian metaphysical speculation.

Once old enough to leave school, Descartes "entirely abandoned the study of letters, and resolved no longer to seek any other science than the knowledge of myself, or of the great book of the world." He acquired a position as a mercenary officer in the Dutch army, putting his mathematical talent to practical use in the form of military engineering. This career took him throughout Protestant Europe, which led him to share Montaigne's view that "the ground of our opinions is far more custom and example than any certain knowledge."

Descartes's mathematical studies suggested, however, that a kind of certain knowledge was in fact possible, contrary to the tenets of Montaigne's

Pyrrhonian skepticism, and he set out to determine just how far such knowledge could extend. In the event, he extended it quite a way: Using the procedures of geometry, in which "long chains of simple and easy reasonings" can be followed to arrive at the "most difficult demonstrations," Descartes proceeded from a point of radical skepticism to a fairly complete picture of the world. He gathered much of his findings into a series of scientific essays, which he published in 1637 alongside an explanation of his philosophical approach, entitled *Discourse on the Method of Rightly Conducting the Reason and Seeking Truth in the Sciences.*

The *Discourse* tells the story of his intellectual development and outlines the rules with which he began his study. The first rule was "never to accept anything for true which [he] did not clearly know to be such." The second was "to divide each of the difficulties under examination into as many parts as possible, and as might be necessary for its adequate solution." The third was to start "with objects the simplest and easiest to know" and move "step by step, to the knowledge of the more complex." The final rule was "to make enumerations so complete, and reviews so general, that [he] might be assured that nothing was omitted."

His initial rejection of uncertain knowledge included not just what comes from our senses, which we know to be fallible, but even the supposedly certain truths of mathematics. It's clearly possible to be wrong about a mathematical fact. I'm confident that one plus one equals two, but perhaps I have miscounted. Or perhaps—as Descartes hypothesizes in a later work, *Meditations on First Philosophy*—some malign deity has tricked me into accepting various mathematical truths that are actually false, even structuring my mind such that I can only ever arrive at the wrong answer when adding one and one.

As Descartes sees it, there is a single point on which such an entity could not possibly deceive me: The moment I think anything at all, even some falsehood I've been deceived into thinking, I can be certain that my thinking self exists. "Cogito ergo sum," as the famous Latin rendering of the *Meditations* goes.

DESCARTES REVERSE ENGINEERS a criterion for truth in general by asking how it is that he knows this one certain truth. He has concluded that "I think, therefore I am" is indubitable, he finds, because its necessity is "clear and distinct," and he arrives at the general principle that "all the things which we very clearly and distinctly conceive are true."

Armed with this epistemological rule, he proceeds to establish (at least to his own satisfaction) the existence of an omnipotent and benevolent God. First he notes the clear and distinct fact that he—that is, the thinking thing—is capable of doubt or uncertainty. This leads to the clear and distinct conclusion that he is a limited and imperfect being, and his awareness of limitation and imperfection puts in his mind the idea of a perfect being. But conceiving of a perfect being is not the same as conceiving of a unicorn or a triangle or some other thing that may or may not actually exist apart from one's own conception of it. Nonexistence is a kind of imperfection, and so a perfect being that doesn't exist is a logical contradiction. If you can clearly conceive of such an entity, there *is* such an entity.

Since Descartes is articulating one of the classic "proofs" for the existence of God, here may be the place to say a bit more about the general form such proofs take. Theology was historically divided into two species—natural and revealed. Natural theology concerns knowledge of God arrived at through reason, while revealed theology concerns knowledge of God arrived at through revelation, whether primary (personal religious experience) or secondary (biblical sources and prophetic testimony). "Natural" arguments for God's existence can be further divided into "a priori" and "a posteriori," depending on whether they argue from general terms or from particular features of our experience.

Descartes's argument that the very concept or definition of God entails existence is a standard a priori move, common enough to have its own name—the Ontological Proof. It dates back at least to Saint Anselm in 1078. (Most medieval theologians, including Aquinas, rejected it.) Setting aside for now how plausible it sounds, this proves an essential step for Descartes, because the existence of a benevolent and omnipotent God is the guarantor that we are not in thrall to some malign deceiver and thus that we can trust at least some of what experience tells us about reality. (You might notice that the "clear and distinct" rule was used to prove God's existence before God's existence was used to undergird the rule, which goes to show how hard it actually is to build foundations on nothing.)

Returning to his "clear and distinct" criterion, Descartes attempts to determine what amid the chaotic swirl of sense experience meets that standard. He concludes that this world is unquestionably spatial—it has "extension in length, breadth, and depth," as he puts it in the *Meditations*—and that within this extensive space are "many diverse parts" with "all sorts of sizes, figures, situations, and local motions."

Descartes hypothesizes that differences in extension and motion lead to differences in how bodies are perceived, but that the "stuff" in motion is uniform. We do not have the famous four elements of classical physics; fire, water, earth, and air are all the same sort of matter. When this matter takes on a particular shape and moves in a particular way, it produces in us the perception of a particular color, taste, texture, or temperature. If we want certain knowledge, we must remove these subjective attributes from consideration and attend to the objective facts of motion and shape.

So we have a reality composed of two very different substances. On the one hand, the res cogitans, the thinking thing—an incorporeal mental substance that has no extension and thus no place in the physical world. On the other hand, the res extensa, the plane of physical reality, in which a singular corporeal substance takes on various forms as its divergent parts move around in a highly mechanized fashion. Within this world, even the human body can be understood as "a kind of machine." But there's one difference between our bodies and all other bodies, from rocks and dirt up to the most complex nonhuman animals: Ours are occupied by minds; we are each "lodged in [our] body as a pilot in a vessel."

Descartes meant his dualism to create a space for the study of the physical world untouched by spiritual belief. He intended to include his treatise on physics, *The World*, among the works published alongside the *Discourse*, but he suppressed it after the Inquisition convicted Galileo for publishing similar views. The work proceeds by adopting the more or less Deist view that God's participation in the physical world is limited to creating it, setting it into motion, and imposing the laws by which it runs. This is presented as a methodological claim, not a theological one: Like Bacon, Descartes simply wants to set aside fruitless philosophical speculations by confining himself to efficient causes. But the fact that doing so can give us a complete picture of reality must tell us something about reality itself. The "why" of things can always be explained by the "how"—that is, by reference to some prior physical state and the laws that govern physical behavior. It is not just (as Bacon has it) that final cause is best studied by metaphysicians rather than physicists, but that the physical order (as opposed to the mental one) shows no sign of purpose and thus teleological thinking has nothing to teach us about it.

DESCARTES'S WORKING TITLE for the *Discourse on Method* was *Plan for a Universal Science Capable of Raising Our Nature to Its Highest Degree of*

Perfection. If all matter is ultimately the same—there is no unchanging heavenly ether, but nor are there fundamental differences between earthly elements, or even between animate and inanimate objects—then astronomy, chemistry, and biology all ought to be reducible to physics. This reduction is the first step toward that universal science.

But there's more reduction to be done. Descartes's version of physical reality—an extended field of uniform points organized into shapes in motion—allows the physical world to be "comprehended in the object of speculative geometry." In "The Geometry"—one of the essays he *did* publish alongside the *Discourse*—Descartes describes the Cartesian coordinate plane (i.e., the X and Y axes), which remains among his greatest intellectual legacies. With it, geometric forms can be expressed as algebraic equations. Having reduced all the natural sciences to physics and physics to geometry, we can further reduce geometry to algebra.*

This mathematical model is a radical simplification of the reality that our senses present to us, but this is a point in the method's favor. Although he believed in studying the "book of the world," Descartes was no empiricist. Our fallible senses can't possibly be the true source of knowledge, as he saw things: "Bodies themselves are not properly perceived by the sense nor by the faculty of the imagination, but by the intellect alone." It's not just that setting aside certain features of reality allows us to study it more exactly. Descartes seems to believe that this simplified, geometric scheme is what physical reality is *actually like*. All of the confusions and contradictions come from the imperfection of our senses, not from reality itself.

The mathematical view of nature relates directly to the belief that we apprehend reality primarily through reason rather than through our senses. To return to some philosophical language that will be coming up a fair

* In the generation after Descartes, Newton and Leibniz would develop differential calculus as a better means of quantifying reality, but Descartes precedes them in the assertion that all of reality ought to be expressible in mathematical form.

amount, mathematical truth is a form of a priori rather a posteriori knowledge; it comes through proof and demonstration, prior to and apart from experience of the world. In practice, most people learn mathematical basics through counting actual objects, and in almost every case, you ought to be able to "do" math in this way, but if I add one apple to two apples and find that I still have only two, I know that I've done something wrong. Mathematical truths aren't provisional. No experimental result could convince me that two plus one is two.

If you believe that the world is fundamentally mathematical in nature, it's natural also to believe that we can have a priori knowledge about the world. If you are seeking certain knowledge and are especially struck by the fallibility of our senses, you might think that a priori knowledge is in fact the only real knowledge there is. The truths of Cartesian physics ought to be consistent with our experience of the physical world, just like mathematical truths, but reason rather than experience is their ultimate source and guarantor. In philosophical terms, Descartes is a "rationalist" where Bacon is an "empiricist," and their two distinct responses to Montaigne's skepticism will become the two major options for modern philosophy.

In the story I'm telling, Descartes's rationalism is best understood as the starting point of the tradition that will culminate in the other major modern-day atheist worldview, which I'm calling romantic idealism. But he's such an important philosophical thinker that neither tradition can be understood without him. He matters to scientific materialism because he rejected tradition and revelation without falling into Pyrrhonian skepticism. While he disagreed with empiricists about how we best acquire knowledge about physical reality, he shared their goal of quantifying this knowledge. His method of breaking problems up into their smallest possible constituent parts would be the foundation of the analytic approach that would eventually emerge from philosophical empiricism. Finally,

Descartes expressed the tradition's greatest aspiration: to develop a "universal science," and to put that science to the use of human perfection.

Because Descartes is so important to the modern tradition, and because his most significant philosophical texts are short and relatively straightforward, he is one of the few thinkers in these pages whose work I knew well from introductory undergraduate philosophy courses. I thought of him as one of the first great secular thinkers. When I began reading modern-day atheists, I was surprised to note their hostility toward him, particularly toward his mind-body dualism.

Scientific materialists are quick to note the obvious problems with Cartesian dualism, not least of them being how exactly the wholly immaterial thinking thing and the extended material world could ever possibly interact with each other. (Descartes's answer—that the soul is lodged in the pineal gland—doesn't inspire much confidence.) Many modern commentators treat this criticism of dualism as applying equally to theist spiritualism, which also surprised me, because I recognized Descartes's radical mind-body separation as a major break from the traditional Christian view of the physical world as everywhere permeated by spiritual reality. I had often prayed the Apostles' Creed, in which I expressed belief in the "resurrection of the body," a belief grounded in the Catholic understanding that our soul is not just the "pilot of the vessel," sitting behind the controls somewhere, but the body's animating force, intimately bound up in it.

Descartes takes a step away from orthodox Christianity with his separation of mind from body, allowing the body to be studied as a purely physical object. Modern-day atheists take a further step with their rejection of the possibility that there is anything at all that needs to be separated out, anything that can't be understood in physical terms. For all its very real shortcomings, Cartesian dualism attempts to give a nonspiritual solution to what I was quickly coming to recognize as atheism's greatest challenge: what to do with the human mind.

Four

THE RESTLESS DESIRE OF POWER

In their different ways, Bacon and Descartes both separated the physical from the mental, applying their objectifying methods only to the first. Both left metaphysics to rule those subjects we now assign to the social sciences—human customs and behavior, political and social arrangements—which were then collectively called "morals." It doesn't seem immediately possible to remove consideration of human minds from such matters, which are defined by intentions, desires, final causes. Yet the decline of the old certainties posed perhaps its greatest challenges in precisely these areas, so it was a major shortcoming of any secular philosophy to leave them untouched.

The first great secular social theorist was also one of the first modern thinkers explicitly charged with atheism. Thomas Hobbes was born in 1588, and he lived long enough to witness (and participate in) nearly a century of political unrest. As a young man, he worked briefly as Bacon's secretary, but he spent the bulk of his early adult life as tutor to an aristocratic family, which brought him into contact with many of the era's greatest minds. The English civil wars forced him into Parisian exile, where he corresponded at length with Descartes and briefly tutored the exiled

English king in waiting, Charles II. There he also wrote his most famous work.

Though its stated subject is "The Matter, Forme, & Power of a Common-Wealth Ecclesiasticall and Civill," Hobbes's *Leviathan* begins with a lengthy consideration of human thought and behavior. The book aims to develop a political science that meets the Cartesian standard of clear and certain knowledge, which means collapsing the distinction between the human as thinking thing and the human as bodily object. Hobbes does this by rejecting Cartesian dualism in favor of materialism. Simply put, he tells us that the Cartesian res extensa—the physical world of matter in motion—is all that exists. Everything is matter.

For Hobbes, animate matter differs from inanimate only in being capable of internally generated motion: "Life is but a motion of Limbs, the beginning whereof is in some principall part within." Human beings are essentially indistinguishable not just from other animals but from the self-moving machines like clocks and engines that were the great technology of the day: "For what is the *Heart*, but a *Spring*; and the *Nerves*, but so many *Strings*; and the *Joynts*, but so many *Wheeles*, giving motion to the whole Body, such as was intended by the Artificer?" The soul is simply that which gives "life and motion to the whole body." Anything that is self-moving, and therefore has life, must also have a soul of some sort. The tension wound into its springs is the "soul" of the watch—the internal force that sets it going.

This doesn't solve the mind-body problem, which concerns not just how internally generated movements happen but how they are accompanied (and, at least apparently, driven) by conscious thought. In Hobbes's account, perception occurs when an external object presses itself against our sense organs. In the case of taste and touch, this pressure is direct; in the case of other senses, it is indirect. A book falls from the pile on my desk. This motion disturbs the air, and this disturbance makes its way to my eyes and ears, by way of which it causes motion within my body: "By the mediation of Nerves, and other strings, and membranes of the body, continued inwards to the Brain, and Heart, [this disturbance] causeth there a resistance, or counter-pressure, or endeavour of the heart to deliver itself: which endeavour because *Outward*, seemeth to be some matter without."

Memories, dreams, and other conscious states are likewise motions taking place within our bodies. The motion caused by the falling book reverberates inside us long after the book has left our sight, and this "decaying sense" is imagination or memory. These fading motions are drowned out by the continuing stream of new motions coming into our bodies, but while we sleep, we stop taking in new motions, which allows various motions earlier set off by waking experience to continue on. Meanwhile, the natural processes of our organs churn up more motion. This combination leads to dreams, in which various qualities of sensory objects are combined in strange and vivid ways.

Hobbes is not simply saying that this motion *causes* our sense experiences. This motion *is* our sense experience. The sensible qualities of external objects are really "so many several motions of the matter," and thus their effects must likewise be internal motion—"for motion, produceth nothing but motion."

The materialist theory of reality has been around at least since the time of the pre-Socratic Greeks, but for most of philosophical history it was treated as fairly eccentric, because it has obvious problems capturing the full range of reality as we experience it. Hobbes's treatment of thought as inner motion lacks the feature that medieval philosophers called *intentio.* In the specialized philosophical sense, "intentionality" indicates not conscious purpose but direction at or toward something. Entities with intentionality point to something other than themselves. They have content; they are "about" something.

When the physical consequences of that book's fall from the table reach my eyes and ears, interior physical motions certainly do result, but the relevant fact for me is that these motions involve a perception *of* the falling book. Hobbes's account gives no explanation for how some physical events inside my body can be "about" external physical events in this way. Accounting for intentionality seems to require some interior mental entity who is experiencing all this bodily motion, above and beyond the fact of the motion itself, and that immediately invites in the specter of dualism.

THE ABSENCE OF intentionality raises too the problem of free will. If there is no Cartesian pilot in the driver's seat, no entity experiencing our experiences, what guides our thoughts in certain directions and puts those thoughts into action through motivated behavior?

In Hobbes's account, the great motivator of action is *desire*. Our body has basic physical desires—e.g., for food and drink and warmth. Speaking more generally, certain internal motions give us pleasure, while others cause us pain. What we call "hunger," for example, is a physical discomfort, which produces the desire to remove that discomfort by satisfying our hunger. In fact, we might do better to think of the discomfort and the desire to alleviate it as the same thing; after all, there is no separate entity experiencing the discomfort and acting accordingly. We naturally seek out pleasure and avoid pain. This is indeed what makes the one pleasure and the other pain. Meanwhile, whatever gives us pleasure we say that we "love" and we call "good." Whatever gives us pain we say that we "hate" and we call "evil."

In addition to the various things we value this way, there is one meta-value: the power to attain goods and avoid evils. This is the greatest good of all, since we can't have any other good without it. For this reason, the "general inclination of all mankind" is "a perpetuall and restlesse desire of Power after power, that ceaseth onely in Death."

All these desires—which must themselves be just motions in the body—cause other motions that are thoughts of how our desires might be met. We want to know what goods might satisfy our desires and what actions might bring us these goods. Our search for knowledge about the world is inevitably a search after causes, and this search is an expression of our endless desire for power.

IN ITS PUREST FORM, our knowledge of the world is entirely unmediated. The external world quite literally pushes itself on us, producing sense experience. But humans have developed a unique set of tools for organizing these experiences to meet our desires. Those tools are words.

Language allows us to receive reports from others about *their* sensory experiences, dramatically increasing our own store of knowledge, and it allows us to put matters of fact into relationships that dramatically increase our ability to seek out cause and effect. This capability allows us to engage in thinking far more powerful and complex than that of any other animal, but it also causes our thinking to go wrong in often catastrophic ways. It is by language alone that man becomes "excellently wise," but also by language alone that man becomes "excellently foolish."

By mediating experience, language creates the possibility of error. An unmediated experience can never be "incorrect," but the moment we describe it in language, the potential for falsehood arises. This can occur when someone reports as a matter of fact something that isn't the case, but it can also occur when we use faulty reasoning to derive from actual matters of fact unsupported conclusions. Finally, language makes possible statements that aren't even false but nonsensical.

In Hobbes's view, all legitimate speech consists of "Names or Appellations, and their Connexion." That is, we can appropriately use language to describe or name objects and attributes drawn from sense experience, to describe or name these descriptions themselves (as with terms like "general" and "particular"), or to put these names and descriptions into relation with each other.

A key contention of empiricism and of scientific materialism follows from this view of language: All real knowledge concerns either matters of fact or matters of logic. There is no such thing as a priori knowledge in the sense of substantive knowledge that is independent of experience. There is on one hand the basic raw material of experience and on the other the logical operations we perform to turn this raw material into generally applicable knowledge. Whenever language concerns something beyond these two categories, it is essentially meaningless.

The proper purpose of language is to stand in for the facts of experience, so that we may share and manipulate these facts in various ways. Within this scheme, some linguistic steps away from immediate experience are perfectly legitimate. We have experience of particular cats, but we can never experience the class or type "cat." Yet universals of this sort are incredibly useful for the seeking out of cause and effect, provided we don't make the Platonic mistake of treating the type as somehow real. But there are also abstract names—Hobbes gives the examples of "Entity, Intentionality, Quiddity, and other insignificant words of the School"—that seem to refer to reality without really describing anything drawn from sense experience. Here Hobbes anticipates what is still the most common defense of materialism's apparent shortcomings: We don't need materialist explanations of things like "intentionality," because these are just words used by philosophers. The very fact that they don't correspond to any material reality means that we can simply do without them.

Hobbes's criticisms apply particularly to religious language. By the theologians' own account, we can never experience the infinite attributes of God. But then what is it that we are even talking about when we use such words as *God* and *infinity*? "None of these things ever have, or can be incident to Sense," Hobbes tells us; thus they are "absurd speeches, taken upon credit (without any signification at all,) from deceived Philosophers, and deceived, or deceiving Schoolmen."

Naturally, he can't go so far as to say that there is simply no basis for belief in God. He argues instead that our relentless seeking after causes leads us to the legitimate conclusion that there must be some first or original cause of everything, and we call this cause "God," though we can't have any real knowledge about it. He (carefully) concludes that "the Name of God is used, not to make us conceive him; (for he is *Incomprehensible*; and his greatnesse and power are inconceivable;) but that we may honour him."

In placing God at the beginning of an otherwise endless causal chain, Hobbes makes the so-called first-mover argument, one of the most common a posteriori proofs for God's existence. He seems more or less to accept the argument, though it's difficult to tell for sure, since explicit atheism was extremely dangerous at the time, and Hobbes makes it elsewhere very clear that he doesn't think it reasonable to risk one's life over such matters. Unlike Montaigne, Hobbes invites the suspicion that he is being less than honest about his personal views on the matter. At the very least we can say that for Hobbes the concept of causality was drawn from sensory experience, and thus speculation about the initial cause of all things was not in his view necessarily empty or nonsensical.

But the first mover is an extremely minimal concept of God. As soon as we apply attributes to this entity—when we call it infinite, omnipotent, omniscient, or incorporeal (i.e., spiritual rather than physical)—we are dealing with concepts about which we have no possible experience, and thus we've entered the realm of absurd speech. Religious conceptions of

God are obviously much more robust. In Hobbes's account, these too come from our concern with causality. Firstly, man—who is constantly thinking of his own pleasure and pain—wonders at the cause of his good or bad fortune, especially relative to others'. He also wonders about his future state, which is subject to unknown causes outside his control and thus a source of anxiety: Man "hath his heat all the day long, gnawed on by feare of death, poverty, or other calamity and has no repose, nor pause of this anxiety, but in sleep." This anxiety—along with a more general desire to understand the causes of events whose physical causes are obscure to us—encourages a belief in gods as invisible powers capable of acting in the world, and the desire to curry the favor of these powers through praise, gifts, and obedience.

THIS ALL LEADS to Hobbes's central concern: political power. Earthly sovereigns claim to rule with divine consent, or even to be divinities themselves. They claim to root their laws in religious commandments, and they tell religious stories that serve their mundane needs. In Hobbes's view, none of these claims can be justified. But then, what *is* the rational justification for terrestrial authority?

We don't need an explanation for why some people assert power over others, which is entirely natural. But why do the rest of us submit to these assertions—insofar as we do—and when is it appropriate to resist them? While political science is not my subject, the emergence of modern atheism required the development of secular theories of power, and Hobbes is one of the first to offer one. Furthermore, his particular version rests on an understanding of human nature that will be incredibly important to the development of materialist ethics, so I'm going to take a moment with it.

Hobbes seeks the legitimate basis of political authority by considering man's condition in the absence of such authority. The primary alternative to religious accounts of legitimate political power had long been the idea of a natural-born hierarchy. Most ancient Greeks, for example, took it for granted that some people were simply born to rule and others to serve, just as some were born to be philosophers and others soldiers or craftsmen. But in Hobbes's "state of nature," most people are basically equal in their powers. This sounds like a good thing, but equality creates a major problem. All people naturally strive after the same goods, creating inevitable conflict. In the absence of any clear competitive advantage, this battle over goods is endless. Thus the state of nature is a state of "such a warre, as is every man, against every man." In this state, as Hobbes's famous phrasing goes, "the life of man [is] solitary, poore, nasty, brutish, and short."

The state of war is not caused by human evil. It arises when we each act for our own good. Since the only inherent good is one's own pleasure and the only inherent evil is one's own pain, we don't commit any inherent evil when we harm another in pursuit of our own good. In the state of nature, other people do not have rights that we are bound to respect. The only right we naturally recognize is our own right to any good it is in our power to acquire.

Nonetheless, when everyone exercises this right, the result is bad for all. Our very lives—the source of all our power and thus the greatest good—are under constant threat. Reason therefore dictates certain natural laws. (For Hobbes, a natural law is just a precept discoverable by reason that dictates behavior preserving of life.) Since the state of war is a constant threat to life, the first natural law is that one ought to create the conditions for peace. The most promising conditions for peace are clear to human reason, and so a second law emerges from the first: You ought to be willing to trade your own right to pursue your ends, accepting only as much liberty as you allow others against you.

This "mutuall transferring of Right" is a contract, but contracts are useless if people don't keep their word, and so there emerges a third natural law: "That men performe their Covenants made." With the arrival of this law, justice appears, for it is only with this law that we can reasonably make demands on the behavior of others and reasonably accept limits on our own.

Other natural laws emerge from these three, all reasonably summarized by the rule propounded by nearly every major religion: "Do not that to another, which thou wouldest not have done to thy selfe." These laws apply wherever we have a reasonable expectation that others will be bound by them, for it is only under such conditions that they will have their life-preserving effect. However, they *are* laws, in the same manner as the laws of mathematics: They are fixed and eternal, drawn not from the changing mores of human culture but from enduring axioms of reason.

Our own self-interest dictates obedience to these laws, so long as we have a reasonable certainty that others will likewise obey. Yet the laws themselves run contrary to our natural impulse to expend all our power in pursuit of our own ends, without concern for the good of others. This dynamic creates one of those collective-action problems beloved by modern-day game theorists. For any given individual, the best possible outcome is one in which everyone *else* obeys the law, while the individual preserves maximal liberty. Yet if everyone pursues this outcome, the result is the state of war, which is the worst possible condition for all.

The solution is that we all submit to a unitary power capable of ensuring widespread obedience. The collective powers of all the individuals in a particular place are put at the disposal of a single sovereign who uses these powers to protect his subjects' lives. The result is "the Generation of that Great LEVIATHAN, or rather (to speake more reverently) of that *Mortall God*, to which wee owe under the *Immortall God*, our peace and defence."

THE RESTLESS DESIRE OF POWER

WHILE HOBBES IS remembered primarily as a political thinker, his importance for my story is his status as perhaps the first modern materialist, and his political thought shows clearly some of the enduring implications of this metaphysical view. Hobbes argues that a materialist ethic must be grounded in the physical sensations of pain and pleasure, and that "good" and "evil" can be comprehensible only as names for these sensations. But since the only pain and pleasure we can possibly experience is our own, it follows that any rational individual will be concerned for his or her *own* good.

Many modern materialists find Hobbes's view of the human condition needlessly dim. As an empirical matter, they say, it is simply not true that the natural human state is a war of all against all. In fact, humans have a natural tendency to cooperate. But as a theoretical matter, these materialists still generally seek to identify some deeper self-interest at work in our cooperation. And necessarily so, for it is difficult to explain in material terms any behavior that isn't grounded in self-interest. In this view, the basis of all apparently selfless behavior must be some arrangement that rewards us for this behavior. Later materialists don't share Hobbes's preference for an absolute sovereign to serve this function, but they are all faced with the question of how a natural concern for one's own interests can be made into a rational concern for the interests of all.

Five

THE EMPTY CABINET

In one of the great ironies of philosophical history, Hobbes's defense of absolute power ran him afoul of the absolute powers in France (and his fellow English royalists in exile), who did not appreciate his treatment of religion. After *Leviathan*'s publication in 1651, he returned to England, then a republic under the control of Oliver Cromwell, with whom he struck a very Hobbesian deal, giving up writing on politics in exchange for his life.

The 1660 Stuart restoration didn't much change his circumstances. Charles II brought Hobbes back to court and gave him a small pension but refused him the right to publish *Behemoth*, his history of the civil wars. Parliament subsequently investigated his work for tending to encourage "atheism, blasphemy and profaneness," and he was forced to stop publishing entirely. He occupied the remainder of his years with topics unrelated to politics, translating Homer into English and attempting to solve the geometric problem of squaring the circle. He also got involved in what might seem an odd intellectual dispute for a protoempiricist.

Soon after the restoration, Charles gave a charter to the Royal Society of London for Improving Natural Knowledge. Founded by the chemist Robert Boyle on the model of Bacon's Salomon's House, the Royal Society became the more or less official home for the emerging experimental approach to natural philosophy, an approach that Hobbes spent the last years of his life attacking relentlessly.

Hobbes objected first of all to the artificial nature of Boyle's laboratory experiments, but he objected more generally to the necessary starting point for inductive knowledge, the collection of "grosse experience" through trial and error. Because nature consists in physical bodies in motion, he argued in Cartesian style, the foundation for our study of it must come from the "Mother of all Naturall Sciences": geometry. Without it, there is "no Sowing, nor Planting of Knowledge by it self, apart from the Weeds, and common Plants of Errour and Conjecture." In other words, Hobbes believed that his materialist conception of reality demanded a deductive epistemology.

Boyle engaged Hobbes in debates on the subject, but he was generally more interested in practice than in theory. It was mostly left to another Royal Society member, Boyle's former student John Locke, to provide the philosophical underpinnings to the Society's approach. Locke was a less distinguished practitioner than fellow Society members like Boyle, Newton, and Edmond Halley, but his theoretical writing brought experimental empiricism into its own.

As he describes it in the early pages of his *Essay Concerning Human Understanding* (1689), Locke was in conversation with a group of friends, "discoursing on a subject very remote" from epistemology, when they "found themselves quickly at a stand, by the difficulties that rose on every side." Before going any further, Locke proposed, they needed to "examine [their] own abilities, and see what objects [their] understandings were, or were not fitted to deal with." He wanted to ask questions in some sense even more fundamental than Montaigne's "What do I know?": What can I *possibly* know? What *is* human knowledge?

His answer took nearly twenty years and more than six hundred pages, but the short version is that knowledge consists of *ideas.* Locke uses this term in a specialized sense, to describe the basic building blocks of all mental activity. "Simple" ideas are the irreducible elements from which mental life is constructed—colors, smells, the feel of hardness or softness, hot or cold, but also pleasure and pain, as well as seemingly more abstract concepts like existence, unity, and sequence. All our thoughts are built from ideas; they are the objects our understanding is "fitted to deal with."

The mind begins as an "empty cabinet," and we gather through experience a storehouse of ideas with which we fill its shelves. Ideas come into the cabinet through two means: Sensation gives us ideas of the qualities of external objects, and reflection gives us ideas of the operation of our own mind. It is impossible to invent a simple idea or to reason one's way into one; they can only be impressed upon us by one of these two forms of experience.

Once the mind has built up a store of simple ideas, it operates on them, combining them, relating them to each other in various ways, and abstracting them "from all other ideas that accompany them in their real existence." All real knowledge is either knowledge of simple ideas drawn immediately from experience or knowledge of complex ideas created through the combination of simple ones. Specifically, Locke defines knowledge as "the perception of the connexion and agreement, or disagreement and repugnancy of any of our ideas."

Sometimes two ideas stand in such close relationship that their agreement or disagreement is immediately apparent to us. A person who possesses the simple ideas "black" and "red" knows intuitively that they "disagree"—an object can't have both characteristics at the same time. Just as we can't describe simple ideas to another person who has not experienced them, we can't demonstrate an intuitive truth about their immediate relationship. There is no "proof" that black is black or that black is not red. A person simply possesses this knowledge or not.

Since most ideas do not stand in such immediate relationship, reason must arrive at their agreement or disagreement through the use of intermediate steps. When this process is conducted scrupulously, we establish the intuitive truth of each step so that our conclusion has something like the same self-evident certainty. The result is demonstrative knowledge. The classic model of demonstration is mathematics, where we connect a series of propositions that are each self-evidently true to prove a truth that was not initially self-evident.

When Hobbes and Descartes treat clear certainty as the criterion for truth, they are saying that all knowledge is either intuitive or demonstrative. Locke agrees that all knowledge about the *relationship* between ideas falls into these categories. But this isn't the kind of knowledge with which natural philosophy is most concerned, which is why Descartes and Hobbes are wrong to make mathematical certainty the model for knowledge about the natural world, and thus wrong to insist on rationalism rather than empiricism as the route to such knowledge. What we want here is knowledge of the agreement or disagreement of our mental ideas with the external world—that is, knowledge of whether an idea "has a real existence without the mind."

This is not a simple matter. Locke's account of human thought improves upon Hobbes by allowing for intentionality. His ideas are ideas *of* the objects we perceive, rather than simply the internal physical results of perception. But he solves this problem at the cost of a retreat into dualism. His ideas are not physical occurrences within the material world but mental representations of it. But if the ideas themselves are all we can ever know, how could we possibly judge whether they accurately render whatever it is they are trying to represent?

Descartes solved this problem with his a priori proof of the existence of a benevolent God that would not systematically deceive us, but that option is obviously closed to an empiricist who rejects the possibility of any a priori knowledge. Meanwhile, a posteriori proofs of God's existence that rest on features of the physical world must already assume that our experience connects up with this world.

In practice, of course, we have perfectly good reasons to believe as much. Some ideas present themselves to us insistently, quite against our will. I can close my eyes and imagine I'm sitting on a pristine Caribbean beach, but when I open them again, I see a desk and a lukewarm cup of coffee. Conjuring that beach requires an act of will, but this desk imposes itself on me, and there is an undeniable qualitative difference between the taste of this coffee and the "taste" of the tropical drink I imagine for myself.

Such experiential distinctions could not be offered as proof to someone who refused to acknowledge the reality of the external world. If a person insists that nothing outside his own mind is real, that his life is a dream (or a cave wall shadow show or a computer simulation), Locke says that we must leave him to this belief: "'Tis not great matter, whether I remove his scruple, or no: where all is but a dream, reasons and arguments are of no use, truth and knowledge nothing."

Not every empiricist agrees on this point. The Anglican bishop George Berkeley—the next great empiricist philosopher after Locke—argued that ideas were not representations of a material reality but rather that they comprised reality itself. He did not think that holding this view meant giving up on reason and argument. As counterintuitive as it might be, this idealist view solves many of the problems associated with Hobbes's materialism on the one hand and Locke's dualism on the other.

For now, though, we'll stick with Locke's view and simply presume that there is an external world to which our ideas correspond in some way. There remains the problem of what kind of correspondence our ideas have to this world. What is the *nature* of the reality we approach by way of experience? Locke draws a distinction between "primary" qualities like size and shape and motion, which inhere in the objects of the external world, and "secondary" qualities like color and taste and temperature, which we perceive on the basis of the way those objects act upon us. But he rejects the notion—common to Descartes and Hobbes—that primary qualities constitute reality as such, and that reason can deliver demonstrative mathematical truth about this reality.

At any given moment that our senses are impressing ideas on us, we can be certain "that there doth something at that time really exist without us which doth . . . actually produce that idea," but we can never have certain knowledge about that "something," because our knowledge is always knowledge of our ideas, not of things themselves. There's an unbridgeable gap between ideas and the objects giving rise to them. We can never "check" our ideas against those objects, but we can be fairly sure that our picture of reality is radically incomplete. "The comprehension of our understandings," Locke says, "comes exceeding short of the vast extent of things."

Does this mean that we can never arrive at any truths about the world outside our heads? Well, yes—if our criterion for truth is certain knowledge. But that is not how "truth" actually works in practice. Skepticism's great mistake, in Locke's view, is the assumption that we must choose between absolute certainty and absolute ignorance. In practice the vast majority of propositions fall into a third category. "God has set some things in broad daylight," Locke writes. That is, he has allowed us to have certain intuitive knowledge in some areas. For the rest "he has afforded us only the twilight, as I may so say, of *probability*."

Everything that we consider knowledge about the sensible world is really *probable* knowledge. It is a mistake to think (as Descartes and Hobbes did) that we can have mathematical certainty in this area, but it is equally a mistake to think (as Montaigne did) that the only alternative to mathematical certainty is radical skepticism. Natural philosophy can never rise to the level of science, in the sense that Locke understood that term, as a field of study like geometry or algebra that concerns demonstrative knowledge. Furthermore, it can never penetrate to the ultimate reality of things. But through it we know enough to serve our most urgent needs: "'Tis of great use to the sailor to know the length of his line, though he cannot with it fathom all the depths of the ocean."

"Great use" here can be understood partly in Bacon's pragmatic sense. Through "experiments and historical observations . . . we may draw advantages of ease and health, and thereby increase our stock of conveniences for this life." But we can also use probabilistic knowledge to answer the most important practical question: how we ought to live.

LIKE HOBBES, Locke believes that the experience of pleasure and pain is the only possible empirical basis for ideas of good and evil, and he agrees that this empirical sense is entirely self-interested: We have no rational basis for caring about the suffering of others; there is no justice or injustice in the state of nature. The drive for our own good naturally causes us to reward those who cause us pleasure and punish those who cause us pain. Such punishments and rewards take the form of imposing pleasure and pain, thus bringing the natural self-interest of others into alignment with our own. This view leads to Locke's version of the social contract—not a Hobbesian contract with an absolute sovereign but one between fellow citizens.

Because the contract is grounded in rational self-interest, it must be one into which a rational person would enter. Since our greatest personal good is the freedom to pursue pleasure in our own fashion, no rational person would consent to give up life, liberty, or the right to property. Everything else is a matter of negotiation, but these are inalienable goods, because it would be irrational to give away in a contract the very things the contract exists to protect. Better to take your chances in the state of nature.

Without an absolute sovereign to enforce it, this contract seems less reliable that Hobbes's version. How are we to deal with the freeloader problem, which is inevitable even under the most robust enforcement regime? Of course, if we knew that the selfless behavior required by the social contract would bring endless rewards from an immortal god, we would not need the "Mortall God" Leviathan to keep us in line. But how could we ever arrive at such knowledge through empirical means?

Locke treated the existence of an "eternal, cogitive, immaterial" God as a demonstrable truth that can be established through a posteriori proof. However, such proof can't tell us whether this God wants us to obey certain laws or whether it will reward our obedience. That kind of knowledge relies on revealed theology, and it doesn't seem like empiricism allows for such things.

Certainly the validity of revelation can't be established intuitively or demonstratively. Nor is it subject to the kind of experimentation that usually justifies assent to probable empirical truths. At the very least, we must treat claims of divine revelation with extreme skepticism. Under many conditions, Locke tells us, we can confidently reject revelation as a source of truth. The first is whenever certain or probable knowledge is available by way of reason. One could imagine, for example, the laws of motion coming to Newton from God—perhaps in the famous moment of seeing the apple fall from the tree—but God's authority does not compel our assent to these laws. They can and therefore must be tested against experience.

Wherever reason is available to us as a source of knowledge in this way, it ought to be relied upon. Relatedly, any truths given to us by revelation must be concordant with reason. God would not reveal an untruth to us, and so no logical absurdity or impossibility could ever come from genuine revelation. Locke clearly thought a great deal of widespread religious beliefs ought to be rejected on this basis.

Even in cases that pass these tests, we may be rationally permitted to assent to such revelations but never rationally *compelled* to do so. Most supposed revelations are almost certainly false, and there is no simple rule for how to apply our judgment to these questions. Luckily, we don't need to apply our judgment in most cases, for it is a key empirical principle that we don't need a comprehensive metaphysical view of reality. "Our business here is not to know all things," Locke tells us, "but those which concern our conduct."

Now, the question of our eternal state clearly concerns us, and if our conduct here on earth will ultimately determine that state, then the question clearly concerns our conduct. Furthermore, it doesn't seem to be a question we can answer by way of reason, which makes it just the sort of case where we might consider assenting to claims of revelation. In doing so, we are acting within the "twilight of probability." Do the claims of the Bible—particularly those relating to eternal punishment and reward—seem probable? Most empiricists would probably say not. But Locke believes we have a very good reason to assent to such claims.

When deciding upon a course of action, we must inevitably consider the consequences, and when we do so in this area, we are struck by the disproportion of the possible outcomes. If the Bible is correct, then "infinite happiness is put in one scale, against infinite misery in the other." In such a case, goodness—that is, obedience to God's law—is the obvious correct course. If the Bible is false, if there is no afterlife, then the good and the wicked receive the same eternal reward, which is annihilation. And so it is unquestionably good to follow God's commandments as we best understand them, for the probabilities tell us that we will enjoy pleasure if we do and suffer pain if we do not—which is all we can ultimately mean when we speak of the good: "Must it not be a most manifest wrong judgement, that does not presently see, to which side, in this case, the preference is to be given?"

While I read some of Locke's political writings as an undergraduate, I was into my twenties and well along my wanderings through the cave before I read the *Essay*, and I quickly recognized this argument as "Pascal's wager," a source of great sport among knowing atheists. Blaise Pascal was roughly a contemporary of Locke's, a distinguished mathematician who had a religious experience that led him to the Catholic sect of Jansenism. His posthumously published *Pensées*, a classic of religious literature, contains his version of the wager: "Wherever there is infinity and where there are not infinite chances of losing against that of winning, there is no room for hesitation, you must give everything."

I was already very familiar with the common arguments against the wager, which seems—according to its atheist critics—to misunderstand the way belief actually works. "Believing in God is not something I can do as a matter of policy," as Richard Dawkins puts it. "Pascal's wager could only ever be an argument for feigning belief in God." It was therefore surprising to find the father of empiricism making the argument, and even more so to find him making it on strictly empirical grounds.

In the twilight of probability, Locke tells us, belief is precisely something we do "as a matter of policy." We can't possibly have certainty in such areas; we can only weigh alternatives. Furthermore, because empiricism doesn't sound the metaphysical depths, there is no important difference between feigning belief in the biblical God—consistently acting *as though* you believed—and actually believing in that God. After all, conduct is all that concerns us here.

Locke's empiricism likewise tells him that belief in the Bible's historical claims—including its descriptions of miracles—can be reconciled with reason. Because the laws of nature are derived from experience rather than a priori demonstration, no empirical state of affairs is rationally impossible. We may find reports of Moses parting the Red Sea or Jesus walking on water highly improbable, but we can't say, for example, that our knowledge of the essence of water makes such events contrary to reason. Once we have entered the realm of probability, we must allow for considerations like those in the wager.

LOCKE ISN'T SIMPLY one of those transitional figures who can't quite see far enough to abandon belief entirely, or an early atheist who allows himself a bit of self-protective hypocrisy. Unlike Bacon and Descartes, he doesn't seek to insulate his philosophical innovations from religious belief. His theological views are at once distinctive and central to his work.

Most notably, Locke's theology is essential to the arguments for liberalism for which he is best remembered. The fact that we can reason our way to probable knowledge about our eternal conditions places a natural limit on political power. It can never be rational to obey an earthly sovereign when his demands conflict with God's laws as you understand them, since God has far more power to cause pleasure and pain than any earthly sovereign could. That fact makes it naturally unjust for the sovereign to demand defiance of God, and this is the basis of Locke's famous argument for religious tolerance.

Given that basis, Locke's tolerance had its limits. It didn't extend to Catholics, who (he thought) did not reason their way to moral knowledge but instead accepted the authority of Rome. This made them essentially loyal subjects to a competing earthly sovereign, and it was not rational to tolerate dual loyalty. Tolerance likewise did not extend to atheists, because liberalism as Locke understood it required subjects who believed in God.

For our purposes, Locke may be best understood as taking a major step in what would become the ongoing Enlightenment effort not to move beyond religion but to place religion *itself* on rational ground. This effort resembles the classic post-Reformation impulse to free individuals to answer questions of belief by their own light. Yet Locke is hardly a conventional Protestant Christian. Martin Luther and John Calvin both insisted that reason must be subservient to faith. In Luther's infamous formulation, reason is "the Devil's whore"—by which he meant not that it was inherently evil but that it could be prostituted to justify the good and the bad alike. Both men believed we must begin with faith, particularly faith in biblical truth, and apply our reason from there.

Medieval Scholastics insisted that reason and revelation were wholly consistent, but in practice they implicitly favored revelation. When apparent conflicts arose, they assumed that reason had gone awry—much as we assume, when numbers don't add up, that we have miscounted, rather than assuming that we have arrived at a rare case where one plus two equals two. Locke reverses this position, putting the burden on belief to show itself consistent with reason.

In fact, he goes quite a bit further than this. He tells us first that we can safely set aside most of the questions that faith claims to answer as irrelevant to the conduct of our lives. We do not need to sound the depths. When it comes to the questions we *do* need to answer, faith is necessary only if reason doesn't suffice. Not only must we reject faith wherever it conflicts with reason, but we can safely ignore it wherever reason alone gets the job done.

In the *Essay*, Locke even suggests that we might arrive at moral knowledge through reason. Given demonstrative certainty about the existence of "a supreme being infinite in power," he says, we ought to be able to "place morality amongst the sciences capable of demonstration"; in other words, we should be able to develop something like mathematical certainty about moral questions. To do so would seem to make revealed religion wholly irrelevant, leaving perhaps only a vague piety and a few cultural niceties. More than outright atheism, this would become the prevailing Enlightenment hope for religion.

But Locke is frustratingly obscure on the point of demonstrative morality, and he never published a work devoted solely to the subject. One thing he does say very explicitly about moral knowledge is that secondary revelation—that is, testimony from others about communication with God—can't be a source of simple ideas, which can come only through direct experience. That means that our own pleasure and pain must inevitably remain the basis for our knowledge of good and evil.

What is true of earthly law therefore holds for divine law: The only rational cause for obedience to it is the promise of reward and the threat of punishment. There is no intelligible conception of the good that does not relate to our self-interest. Whatever the demonstrative science of morality ultimately involves, it will have to start there.

Six

PASSION'S SLAVE

Although he's remembered among the great modern thinkers, Locke was modest about his achievements. "In an age that produces such masters, as . . . the incomparable Mr Newton," he wrote, "'tis ambition enough to be employed as an under-labourer in clearing ground a little, and removing some of the rubbish that lies in the way to knowledge."

Philosophers in Locke's line have largely embraced the job of clearing ground for the experimental sciences, creating the space where others can do the real work of building up proper knowledge. One key part of this job is providing the rational justification for science's methods. On this front, many people find Bacon's instrumental case sufficient: The empirical sciences just work, and if you are willing to enjoy their fruits, you owe them a certain epistemic allegiance. But if you want to claim not just (as Bacon did) that empiricism is a powerful source of knowledge within its own realm, but (as modern thinkers increasingly came to claim) that it is the *only* proper source of legitimate knowledge, you will probably need stronger justification than this.

Such justification has proved surprisingly hard to find. The philosophical effort to legitimize empiricism on rational grounds was radically undermined almost as soon as it began—not by any Aristotelian "schoolman" or even by some Cartesian rationalist, but by one of the greatest of all philosophical empiricists, widely beloved by modern-day atheists. A mere generation after Locke set the course for philosophical empiricism, David Hume ran the ship aground.

If you've read many atheist polemics, you may know Hume as perhaps the greatest of modern skeptics, a man who relentlessly attacked religious dogma with the power of common sense, leaving no reasonable case for belief standing in his wake. That is certainly how I came to know him in my earliest days of disbelief. Every atheist anthology includes his famous case against miracles, and nearly every atheist tract quotes from it. But few mention that Hume applied the same withering analysis to the claims of empirical knowledge or that he turned his skepticism on reason itself. "Reason," he wrote, in a declaration that seems to fly in the face of all that contemporary atheists believe, "is and ought only to be the slave of the passions."

HUME WAS BORN in Scotland in 1711, nearly a century after Bacon's death, and he consciously understood himself as working within the well-established philosophical tradition that Bacon founded and Locke furthered along. While still in his twenties, he published his first work, *A Treatise on Human Nature*, which applied the experimental method of natural philosophy to "moral subjects." In Hume's view, this category included nearly everything. "Even *Mathematics, Natural Philosophy, and Natural Religion* are in some measure dependent on the science of Man," he wrote, "since they lie under the cognizance of men, and are judged of by their powers and faculties."

Hume expected the book to make him a celebrity. Instead, as he later wrote, it "fell *dead-born from the press*, without reaching such distinction as even to excite a murmur among the zealots." Blaming this failure on his abstruse style,* he embarked on a series of shorter works designed to make his ideas more accessible. The first of them, which dealt with epistemological questions, he called *An Enquiry Concerning Human Understanding*, a title nearly identical to that of Locke's major study.

While his terminology differs slightly from Locke's, Hume holds all the requisite empiricist views: We have no innate knowledge; human cognition operates by gathering a stock of ideas from sense experience, combining these simple ideas into complex ideas, and relating them mentally; so long as we limit ourselves to mental relations, our knowledge is susceptible to intuitive or demonstrative certitude; when it comes to the relation of our ideas to external reality, we must be satisfied with probable truth. But he believed that Locke had given far too little attention to the question of how we actually arrive at this probable truth, and that he had allowed into his picture a great deal of knowledge that could not be empirically derived.

Hume was particularly concerned with how we arrive at knowledge about "real existence and matter of fact" that we don't experience directly. How do we get from "the present testimony of our senses, or the records of our memory" to the kind of general principles about the way the world works that allow us to make predictions about future events and to judge the probability of secondhand testimony?

Everyone who has spent any time on the question agrees that we need such principles to order the flow of sensory experience into meaningful knowledge. Rationalists believe that we can generate these principles through abstract reasoning and apply them deductively to the facts of experience. Empiricists advocate the opposite route, deriving general principles from the study of the particulars. Baconian induction demands that

* The *Treatise* is remarkably lucid compared with today's academic philosophy.

we be very circumspect about moving from particular case to general rule, but if we don't *ever* make the move, we have nothing but a collection of unordered and unrelated data points. The problem is that experience itself—the supposed source of all knowledge about the external world—can't tell us when we are justified in taking this step. In fact, experience can't tell us that deriving general inferences from particular cases is ever justified. Nor is the movement from the particular to the general a simple logical operation subject to mathematical demonstration. Where does this justification come from?

Like Aristotle, Hobbes, and many others, Hume identified causation as the central concept by which we organize reality into usable knowledge. And it's tempting to rely on our sense of cause and effect to solve our problem here. When we see two events related in this way, we know we are dealing not with random occurrences but with something predictably repeatable, something about which we can generalize. But how is our belief in causation itself justified?

Let's return to that book falling off the table. If I push the same book off my table now, I know with something approaching certainty that it will again fall to the ground. How do I know this? Is it only because that's what happened last time? That hardly seems sufficient. I might add that I know the book will fall because I know the "why" of its falling, what causes it—i.e., the force of gravity acting on the book. But what is our experience of this rather occult force? It is just our experience of heavy objects falling. We have no experience of something "causing" the book to fall; we just have experience of things like books falling when nothing is there to support them.

Aristotle's assumption that our study of the physical world should be guided by our prior metaphysical understanding of causality was the primary target of the empiricist revolution that did away with final causes. Hume tells us that reliance on efficient cause—the simple temporal relationship of cause and effect—is similarly unjustifiable. What would it mean to *experience* an efficient cause? We see one event following quickly after another, but how do we know they bear the relationship we mean by causality?

I flip a switch on the wall, and at once a light goes on. At the same time, a car horn honks outside. I take the first result as caused by the switch and the second as coincidence. I expect that the next time I flip the switch, the light will again go on but no horn will honk. Is that only because the light has gone on every other time I flipped the switch, and this is the first time the car has honked this way? Hoping to do better than that, I might say that I know *how* the switch causes the light to go on—by completing a circuit that runs electricity through a filament in the bulb. But how does completing the circuit make electricity run this way, and how does the electricity heat the filament, and how does being heated make the filament light up?

A chemist or a physicist could offer granular descriptions of these events, but ultimately they will be just that—descriptions of events. No matter how closely we study a singular series of events, we will never identify the special relationship between successive events that we call "causality." It is only when we have multiple instances of one event preceding another that we begin to call the first a cause and the second an effect. We are, finally, not much better off than when we said that we know the switch causes the light to go on because every time we flip the switch the light does go on.

In that case, our ideas of causation are best understood as a matter of habit. When we call one thing the "cause" of another, all we mean is that "we are determined by custom . . . to expect the one from the appearance of the other." Over time, we get used to things being a certain way, and we expect them to continue to be so. We can't justify this tendency; it's just how we are.

But remember that we were looking for an empirical basis of causation because we wanted some grounds for inferring general rules from particular cases. The empiricist wants to say that once we experience a process of cause and effect at work, rather than simply a succession of unrelated events, we can begin to generalize. But we can never experience such a thing. All we can say is that because we have seen one event follow another in the past, we expect them to go together, and that is precisely the kind of generalized conclusion we wanted causality to justify in the first place.

The upshot is that purely inductive reasoning—the gathering from individual experiences of generally applicable rules, without the assumption of any premise or rule that can't itself be checked against experience—is simply impossible. It's not just that matters of fact are not susceptible to demonstrative certainty but that our method for turning probable matters of fact into even the most provisional sort of general knowledge cannot be rationally justified.

Custom—rather than reason—is not just the source of our understanding of causality but the source of "all inferences from experience." Custom is "the great guide of human life," the one thing that "renders our experience useful to us, and makes us expect, for the future, a similar train of events with those which have appeared in the past." In the absence of custom we could have knowledge of those matters of fact "immediately present to the memory and senses," but all our knowledge would end at the limits of our personal experience.

IF WE CAN'T RATIONALLY justify physical laws, it probably goes without saying that we can't rationally justify human laws. Custom is likewise the basis for morality—in both the broad sense of social and political norms and the narrow sense of personal ethical judgments.

All reasoning, empiricism tells us, concerns either the logical relation between ideas or the relation of ideas to matters of fact. In order for moral reasoning to consist in the relation of ideas (for example, the resemblance between some action and some value), one must already have moral ideas delivered up by experience. Demonstrative moral reasoning can be used to apply moral laws but never to prove or to generate them. But sense experience is similarly helpless on this front, because moral values are not facts in the world.

If you examine any action taken to be immoral, Hume tells us in the *Treatise*, you will never perceive in the action itself "that matter of fact, or real existence, which you call *vice.*" Only when you turn inward do you find a negative sentiment or emotion that you feel toward the action, and this feeling is all you're describing when you call that action "evil."

The existence of such internal moral sentiments is itself a matter of fact, and thus these sentiments can be the subject of reasoning, but they can't be rationally *judged*, for this will always involve bringing some other equally subjective sentiments into play. We can say that a person's moral sentiments are not consistent with ours or those of society at large, or even with the person's own actions, but we can never make the rational judgment that they are better or worse than some other sentiments.

In a famous passage, Hume complains of reading moral philosophers who begin with some form of reasoning about the workings of the world, in which propositions are held together by *is* and *is not*, only to find himself suddenly reading a string of sentences containing instead *ought* and *ought not*. It seems like a subtle change, Hume says, but the gap between these two is actually uncrossable. A normative statement (an "ought") can never be derived from a factual statement (an "is"). If we want to develop a "science" of morality, it must be resolutely descriptive, like any other science.

Hume's own moral philosophy is based on an examination of the traits that humans actually find estimable in one another. Chief among these, he writes in the *Enquiry Concerning the Principles of Morals*, are the "benevolent or softer affections": "The epithets *sociable, good-natured, humane, merciful, grateful, friendly, generous, beneficient,* or their equivalents, are known in all languages, and universally express the highest merit, which *human nature* is capable of attaining."

The one characteristic uniting these virtues is that they are conducive to "happiness and satisfaction." We naturally value the "social virtues," prior to any "precept or education." Many of them—things like "chearfulness," wit, and taste—are not generally considered moral goods, but it does seem unquestionably true that we value them. Meanwhile, Hume leaves out a great deal of traditional morality, specifically "celibacy, fasting, penance, mortification, self-denial, humility, silence, solitude, and the whole train of monkish virtues." While we sometimes pay lip service to such supposed goods, Hume tells us, we do not value them in practice, except where "the delusive glosses of superstition and false religion" hold sway: "A gloomy, hair-brained enthusiast, after his death, may have a place in the calendar; but will scarcely ever be admitted, when alive, into intimacy and society, except by those who are as delirious and dismal as himself."

It's tempting to say that for Hume the virtuous person is simply one who is pleasant to be around. Indeed, Hume says as much himself, and he thinks this view entirely natural. "But why, in the greater society or confederacy of mankind," he asks, "should not the case be the same as in particular clubs and companies?" He concludes that "personal merit consists altogether in the possession of mental qualities, useful or agreeable to the person himself or to others." In the absence of any rationally derived natural laws or rights, without any hypothetical social contract to which we are rationally obliged to consent, this same standard of usefulness is likewise the basis for more formal legal codes: "The *sole* origin of justice [and] the *sole* foundation of its merit is public utility."

Many people who share Hume's rejection of religious asceticism would still not elevate being clubbable to the greatest human good. It is clearly Hume's *own* greatest good, but that does not seem to be a fact about the nature of humans in general so much as one about the nature of Hume in particular and the people whose company Hume enjoyed. Is it actually true, as an anthropological matter, that the epithets *sociable* and *good-natured* express in every language known to man the highest merit one can attain? Is religious superstition really the only thing that leads people to value self-denial, humility, silence, or solitude over cheerfulness?

Hume believed that the passions ultimately rule our reason, but he found the passions themselves surprisingly rational. While attempting to establish the universality of the social virtues, Hume asks a rhetorical question: "Would any man, who is walking along, tread as willingly on another's gouty toes, whom he has no quarrel with, as on the hard flint and pavement?" To which most of us, I think, whether we like it or not, would have to answer that *some* men would. And we'd like to have some rational basis for stopping them.

THOUGH HUME AUTHORED some of the most devastating critiques of the rational proofs for God's existence, and he extended these critiques to the a posteriori proofs favored by earlier empiricists, his work poses a significant challenge to the major strain of a modern-day atheism in its most self-confident mode. If this tradition has a defining attitude, it is: *Custom, tradition, faith in the power of invisible forces—that is the stuff of religious superstition; we rely instead on evidence and reason.* Hume radically undermines this distinction, bringing us back two hundred years to Montaigne's view that the base of knowledge is grounded in faith, however much we might reason about the branches.

Hume is also beloved by modern atheists for writing one of the earliest examples of a favorite atheist genre, the explanation of religion as a natural phenomenon. His *Natural History of Religion* traces belief back to "the ordinary affections of human life; the anxious concern for happiness, the dread of future misery, the terror of death, the thirst for revenge, the appetite for food and other necessities." Many atheist thinkers who embrace Hume's view that religion originates in human vulnerability and ignorance have concluded that religious belief is destined to wither away in advanced societies, where technology and material wealth increasingly shield us from vulnerability and the sciences increasingly dispel our ignorance. But Hume did not share this belief.

First of all, he didn't think that science could ever dispel our ignorance about the ultimate workings of reality. "Doubt, uncertainty, suspence of judgment," he writes at the conclusion of the *Natural History*, "appear the only result of our most accurate scrutiny, concerning this subject." He also knew that this "deliberate doubt" was inconsistent with human nature, and he did not think for a moment that most people would one day give up on religion.

For the lucky few, he proposed an "escape into the calm, though obscure, regions of philosophy." The best alternative to religion, in Hume's view, is a "mitigated" form of skepticism. As he explains in the *Enquiry Concerning Human Understanding*, this is not the "speculative" skepticism of Descartes, which begins with a "universal doubt" but ultimately arrives at certain knowledge. Nor is it the Pyrrhonian skepticism of Montaigne, which treats this universal doubt as insurmountable. As a theoretical matter, Hume argues, Pyrrhonism is correct. Cartesian doubt, once attained, "would be entirely incurable," since there *is* no original principle from which the veracity of our faculties can be deduced.

Fortunately, this level of doubt is impossible in practice. No person could ever *actually* embrace universal doubt as a starting point. All people are "carried, by a natural instinct or prepossession, to repose faith in their senses." If we were to base our worldview entirely on reason, Hume says, we would have to satisfy ourselves with the most extreme skepticism. We simply don't have a rational warrant to believe anything about "matters of fact" in the world. The inductive belief that the sun will rise tomorrow can't be rationally justified, but nor can the belief that the sun is shining while I stand in its light today. I have mental images and sensations; that is all I have. There is no rational warrant for supposing that these images and sensations relate to anything outside my own mind.

Yet the very extent of reason's limits offers a way out of this skepticism. Truly basing our actions on reason would result in paralysis, but paralysis runs contrary to our nature, and "nature will always maintain her rights, and prevail in the end over any abstract reasoning." Just as we have a natural tendency to trust our senses or to become accustomed to certain causes having certain effects, we have a natural tendency to act in the world, and this tendency needs no rational justification. In your quiet moments, you might talk yourself back into skepticism, but eventually your stomach will growl. You will apply your reason to get yourself fed, and it will not matter that your reason itself cannot be put on rational grounds.

We have wants and needs and natural preferences, and we act to fulfill them, whatever reason tells us: "The great subverter of Pyrrhonism or the excessive principles of skepticism, is action, and employment, and the occupations of common life." Still, Hume believed, we ought to be ever mindful of how limited our capacities actually are. This is the great value of skepticism mitigated by common sense. Whenever our natures compel us toward dogmatic reasoning, we should apply "a small tincture of Pyrrhonism," reminding ourselves of the "universal perplexity and confusion, which is inherent in human nature." Wherever our understanding leads us, we ought to be accompanied by "a degree of doubt, and caution, and modesty." Finally, mitigated skepticism encourages "the limitation of our enquires to such subjects as are best adapted to the narrow capacity of human understanding."

Hume draws these limitations most famously in the closing pages of the *Enquiry*:

> If we take in our hand any volume; of divinity or school metaphysics, for instance; let us ask, Does it contain any abstract reasoning concerning quantity or number? No. Does it contain any experimental reasoning concerning matter of fact and existence? No. Commit it then to the flames: for it can contain nothing but sophistry and illusion.

To a remarkable degree, philosophers after Hume followed this practice. The complaints about Aristotle and the "schoolmen" so often found in Bacon, Descartes, Hobbes, and Locke become far less frequent in the hundred and fifty years after Hume's death in 1776. For the time being, at least, Scholasticism seems to have been safely consigned to the past.

At the same time, philosophical empiricism never entirely recovered from Hume's attack. One school of thought attempted to pick up the pieces, but others simply took for granted that empirical science in the strictest sense—in which every general principle is inductively justified by experience—was theoretically impossible. In practice, it was understood, scientists made ad hoc use of quasi-metaphysical principles and concepts whenever such use was expedient. The justification for this practice was the justification empiricism had always relied upon: It worked.

Is this justification enough? This question can't be answered objectively. Some feel a distinct vertigo at the notion that all our technical advances have no solid foundation beneath them. Others find it bizarre to demand a theoretical defense of an approach that has brought us such unquestionable improvements in material wealth and quality of life. When it comes to settling the question, the latter camp has a great resource at its disposal, namely a modern ethic that raises utility to the highest possible good.

Seven

EXPERIMENTS OF LIVING

The proper construction of this morality began almost immediately after Hume's death, with the 1780 publication of Jeremy Bentham's *Introduction to the Principles of Morals and Legislation.*

Although he founded one of the most significant schools of moral thought, Bentham didn't think of himself as a philosopher. He was a legal theorist and social reformer. Trained as a lawyer, he became frustrated by the Byzantine English common law, and he set out to develop a rationally ordered criminal code to replace it. He soon found himself "entangled in an unsuspected corner of the metaphysical maze," and he concluded that he couldn't design a legal system without answering basic questions about the nature of justice.

Bentham shared the view of Hobbes and Locke concerning the empirical basis of our ideas of good and evil. "Nature has placed mankind under the guidance of two sovereign masters, *pain* and *pleasure*," he writes at the beginning of the *Introduction*. "It is for them alone to point out what we ought to do, as well as to determine what we shall do." But he also shared Hume's view that we could not derive from these ideas of pain and pleasure some universally binding natural law. In place of such a thing, Bentham offers what he calls the "principle of utility": "that principle which approves or disapproves of every action whatsoever, according to the tendency which it appears to have to augment or diminish the happiness of *the party whose interest is in question*."

The emphasis on those last words is mine: For each of us as individuals, the "party whose interest is in question" is ourselves. Our natural goal in life is maximizing the sum total of our individual pleasure and minimizing the sum total of our individual pain. Here the words *pleasure* and *pain* should be understood in their most basic and immediate sense. While we are capable of enjoying rather complex and sophisticated pleasures (and suffering rather complex and sophisticated pains), they can all be reduced to the simple physical experience of what Bentham calls "interesting sensations."

Bentham believed that such sensations could be precisely quantified, and he developed a system for doing so on the basis of their intensity, duration, certainty, remoteness, fecundity (i.e., the likelihood of the sensation's being followed by sensations of the same kind), and purity (i.e., the likelihood of the sensation's *not* being followed by sensations of the *opposite* kind). Putting these together, one could "take an exact account" of the value of any action: "Sum up all the values of the pleasures on the one side, and those of all the pains on the other. The balance, if it be on the side of pleasure, will give the *good* tendency of the act upon the whole, with respect to the interests of that *individual* person; if on the side of pain, the *bad* tendency of it upon the whole."

With this method, Bentham laid the groundwork for that great Enlightenment dream—an objective science of morality. The most important feature of this science is that it is resolutely consequentialist: It judges behavior solely on the basis of its tendency to produce pleasure or pain. This doesn't quite mean that *intentions* don't matter. If I run into a burning building with the aim of saving your life, and through no fault of my own I trip on the way in and block the doorway, it doesn't make sense to hold me responsible for the pain you then suffer. But supposing that I do save your life as intended, my *motive* for doing so doesn't matter. I might have entered that building for the prospect of heavenly reward or in order to look good in the eyes of others or because you owed me money that I would never recover if you were dead. From the standpoint of moral accounting, all that matters is that I have saved your life.

Part of the reason that we can't judge actions on the basis of motives is that, again, we all ultimately act from the singular motive of maximizing our own pleasure. This brings us to another important point: If acts are to be judged entirely according to the pleasure or pain they cause, it would be circular to judge our pleasure or pain on the basis of the acts that cause them. One person gains utility from helping old ladies across the street (Bentham calls this "the pleasure of benevolence"), another from pushing them into traffic ("the pleasure of malevolence"). For the individual pleasure-seeker, the distinction is irrelevant, and Bentham's system makes no judgment between them.

For the old lady, of course, the matter is quite different. She clearly has an interest in not winding up under the bus. But what business is this of the malevolent actor, if his interest is served by putting her there? Bentham believed it was the purpose of a legal regime to make it the actor's business. In the political context, the "party whose interest is in question" is the community at large, which is to be understood as a collection of individuals rather than a singular entity with its own interests. The purpose of government is to maximize the sum total of pleasure and minimize the sum total of pain among its members. States exist to "secure the greatest happiness of the greatest number." With this guiding insight, politics becomes an engineering problem, a matter of technical management.

Bentham's application of the utility principle led him to positions that were radical for his age and surprisingly progressive even for our own. His great cause was criminal justice reform, limiting sentences to the minimum required for effective deterrence, which meant eliminating corporal and capital punishment. He also opposed slavery and imperialism. He wrote (though never published) a defense of homosexuality, and generally argued that sexual relations between consenting adults tended to increase their own happiness with no harm to society, so that virtually any attempt to regulate sexual morality was unjust. He argued strongly for the legal equality of women, and he insisted that the ability of nonhuman animals to experience pleasure and pain ought to include them in our moral calculus.

But he did not use the language of universal rights and natural equality that generally motivates supporters of these causes today. Instead he justified all his positions strictly on the basis of utility, for he shared with Hume the belief that no other justification made sense. The concept of inalienable rights, as he famously put it, was "nonsense," and the concept of *natural* inalienable rights was "nonsense on stilts."

WHEN DIVORCED FROM any underlying notion of rights, however, the greatest-happiness principle delivers some strange results. Take again the pleasure of malevolence. If the pleasure I get from pushing a lady into traffic outweighs the pain she suffers, then the action is socially beneficial from Bentham's standpoint. Absent any countervailing idea that this woman has a fundamental right to be left alone by me, there is no reason not to allow it.

There is also the problem of compliance. Benthamism assumes that the threat of punishment is our only rational reason for obeying the law where doing so conflicts with our own desires, but he allows himself neither Locke's supernatural divinity nor Hobbes's all-powerful "mortall god" to enforce these laws. The power of the state is limited by the principle of utility, which means that it must be ruthlessly efficient in exercising what power it has.

Like many people who earned undergraduate humanities degrees in the age of critical theory, I came to know Jeremy Bentham first of all as the inventor of the "panopticon," a prison plan that was put into use throughout the nineteenth century. Developed a few years after the publication of the *Introduction*, the panopticon is designed so that any cell can be watched at any moment from a single vantage point. At the same time, the prisoners can't see their guards, so they must always assume they are being watched. A hundred years later, the French theorist Michel Foucault took the panopticon as a metaphor for social control in post-Enlightenment societies, and the metaphor has only grown more resonant with the rise of the surveillance state.

Bentham did not call for society at large to be turned into a panopticon, but his ideas point unmistakably in this direction. If the prisoners are not being punished as retribution for having done anything wrong as such* but only to bring their interests into alignment with those of society at large, then there is no important moral distinction between the prisoner and the free citizen. This alignment of interests is required of every citizen, and behaving selflessly is no more natural for the rest of us than it is for habitual lawbreakers, so why should we not all be subject to the same state of constant observation? Without an inherent right to privacy,† we have no obvious basis for objecting to this treatment, provided that it serves the public good.

The final problem with Bentham's ethics plays out on the individual level. While elevating happiness as the sole moral good, his system can't ever tell us anything about what will in fact make us happy. This proves to be a much more difficult question than some people allow. It would be nice to believe that most of us know instinctively what will make us happy,

* There *is* no "wrong as such."

† There are no "inherent rights" either.

that we will naturally pursue this happiness if left to our devices, but experience tends to suggest otherwise. Following our instinct on such matters often leads to catastrophic results, and following reason does not do much better.

Of course, Bentham knew that individuals did not really calculate the intensity, duration, certainty, remoteness, fecundity, and purity of the pleasure that would result from each action before engaging in it. Life faces us with far too many choices for that. But even on the big questions where we do take time to calculate costs and benefits, we very often get things wrong. More profoundly, many of us suspect that a life dedicated to seeking our own happiness would ultimately be an empty and, paradoxically, unhappy one. This problem was vividly demonstrated by a radical experiment in Benthamism conducted by his leading acolyte.

JAMES MILL WAS a Scottish economist and political theorist who worked for a time as Bentham's secretary and became one of his chief popularizers. Though a major intellectual figure in his own right, Mill is mostly remembered for the education he gave his firstborn child, John Stuart, which was heavily influenced by Bentham's sense that life could be rationally organized to maximize efficiency.

As described in his *Autobiography*, John Stuart Mill spent the bulk of his childhood seated at a desk beside his father, who directed his reading while he worked. (Mill's mother, Harriet Barrow, goes almost entirely unmentioned in his account of his upbringing.) He could not remember a time when he didn't know Ancient Greek. By age eight, he'd read "the whole of Herodotus, and of Xenophon's *Cyropaedia* and *Memorials of Socrates*; some of the lives of the philosophers by Diogenes Laertius; part of Lucian, and Isocrates' *Ad Demonicum* and *Ad Nicoclem*. I also read, in

1813 [i.e., at age seven], the first six dialogues (in the common arrangement) of Plato, from the *Euthyphron* to the *Theaetetus* inclusive: which last dialogue, I venture to think, would have been better omitted, as it was totally impossible that I should understand it."

That final clause sounds like a dry joke but seems to have been entirely sincere. Mill thought of himself as intellectually unexceptional and believed that his education—which quickly came to include Latin and history and differential calculus—could be as easily given to nearly any young child. Thus his experience "proved how much more than is commonly supposed may be taught, and well taught, in those early years which, in the common mode of instruction, are little better than wasted."

The morally tinged sense of frugality in the word *wasted* is typical. The elder Mill made every effort to impress upon his son the "utility" of everything he learned, but no effort to impress upon him a love of learning or any sense that one might take pleasure in it. James Mill himself took very little pleasure in anything, which was ironic given the philosophy he espoused. "He thought human life a poor thing at best," the younger Mill wrote of his father. "He would sometimes say, that if life were made what it might be, by good government and good education, it would be worth having: but he never spoke with anything like enthusiasm even of that possibility."

This sort of dour, joyless atmosphere is often associated (fairly or not) with religious upbringings, but Mill also described himself as "one of the very few examples, in this country, of one who has, not thrown off religious belief, but never had it." James Mill was himself born into a devout Presbyterian family and studied for the ministry, but by the time he was licensed to preach, he had already lost his faith. He gave up the ministry and set out to make a living as a writer and editor, at which point he fell under Bentham's influence. As his son later stressed, even James's rejection of religion had a strong moralistic streak to it: "He regarded [belief] with the feelings due not to a mere mental delusion, but to a great moral evil."

AT EIGHTEEN, the younger Mill traveled to France, where he stayed with Jeremy Bentham's brother, Samuel. Ironically, it was only at this time that he began to read Bentham seriously (in French translation) and to become a committed Benthamite himself. He also became acquainted with the circle of French thinkers surrounding the socialist theorist Henri de Saint-Simon, among them Auguste Comte, who would have a major influence on his thought.

Comte believed himself to have discovered a "great fundamental law" that governed the "total development of human intelligence," which was that all branches of knowledge pass successively through a "theological," a "metaphysical," and a "positive" stage. The last fifty pages should have given you a fairly good sense of what these terms indicate. In the theological stage, we understand observable phenomena as expressions of the will of conscious supernatural agents. We seek to exert control over the physical world through prayers, sacrifices, and other tributes to these agents, and we make sense of the past and predict the future through reference to their personalities. In the metaphysical stage, "the supernatural agents are replaced by abstract forces, real entities or personified abstractions, inherent in the different beings of the world." This is the stage that understands the behavior of objects in terms of final causes or the natural tendencies of different elements. Gone are the invisible gods at work in the world, but there remains a sense that observable phenomena are reflections of some deeper truth about reality. Our goal in studying the phenomenal world is transcending phenomena to approach this truth.

The positive approach recognizes "the impossibility of obtaining absolute truth" and thus "gives up the search after the origin and hidden causes of the universe and a knowledge of the final causes of phenomena." At this stage, humanity satisfies itself with knowledge about the phenomena themselves. This knowledge takes the form of general laws derived from observation. Importantly, these laws are not to be understood as causing or influencing phenomena but merely as describing them.

Comte insisted that this progression would inevitably occur in every realm of human knowledge. The passage from theological to metaphysical to positive knowledge was not a historical accident or even a general tendency but an "invariable necessity" dictated by the very structure of the human mind.* Bacon had brought positivism to natural philosophy, but other areas of thought, particularly those concerned with humanity itself, remained stuck in earlier stages of development. A field like psychology, for example, still depended heavily on introspection—that is, on the mind's understanding of its own workings. Comte found this unacceptable. What is true of all other phenomena is true of the human passions: "The best way of knowing [them] will always be to observe them from the outside."

If individual consciousness can't be observed from the outside, this only goes to show that consciousness has no place in a truly positivist psychology. "The mind" is a piece of metaphysics. We must study human behaviors as observable phenomena subject to general laws, and these laws must be derived from the behaviors themselves, without any reference to human motivations, which are final causes grounded in subjective reports about conscious states. The study of human beings can't invoke the will of human agents any more than the study of an acorn can invoke the acorn's will to become a tree.

Comte believed that political theorists made a similar mistake when relying on metaphysical concepts like "the sovereignty of the people,"

* There seems to me something deeply *metaphysical* about the idea that human intellectual development has this kind of teleological thrust.

which were barely improvements over theological concepts like "divine right." A positivist study of society would require an understanding of the laws that determined the behavior of individuals in society and the development of societies themselves. Once these were discovered, one could have a truly positive "social physics," for which Comte coined the term *sociology*.

As you may have already noticed, Comte's philosophy was perfectly matched to Bentham's ethic. The removal of motive from considerations of human behavior represented the banishment of an outdated metaphysical entity. Indeed, the progression from the metaphysical state to the positive state in any discipline could be defined precisely as the process by which one stops understanding observable phenomena—whether that means an apple falling from a tree or a person breaking into an orchard to steal it—in terms of motivation. The utility principle also provided the study of human behavior with the sine qua non of positive science: a generally applicable law. This is the light in which Mill would forever view Benthamism, even after he had modified many of his views on the subject. "What Bacon did for physical knowledge," Mill would write, "Mr. Bentham has done for philosophical legislation."

UPON HIS RETURN to England, Mill started a weekly reading group of young Benthamites, which he called the Utilitarian Club. (He was the first to apply this term to Bentham's philosophy.) In advancing the cause of utilitarianism, the young Mill found "what might truly be called an object in life; to be a reformer of the world." He spent the next several years working tirelessly to advance that object, until he was brought to a dramatic stop by a mental collapse that he later described in his *Autobiography*:

> I was in a dull state of nerves, such as everybody is occasionally liable to; unsusceptible to enjoyment or pleasurable excitement; one of those moods when what is pleasure at other times, becomes insipid or indifferent; the state, I should think, in which converts to Methodism usually are, when smitten by their first "conviction of sin." In this frame of mind it occurred to me to put the question directly to myself: "Suppose that all your objects in life were realized; that all the changes in institutions and opinions which you are looking forward to, could be completely effected at this very instant: would this be a great joy and happiness to you?" And an irrepressible self-consciousness distinctly answered, "No!" At this my heart sank within me: the whole foundation on which my life was constructed fell down. All my happiness was to have been found in the continual pursuit of this end. The end had ceased to charm, and how could there ever again be any interest in the means? I seemed to have nothing left to live for.

The resulting depression lasted several years, during which Mill considered suicide. What finally brought some relief was a chance reading of the memoirs of the French encyclopedist Jean-François Marmontel. While reading a description of Marmontel's father's death, Mill found himself moved to tears. "I was no longer hopeless," he wrote of the experience. "I was not a stock or a stone."

A piece of sentimental literature—rather than any philosophical argument—finally brought Mill relief from his condition. He had not turned to the book seeking such a breakthrough; he had picked it up "accidentally," as a diversion. From these facts, he took the lesson that happiness could not be approached self-consciously, as an end in itself. He still believed it rational to place individual human happiness at the center of life, but he did not believe that happiness could be attained by rational means. On this point, he had the powerful example of his father, who took so little pleasure in his dedication to philosophical hedonism.

When I first read Mill's *Autobiography* as an undergraduate, it didn't leave much of an impression on me. I returned to it in my late twenties, and this time I found it thoroughly shaking. (The different effects that the same words can have at different times in life is part of the point being made.) My life was lacking in meaning and happiness, and I still had some trust in the idea that I could outsmart this problem with sufficient learning. That idea had returned me to Mill in the first place. But his work complicated the picture for me, and I came to see his own breakdown and recovery as one of the clearest arguments against the ethic with which he is so closely associated.

After these events, Mill came for the first time to place the "internal culture of the individual" among the central concerns of life. Having been raised squarely within an Enlightenment tradition that judged individuals entirely on the basis of externally observable behavior, he began to take up the reactionary English Romantics—particularly Thomas Carlyle and Samuel Taylor Coleridge—who thought the great significance of a person's life might rest in interior emotional events invisible to the larger world.

Around this time, one such event occurred for Mill: He fell in love. In 1831, he met the young writer and social reformer Harriet Taylor. The two felt an immediate intellectual and emotional kinship, but Taylor was the married mother of three children. Mill and the Taylors came to an understanding that allowed the pair to spend long stretches together while writing to each other almost constantly. This arrangement lasted almost two decades, until the death of Taylor's husband. As this point, the pair finally married, but Taylor too died soon after. For the rest of his life, Mill described her as the decisive force on his personality and his thought and a coauthor of most of his mature work.

Mill's arrangement with Taylor was an ongoing public scandal that badly strained his relationship with his surviving family members—James Mill had died in 1836—and many within his intellectual circle. This experience echoed throughout his later writing, particularly in his most famous essay, *On Liberty*, published soon after Taylor's death and dedicated to her. In it, Mill* takes up the familiar Enlightenment problem of the circumstances under which a society can justly coerce its members, and he offers the classical liberal answer: "The sole end for which mankind are warranted, individually or collectively, in interfering with the liberty of action of any of their number, is self-protection." Starting from this negative limit, Mill maps out a positive "region of human liberty" that includes complete freedom in the "inward domain of consciousness"—thought and belief and, by extension, expression—as well as a broader freedom to "fram[e] the plan of our life to suit our own character." Perhaps most personally relevant for Mill, he insists on the freedom of any number of individuals "to unite, for any purpose not involving harm to others."

Mill's essay has become a cornerstone political text, articulating the principle that government should stay out of citizens' private affairs, but Mill's own experience had made him more concerned with the power of informal social forces—what he called "the despotism of custom." (No formal law had prohibited Mill's mother from accepting Harriet Taylor as a guest in her home.) Mill recognized that every age was governed by custom, but he felt that the particular custom of his time encouraged a conformist mediocrity. For most of history, he wrote, "the individual was a power in himself; and if he had either great talents or a high social position,

* Mill counted this essay among those on which he and Taylor collaborated. I'm following the general convention of treating the works published under Mill's name as his own, which isn't meant to minimize the role that Taylor played in their composition.

he was a considerable power." In the democratic age, by contrast, "individuals are lost in the crowd."

Even as Mill celebrates the energetic, great-souled individual who stands out from the crowd, his ultimate defense of liberty remains thoroughly utilitarian. As Locke had earlier argued, we are each the best judge of what actions will bring us happiness, and so the greatest-happiness principle requires the maximization of personal choice. Mill also saw a larger social benefit. Just as Bacon viewed the chief purpose of scientific experimentation as technological advancement, Mill saw human choice as a means of social progress.

His own experience synthesizing the Enlightenment and Romantic traditions had taught him that arriving at truth often means "reconciling and combining opposites," a process that occurs through "the rough process of a struggle between combatants fighting under hostile banners." And so he advocated what we would now call the "marketplace of ideas"—a space of robust disagreement and free expression—as the best means of arriving at the truth. But he carried the idea from the realm of opinion to the realm of morality: "As it is useful that while mankind are imperfect there should be different opinions, so is it that there should be different experiments of living. . . . The worth of different modes of life should be proved practically."

In order for such experiments to be properly carried out, people must make choices about what will bring them happiness, but "he who does anything because it is the custom, makes no choice." Custom and progress are inevitable antagonists, and "the contest between the two constitutes the chief interest of the history of mankind."

Mill's emphasis on progress or development as itself a sort of highest good of human life is one of the major ways he modified the utilitarianism he inherited from Bentham and his father. Another important break concerns his application of the greatest-happiness principle. Bentham emphasizes "the party whose interest is in question." Because his primary concern was legislation, he took the community at large as the relevant party in his own work, but he didn't think there was any justification for expecting individuals to take the community's interests over their own. This was precisely why it was necessary to design laws to align conflicting interests. But Mill means to construct an individual ethic while limiting as much as possible the state's coercive power.

As individual ethics go, "do what feels good" is paltry stuff, and Mill's own experience had taught him that seeking pleasure directly was not apt to produce happiness anyway. So he simply universalized the greatest-happiness principle: "The happiness which forms the utilitarian standard of what is right in conduct, is not the agent's own happiness, but that of all concerned. As between his own happiness and that of others, utilitarianism requires him to be as strictly impartial as a disinterested and benevolent spectator."

Part of the power of Bentham's approach was that it seemed to rest on a purely descriptive account of human wants. While it made prescriptions on the community level, they were something like an engineer's blueprints. Given what we know empirically to be our desired ends, Bentham's political reforms aimed to achieve those ends for as many of us as possible. It did not impose any ethical "oughts" on individuals, who were expected to go right on maximizing their own utility.

By contrast, Mill asks us not just to consider the interests of others but to treat them as indistinguishable from our own. This is closer to the impossible mandate that Jesus laid upon his followers than it is to any description of actual human behavior. And Mill does not even attempt to justify the move: "No reason can be given why the general happiness is desirable, except that each person, so far as he believes it to be attainable, desires his own happiness." Of course, this is no reason at all; it is simply a restatement of Benthamite self-interest.

Mill acknowledges the problem but insists that it is "inherent in every attempt to analyze morality and reduce it to principles": "It arises, in fact, whenever a person is called on to *adopt* a standard, or refer morality to any basis on which he has not been accustomed to rest it." Mill reintroduces the Humean idea that morality is ultimately dictated by custom rather than reason, which was precisely what Bentham meant to overcome. This seems particularly surprising, given Mill's thoughts on custom, but he didn't think we ought simply to accept the morality that custom hands down. Instead we ought to accustom people to a new morality.

This brings us back to the Enlightenment view of education so powerfully handed down to him by his father. If Locke is right that all ideas—including moral ideas—are acquired rather than innate, then it ought to be possible to inculcate the utilitarian ethic through education—essentially, to *make* it customary. There is obviously something coercive about wielding the "the despotism of custom" for such purposes, but Mill's justification for doing so is something like Locke's social-contract justification for political coercion: No rational person could object to being coerced in this direction. The only moral systems not consistent with utilitarianism are those life-negating ethics that embrace asceticism or sacrifice with no benefit for others, and these are clearly irrational.*

Finally, Mill argues that there is a qualitative distinction between the deeper pleasures of communal spirit and the narrower pleasure of self-interest, one that people will inevitably recognize once they have been taught to appreciate the higher communal pleasures. Bentham had rejected the very idea that we can distinguish "higher" and "lower" pleasures, but this was another one of Mill's innovations, likewise influenced by his brush with Romanticism. "It is quite compatible with the principle

* Mill seems to commit the same circularity as Hume, declaring the utility principle universally valid simply by discarding from consideration any morality that doesn't conform to it.

of utility," he writes in *Utilitarianism*, "to recognize the fact, that some *kinds* of pleasure are more desirable and more valuable than others."

Indeed, he goes further and says that "there is no known Epicurean theory of life which does not assign to the pleasures of the intellect, of the feelings and imagination, and of the moral sentiments, a much higher value as pleasures than to those of mere sensation." As a historical claim, this is nonsense, as Mill certainly knew: Bentham himself drew no such distinction. Mill's reliance on a spurious historical precedent reflects the enormity of the challenge he's set for himself. In order for different kinds of pleasure to be judged qualitatively, one must have some standard other than pleasure itself by which to make qualitative judgments, and this is precisely the thing that utilitarianism denies.

One pleasure can be understood as "higher" than another, Mill says, when a person with sufficient ability to appreciate both chooses the one over the other. Most people lack the faculties and cultivation to appreciate the "higher pleasures," but those who do will reliably choose them over simpler ones: "On a question which is the best worth having of two pleasures, or which of two modes of existence is the most grateful to the feelings, apart from its moral attributes and from its consequences, the judgment of those who are qualified by knowledge of both, or, if they differ, that of the majority among them, must be admitted as final."

There is a circularity here: We educate people to share our values, then we use the fact that educated people share our values as evidence of their "higher" status. Might it not equally be the case that through education we turn people away from what they naturally value? That is precisely the argument that Hume and Mill and countless contemporary atheists make about religious education, and it is hard to see how it doesn't apply equally to Mill's kind of education.

In fact, the Romantic tradition does apply this same critique to Enlightenment rationality, and this critique is expressed by Mill himself in his complaints about democratic mediocrity. Mill insists that the "inward domain of consciousness" should be free, but his educational plan seeks to influence precisely this domain. He tells us that people should determine their own sense of the good rather than blindly following custom, but he also believes that education should make people internalize this particular custom to such a degree that they don't even recognize custom at work.

To Foucault and other postmodern critics of Enlightenment rationalism, the most sinister feature of the Benthamite panopticon is the fact that we are *not* always being watched but could be watched at any time. Eventually we come to internalize the watching; we become our own prison guards. While he describes it in more benign terms, this is exactly the outcome Mill envisions.

All of this, of course, assumes that such radical reformation of human nature is even possible. For all his Romantic suspicions of Enlightenment rationality, Mill embraces the Enlightenment view that human nature is malleable to an almost limitless extent, and that the problem of evil, which had been taken as a permanent feature of terrestrial existence, is really a technical challenge to be rationally managed away: "All the grand sources, in short, of human suffering are in a great degree, many of them almost entirely, conquerable by human care and effort."

Eight

EMBRYO ENGLANDS

I used the slightly anachronistic expression *marketplace of ideas* to characterize Mill's ideal of "experiments of living" and his faith that allowing lifestyles and beliefs to compete for adherents, rather than preempting this process through formal or informal restraints, would ultimately ensure that the best of them won out. Another term comes to mind as well: *survival of the fittest.* This may be more historically appropriate, since *On Liberty* appeared in the same year as Charles Darwin's *On the Origin of Species.*

Evolutionary thinking was commonplace in the intellectual environment surrounding both men, who were nearly exact contemporaries. One of the most significant and controversial scientific works of the first half of the nineteenth century was Charles Lyell's *Principles of Geology*, published in three volumes between 1830 and 1833, which argued that the earth's topography had arisen through a process of steady and gradual change rather than being created all at once or developing through global catastrophes like the biblical flood. In the book's second volume, Lyell took up the question of a similar process of biological evolution, which had been earlier described by the French naturalist Jean-Baptiste Lamarck, who argued in *Philosophie zoologique* that physical adaptations to the environment occurring during a creature's lifetime could be passed on to offspring.

Charles Darwin was born in 1809—the same year Lamarck's study appeared—to a wealthy and culturally prominent family. His grandfather Erasmus was a physician and poet who had proposed his own version of biological evolution. The younger Darwin was expected to follow the family trade of medicine, but he proved an indifferent student, so he was sent instead to study for the ministry at Cambridge, where he developed a serious interest in the natural world. Upon graduation, he was invited to join a multiyear surveying voyage on the HMS *Beagle*.

Accepting this offer was not a repudiation of his earlier career plans; there was a long tradition of Anglican "parson-naturalists," some of whom taught Darwin at Cambridge. By the end of the voyage, however, he had given up plans for the ministry and committed himself to a proper career in the sciences.

Apart from the literary account of his travels that made Darwin famous, his earliest works were monographs on geographical features drawn from his trip. (Lyell's book was among the few that he'd taken along.) But he soon set himself thinking about the variety of organic life he'd seen and the strange precision with which particular species and subspecies (or "races") of plants and animals seemed suited to their local environments. It did not make sense to say that they were created for their environments because—as Darwin's geological studies had taught him—the environments themselves had changed over time.

Darwin believed he could find a better explanation for this phenomenon by "following the example of Lyell in Geology"—that is, assuming a natural process governed by laws still in evidence. He began his search "on true Baconian principles," collecting facts without any theory or principle behind them. Having noticed that domesticated plants and animals showed particular signs of both variability and suitability, he devoted a great deal of time to interviewing "skilful breeders and gardeners." Many of them noted that the general rule that offspring inherit the characteristics of their parents was marked by frequent, unexplained exceptions. Breeders and gardeners produced the great variety of domestic breeds by maintaining the offspring that exhibited adaptive characteristics and destroying those that did not. In other words, the key to "man's success in making useful races of animals and plants" was *selection*. Darwin guessed that a similar principle was at work among undomesticated species. But how did such selection occur in nature, absent intelligent intervention?

The answer came from the economist Thomas Malthus. Decades earlier, Malthus had become famous for his argument that the human population naturally increased at a geometric rate while the supply of resources sustaining that growth increased linearly. Population growth therefore inevitably lowered per-capita output. Throughout human history, infant and childhood mortality had served as a natural check on this problem, but in Western societies that was beginning to change. Malthus argued that people in technologically advanced countries should have smaller families. He also argued that laws protecting the poor from starvation were ultimately counterproductive, since they encouraged behavior that lowered overall standards of living.

In 1839, fifteen months into his "systematic enquiry," Darwin read Malthus's *Essay on the Principle of Population*. "Being well prepared to appreciate the struggle for existence which everywhere goes on from long-continued observation of the habits of animals and plants," Darwin later noted, "it at once struck me that under these circumstances favourable variations would tend to be preserved, and unfavourable ones to be destroyed. . . . Here then I had at last got a theory by which to work."

The core of this theory would be "the doctrine of Malthus applied with manifold force to the whole animal and vegetable kingdoms." For the key to natural selection was the understanding that "a struggle for existence inevitably follows from the high rate at which all organic beings tend to increase." This struggle comprises not just individual survival but "success in leaving progeny." If reproduction weren't checked in some way, the offspring of any given reproducing pair would soon cover the entire earth. What does check them is all the other organic life similarly filling the world with offspring. Creatures feed on other creatures, compete with other creatures for the same food, fight over territory in habitable climates. In the process, nature itself acts like a particularly merciless breeder, destroying the ill-suited before they reproduce.

An important feature of Darwinian competition is that it is fiercest among individuals most similar in "habits and constitution"—not between predators and prey, but between those fleeing the same predators or seeking the same prey. Offspring that enjoy some singular random advantage will thrive precisely at the expense of creatures otherwise most like them, including their own sibling offspring. This dynamic explains why two species descended from the same source may be wildly unlike each other, with no apparent "linking" species: The intermediate species are precisely the ones that would be lost to competition. It also explains why species themselves show great uniformity within closed areas but tend to develop into different "races" as they spread to wider territory.

Darwin developed this idea with great care over two decades, corresponding with others about it but never publishing on it until he learned that a younger British naturalist, Alfred Russel Wallace, was preparing to publish a nearly identical theory. Evolution through natural selection is one of the most famous instances of simultaneous discovery in human history, and the fact that the two discoverers were Englishmen who had previously met each other and shared acquaintances suggests the extent to which the idea was already in the intellectual air. (Wallace too was inspired by Malthus.) In 1858, the two men published a jointly authored paper setting the question of priority to rest. The next year Darwin completed *On the Origin of Species by Means of Natural Selection, or the Preservation of Favoured Races in the Struggle for Life.*

UNLIKE EARLIER EVOLUTIONARY theories, Darwin's was entirely positivistic: It concerned only observable material facts and a handful of laws governing these facts. Again, these laws were not causal forces or explanations but merely redescriptions of the facts themselves: "I mean by Nature," Darwin wrote in response to those who accused him of elevating natural selection to a kind of deity, "only the aggregate and action of many natural laws, and by laws the sequence of events as ascertained by us."

From the positivist perspective, the key breakthrough is Darwin's insistence that adaptation happens by way of random variation, not through the choices of individual creatures. This removes any explanatory role for the outdated metaphysics of interior psychology. Darwinians speak often in terms of the individual motivation to survive and procreate, but like the invocation of "Nature," this is a metaphor, "almost necessary for brevity." It is simply a fact that the things that successfully propagate crowd out the things that don't; no existential drive is necessary. There is no place for agency at all.

This very much includes human agency. Darwin did not initially dwell upon his theory's implications for humanity, but they were obvious to others from the beginning. Because it explains not just physical structure but behavior, evolutionary theory provides a positivist approach to all those human sciences—psychology, sociology, economics, politics, and ethics—that Enlightenment thinkers had dreamed of subsuming under natural philosophy.

Darwin sometimes referred to the principle of natural selection as "utilitarian," and the parallel between Bentham's happiness principle and

Darwin's struggle for existence is clear enough. Both are resolutely consequentialist, and both presume a single, strictly self-interested impulse as the motivating factor in all behavior. But Darwinism could go where Benthamism could not. As even Mill had acknowledged, the great difficulty for the happiness principle is making it the basis for a wholly naturalized normative system. This was a problem Darwin seemed to solve with the idea of "survival of the fittest."

The philosopher Herbert Spencer coined this expression upon first reading *Origin*, but Darwin found it apt enough to give it a prominent place in later editions of the book. (He describes it as a "more accurate" term than "natural selection.") Today we understand evolution as morally neutral and "survival of the fittest" as a kind of poetic tautology: The only kind of "fitness" nature selects is the fitness to survive and propagate. But this is not how Darwin thought of things. While acknowledging the potential grimness of the zero-sum struggle for survival, Darwin noted that in such a system "the vigorous, the healthy, and the happy survive and multiply." Evolution naturally produced superior specimens.

It was as obvious to early Darwinians as it was to their religious opponents that humans were superior to brute animals. The evidence of this fact was that humanity had spread everywhere around the globe, adapted to various climates, and placed nonhuman animals under its dominion. The realization that humanity was not made in God's image did not lower us in the order of beings. And it was just as obvious that certain human "races" were superior to others. Darwin believed resolutely in the biological reality of racial differences, and he believed there to be a clear evolutionary hierarchy among races.

While traveling with the *Beagle*, Darwin often remarked upon the brutality of Western encounters with Indigenous groups, and he was sometimes sensitive to it—particularly in places like South America, where the Westerners in question were continental Europeans. But where his own countrymen were concerned, his feeling was different. "All the fragments of the civilized world which we [i.e., the English] have visited in the southern hemisphere, appear to be flourishing," he wrote. "Little embryo Englands are springing into life in many quarters." This spectacle filled him with an unmistakable pride: "To hoist the British flag, seems to draw with it as a certain consequence, wealth, prosperity, and civilization."

The march of improvement had been an Enlightenment faith since Bacon, but Darwinism brought a new possibility to this dream of progress. Darwinism rejects the idea that human nature is fixed in any way. Indeed, it rejects the idea of human nature. We have progressed from single-cell organisms, and there is nothing about us as we are now that can't be radically changed.

Darwin was under no illusions about what this progress would entail. "Wherever the European has trod," he'd already noted in *Voyage of the Beagle*, "death seems to pursue the aboriginal." At the time, Darwin had seen in this fact a "mysterious agency" at work, but once he'd developed his own theory of natural selection, he had an obvious explanation: As we've already seen, a creature with an advantageous variation poses the greatest threat to precisely those creatures that are otherwise most like it.

IN 1871, Darwin published *The Descent of Man*, his account of human evolution, where he finally states explicitly that *Homo sapiens* share evolutionary ancestors with all the animals on earth, and that what we take to be particularly human qualities—language, reason, emotions—are modifications of attributes visible in other creatures. But the book is just as interested in accounting for differences within the species. Indeed, the two subjects are inseparable: His earlier work had traced the origin of species to the "preservation of favoured races"; *The Descent of Man* takes the competition between human races as the key to our future development.

As Darwin observed throughout his travels, different races or subspecies can survive in isolation from each other—as do the finches on the different islands of the Galapagos. If they find themselves competing within the same environment, however, the inferior strain will soon be extinct. For human subspecies, this would not mean mere cultural extinction, because Darwin understood racial difference to be biological: *The Descent of Man* is full of "scientific" details about variance in "the capacity of the lungs, the form and capacity of the skull, and even in the convolutions of the brain" among different human types. Now that the advanced European race had found its way to every corner of the globe, the verdict was clear. "At some future period, not very distant as measured by centuries," Darwin predicts, "the civilised races of man will almost certainly exterminate, and replace, the savage races throughout the world."

Darwin recognized the brutality of this, but he thought it inevitable and even desirable. The real risk to humanity was that sensitive feelings would tempt civilized men to stop natural selection from doing its work. "With savages, the weak in body or mind are soon eliminated," he remarked, "and those that survive commonly exhibit a vigorous state of health." Civilization undermines this strengthening process: "We build asylums for the imbecile, the maimed, and the sick; we institute poor-laws; and our medical men exert their utmost skill to save the life of every one to the last moment." He even blames vaccination for "preserv[ing] thousands, who from a weak constitution would formerly have succumbed to small-pox."

Darwin's study of plant and animal breeding showed him the likely results of allowing the weak to produce offspring: "It is surprising how soon a want of care, or care wrongly directed, leads to the degeneration of a domestic race; but excepting in the case of man himself, hardly any one is so ignorant as to allow his worst animals to breed." On this matter, he quotes with approval the founders of the eugenics movement, Francis Galton (Darwin's cousin) and W. R. Greg: "The careless, squalid, unaspiring Irishman multiplies like rabbits: the frugal, foreseeing, self-respecting, ambitious Scot, stern in his morality, spiritual in his faith, sagacious and disciplined in his intelligence, passes his best years in struggle and in celibacy, marries late, and leaves few behind him." If a misguided charity protected these squalid Irishmen from starvation, the result would be that "the inferior and LESS favoured race" prevailed "in the eternal 'struggle for existence.'"

A century and a half later, we take for granted that eugenics and the specious racial science that underwrote it were terrible perversions of Darwin's biological theory. But this is not what one naturally concludes when reading Darwin himself. You won't find many scientific materialists recommending *The Descent of Man*. When I finally came to it, I had the same feeling I'd gotten from reading Montaigne and Hume: I was encountering a very different writer from the one who'd been described to me. The study of competition within human societies was not some eccentric, off-brand application of evolutionary theory but a chief inspiration for it. Having been sent by Malthus in the direction of natural selection, Darwin ultimately arrived at the Malthusian view that the forces of scarcity and competition ought to be freed to do the work of elevating humanity—and that this elevation would require the extinction of inferior human races.

Another requirement of this elevating process, Darwin eventually came to suspect, would be the withering away of religious faith. It remained quite rare at that time (at least in England) for a person to declare outright that he didn't believe in God. Even John Stuart Mill, when describing his irreligious upbringing, insisted that his father looked upon "dogmatic atheism" as "absurd." Instead, James Mill "yielded to the conviction, that concerning the origin of things nothing whatever can be known."

It was one of Darwin's most prominent defenders, the biologist T. H.

Huxley, who coined *agnosticism* to describe the view that we should not hold any beliefs for which we do not have scientific evidence, and Darwin would eventually use the term to describe his own religious disposition. The view is a logical extension of Locke's insistence that we should rely on faith only where reason can't do the job. It simply adds the increasingly plausible belief that reason alone could do any job worth doing.

But Darwinism didn't just make agnosticism of this sort a more tenable position. It made the rejection of traditional religious belief an urgent social mandate. After Darwin, religious superstitions came increasingly to seem like those squalid (Catholic) Irishmen, allowed to multiply despite their inability to pay their own way. A false sense of enlightened magnanimity toward these beliefs threatened the health of our entire species.

The search for scientific explanations for the remaining human mysteries would become inseparable from the larger project of material and moral progress, which would in turn become the grand narrative that gave life meaning for many atheists. Progress demanded that religion give way to scientific explanation. One day, Darwin suggested, humanity would reach such a height that it could look back even on civilized Englishmen as "mere Barbarians." Doubtless our remaining vestiges of belief would look particularly primitive to those perfected humans.

Nine

ROBBING THE GODS

Bertrand Russell was born directly into these cultural developments. His parents were "freethinkers," and his father was a member of the radical, Benthamite wing of the Whigs, the liberal political party that one of Russell's ancestors had helped to found in the eighteenth century on Lockean principles. John Stuart Mill and Helen Taylor (Harriet's daughter) served as Bertrand's godparents,* and he seemed destined from birth to be raised along progressive lines. "I do not remember ever being taken to church or having the name of God inflicted upon me," his older brother, Frank, wrote about their early years.

All this changed in 1874, when Russell was two years old. His mother, Kate, and his older sister, Rachel, died of diphtheria within weeks of each other. His father fell into a depression that left him unable to care for his surviving sons and died himself two years later, having apparently lost the will to live. He named two young radicals, Douglas Spalding and T. J. Sanderson, as the boys' guardians. Introduced to the household by Mill, Spalding had lived with the Russell family and had an affair with Kate, undertaken with her husband's encouragement, lovelessly and in an entirely

---

* A secular honorific, but Russell relished both his connection to the radical tradition and the ironic form this connection took.

utilitarian spirit: Spalding was consumptive, and the couple had agreed that it was unjust for him to be denied the pleasures of sex simply because he was not suitable to marry.

In the process of fighting (successfully) for custody, Russell's grandmother discovered all this, and she was suitably horrified. Lady Russell was a devout believer whose home, as Frank would put it, was "full of high principle and religious feeling of the same kind that surrounded Queen Victoria."* Given the tenor of Victorian religiosity, Bertrand would have faced his share of pious repression in any case, but the specific circumstances led to an exceptionally stifling atmosphere in which neither his parents nor sex were ever discussed, and in which these two silences were vaguely understood as related.

When Bertrand was eleven, Frank introduced him to Euclidean geometry. He immediately demanded a justification for Euclid's axioms and received the reply that geometry wouldn't work without them. He later described his dissatisfaction with this answer as "the first thing that led me towards philosophy." Nonetheless he was moved by the sense of certainty that mathematics provided, and he dreamed of expanding this certainty into other areas: "I hoped that in time there would be a mathematics of human behavior as precise as the mathematics of machines."

This ideal of certainty brought Russell his first doubts about God. While still young, he abandoned religious faith, apart from a kind of abstract philosophical theism with which he would flirt all his life. This was not a particularly welcome development, for Russell found that his new worldview was insufficient for living: "My doctrines, such as they are, help my daily life no more than a formula in algebra."

He went on to study math at Cambridge but remained bothered by the question he'd first posed to his brother: What was the foundation on

* Russell's grandfather twice served as prime minister during Victoria's reign.

which mathematical certainty was built? A younger Cambridge contemporary, G. E. Moore, convinced Russell that his troubles were actually philosophical in nature, and Russell changed the focus of his studies.

"I had not read Hume," he wrote later about this period in his life, "but it seemed to me that pure empiricism (which I was disposed to accept) must lead to skepticism." At Cambridge at this time, the prevailing philosophical response to this skepticism was a form of idealism influenced by the German philosopher G. W. F. Hegel, who understood ultimate reality as something eternal, infinite, singular, and perfect, resting outside the bounds of sensory perception. He called this reality *Geist*—"mind" or "spirit"—but the British idealists tended to call it "the Absolute." In either case, the implications are clear: An eternal, infinite, singular, and perfect entity is a god in all but name.

Many British idealists saw in the Absolute an attractive alternative to traditional theism. Russell was briefly among them, but his embrace of the doctrine was short-lived. In 1899, at the age of twenty-seven, Russell delivered a talk to the Apostles, the famous Cambridge intellectual society. While he didn't publish it at the time, the performance was his first more or less public call for the "abandonment of religion." Almost sixty years later, it would be the earliest work included in *Why I Am Not a Christian*. "Philosophy when it was still fat and prosperous, claimed to perform, for its votaries, a variety of the most important services," Russell begins. "It offered them comfort in adversity, explanation in intellectual difficulty, and guidance in moral perplexity." Intellectual difficulties were now the purview of science, while moral perplexity had been given over to "the whimsies of statistics and common sense." There remained only the "power of giving comfort and consolation": "It is this last possession of which, tonight, I wish to rob the decrepit parent of our modern gods."

Even if one accepts the idealist metaphysic, Russell argues, it can't be a rational source of consolation, because we can never hope to experience this timeless and infinite "Absolute," the very notion of experience being bound up with time and space. Metaphysical speculation might offer other kinds of comfort: It was a pleasant way to spend time and, "in this sense, the comfort derived may even, in extreme cases, be comparable to that of drinking as a way of passing our evenings." It could be enjoyed "like poetry or music, as a means of producing a mood, of giving us a certain view of the universe, a certain attitude toward life." But in these cases, the pleasure does not rest on "intellectual conviction."

If we aspire to gain comfort from the *truth* of metaphysics, we will be led astray by wishful thinking. Like scientists, philosophers "ought to be guided by intellectual curiosity alone," not by the hope of finding meaning in the world.

RUSSELL WAS ONCE again helped along here by G. E. Moore, whose own flirtation with idealism had been even shorter-lived. Another inspiration was a series of cutting-edge mathematical breakthroughs occurring on the Continent.

Since the time of Pythagoras, philosophers have had an almost mystical fascination with mathematical truths. Their power rests not just in their seeming certainty, but in the apparent fact that they can be apprehended through both reason and experience, a priori and a posteriori, which suggests that numbers might be our route to the metaphysical reality that orders and undergirds the world of sense experience.

This fact has also meant that grave problems arise when mathematical operations deliver up absurdities, paradoxes, or results inconsistent with experience. Philosophers and mathematicians have fought dramatic battles over the status of irrational, imaginary, and negative numbers, as well as zero and infinity, which can be treated as numbers in some cases but not in others. Many treated the infinite as something more like a philosophical concept than a mathematical entity, but the Copernican revolution presented the universe itself as infinite, rather than bounded, as Aristotle had believed it to be. With the development of calculus, mathematicians came to make frequent practical use of infinity without having eliminated the paradoxes that came with it.

Around the time of Russell's birth, the German mathematician Georg Cantor resolved many of these issues through the development of set theory. A mathematical "set" is a collection of mathematical entities, with inclusion in the set being determined by some logical operation. For example, imagine a set of all the whole numbers. This set would have infinite members, but the "number" infinity would not be contained in the set. Nor would the set itself be a number, any more than a set of five IKEA chairs is itself a chair. You could use the set in place of infinity in various mathematical operations that require it, and in doing so eliminate many of the perplexities that arise from treating infinity as a number like any other.

The details of set theory would be well beyond the scope of this book even if I understood them. The important point for Russell was that Cantor redefined what had been a numerical entity as a logical arrangement, which raised the possibility that *all* quantities could be redescribed as sets, allowing pure mathematics to do away with the metaphysically fraught concept of "number" entirely.

In 1903 Russell published *The Principles of Mathematics*, in which he began the work of getting from a handful of logical inferences to the most complex mathematical operations. He quickly proceeded to a second volume that he hoped would continue the project. Over the course of the next decade, this would become the multivolume *Principia Mathematica*, written in collaboration with Alfred North Whitehead. Though it spanned almost two thousand pages, the *Principia* still didn't complete the job, but it got far enough along to convince Russell and many others that all of mathematics could indeed be redescribed in logical terms.

"MATHEMATICS AND LOGIC," Russell wrote at the outset of these efforts in *The Principles of Mathematics*, "are identical." This identity had implications for logic as well as mathematics. It suggested that logic could be expressed with the rigor of mathematical language and that logical truths could have the full force of mathematical certainty.

Since the time of Hobbes, empiricists had recognized words as powerful tools for relating the facts of experience while also viewing them as a dangerous invitation to spurious metaphysical thought. Words could make the illogical sound logical. They could express sheer nonsense as though it were sensical. Neither of these things is possible in mathematics. Certainly it's possible to say something mathematically false, but there is a very clear method for checking the truth of a mathematical statement, in part because it's always clear what a mathematical statement means to express. Furthermore, Russell believed, there are no mathematical truths that elude expression. Everything that can possibly be true in a properly ordered mathematical system can be expressed in that system's language. In the *Principia*, Russell and Whitehead developed a symbolic logic that treated logical relations as quasi-mathematical operations and allowed variables to be substituted for facts in much the way they are substituted for numbers in algebraic equations. The hope was that expressions of empirical fact and logical relationship—the two kinds of significance that empiricists recognize—could both be sufficiently quantified to do away entirely with words as carriers of truth.

For Russell, the very heart of philosophy was at stake. When Bacon began the work of separating speculative philosophy from what would become the natural sciences, he left the former with the task of metaphysics. With Locke's identification of philosophers as under-laborers, clearing the ground for empirical science, the philosopher's task instead became epistemology. Russell introduced another turn: "Logic is what is fundamental in philosophy."

Philosophy could never say whether a meaningful claim about the world was true—that was an empirical question. But through logical analysis philosophers could determine precisely what meaningful claims about the world were actually being made in various kinds of verbal statements. Very often, the answer was: none at all. That a proposition was meaningless, tautological, or contradictory—these were the kinds of judgments philosophers could make. As we've seen, this had always been a popular philosophical task, but Russell made it essentially the *only* philosophical task. He was once again preceded in this conclusion by G. E. Moore, and the analytic tradition they started remains to this day the dominant strain in Western academic philosophy.

Intellectual sanitation work is a dignified but perhaps not especially inspiring undertaking. As though in compensation for all that's been robbed from them, analytic philosophers have made great sport of puncturing their discipline's grand pretensions. They use the terms *metaphysics* and *nonsense* interchangeably, for example, or compare speculative philosophy—as Russell did in his Apostles talk—to getting drunk.

A certain kind of philosopher finds it scandalous to still be fighting over the same problems that animated the pre-Socratics. What is the point of the discipline, if it can't settle certain questions, in the way that other fields of study—particularly the sciences—seem to do? And the simplest way to put an intractable question to rest is to prove that it's nonsensical.

One of the enduring philosophical controversies that the new dispensation believed itself to have resolved in this way was that between realism and idealism—that is, the question of whether subjective experience is more or less transparently representative of some objective reality. Russell and Moore both professed to be realists of a sort, but the proper analytic response to the controversy was hinted at in the Apostles talk: What difference could it possibly make?

The logical positivist Rudolf Carnap—one of Russell's earliest followers—placed the realism-idealism argument high on his list of "pseudoproblems" that philosophers had created for themselves through linguistic confusion. The theses of both realism and idealism, Carnap insisted, "have no content; they are not statements at all." The very fact that the matter can't be settled either empirically or analytically makes it meaningless.

In practice, of course, most experimental scientists take the subject of their experiments to be material objects arranged in physical space, rather than mental representations arranged in logical space. The modern era in which science is taken to be the primary source of knowledge treats realism as common sense in just the way that Locke did. Anyone who has not been irremediably corrupted by recreational drugs or undergraduate philosophy courses, the prevailing view goes, will reject idealism as a kind of lunacy.

The prevailing modern view actually goes quite a bit further than this commonsense realism. As noted, Locke's realism is dualistic: It suggests that there exist two kinds of things—mental ideas and the physical objects they represent. Dualistic accounts of reality have all sorts of problems, and so it has always been tempting to do away with one or the other of these two sets of corresponding entities. Bishop Berkeley's idealism eliminates the physical. The other option is doing away with the mental.

Though it has had its proponents in every era, materialism was generally unpopular before the twentieth century, because it just seems intuitively the case that mental experience exists. But the positivist turn tells us that the introspection from which such intuitions come is itself not a proper basis for knowledge. This turn made materialism not just tenable but something like the new commonsense view. From the perspective of the positivist philosophers themselves, materialism is thoroughly unscientific; the great positivist project of overcoming metaphysics does not seek to answer such questions in one direction or another but to set them aside entirely, to grow out of asking them. But philosophers have largely lost their self-appointed task of drawing science's proper boundaries. Having handed over the deed to the house, it is hard to declare one room off limits, no matter how strongly you insist that there's really nothing in there.

In the post-Darwinian era, the materialist metaphysic has gone hand in hand with the belief that science *has* no proper boundaries, that it can offer a complete picture of reality. I'm going to use the name *scientism* to describe this view. The term is often pejorative, but it's worth maintaining, because it draws an important distinction: One does not have to accept this totalizing view in order to practice science or to accept the knowledge that science gives us, just as one does not have to be a materialist to be an empiricist. Indeed, the slightest tincture of Humean skepticism will tell you that scientism itself can't be arrived at empirically.

Proponents of scientism disagree over how close we are now to a complete picture of reality and whether we are likely in practice ever to complete the picture, but they agree that there can be no reason in principle why the picture couldn't be completed, given sufficient time and effort. Before Darwin, they note, many people who denied religious accounts of creation assumed that humanity would simply have to live without an explanation for the appearance of complex design in nature. After Darwin, there remained questions to be answered in this area, details to be sorted, but the mystery was resolved. Scientism takes for granted that any remaining apparent mysteries are ultimately subject to an equivalent elucidation. "A mystery," as Daniel Dennett has put it, "is a phenomenon that people don't know how to think about—yet."

Scientistic epistemology and materialist metaphysics depend on each other. The belief that experimental science can complete the picture of reality requires the belief that reality is exclusively composed of the kind of stuff that experimental science can study—i.e., objective matter. Meanwhile, the only empirical way to establish the truth of materialism is implicitly, by providing a picture of reality that is at once comprehensive and wholly material. This may be impossible as a practical matter, but at the very least science must come close enough to completing the picture to show how it could be done in principle.

This effort at complete description relies on another key feature of scientific materialism—physical reductionism.* In the reductionist view, the behavior of living organisms (including the most complex human behavior) can be explained in biological terms, biology explained in chemical terms, chemistry explained in physical terms, and physics explained in terms of a handful of immutable laws.

It took a twentieth-century discovery (or rediscovery) to make reductionism seem widely plausible. Darwin did not have a physical explanation for the inheritance with random variation that drove evolutionary change. That explanation ultimately came from Gregor Mendel's genetic theory of biological inheritance. Almost a century after Darwin and Mendel made their respective discoveries, the discovery of DNA's double-helix structure showed how replication happened and accounted for the mutations that play such a key part in natural selection. Inheritance with variation was another mystery tamed.

The implications of the gene-centered view eventually found their classic expression in Richard Dawkins's *The Selfish Gene*. Dawkins em-

* *Reductionism* (like *scientism*) is a word often used by Darwin-resistant humanists to attack scientific materialists, so it may seem that I am begging the question by making it a defining feature of the worldview. But most scientific materialists proudly admit to being reductionists in the sense I'm describing here.

phasizes a simple point: If genes are the mechanism by which inheritance with variation happens—if they are, in fact, the very entities that are inherited with variation—then it must be on the genetic level that natural selection operates. When we think about survival of the fittest, we must remember always that it is *genes* that survive, and that it is genes whose fitness is being implicitly tested: "They are in you and me; they created us, body and mind; and their preservation is the ultimate rationale for our existence." All living creatures are in fact "survival machines—robot vehicles blindly programmed to preserve the selfish molecules known as genes."

This approach is an incredible boon to the reductionist project. The fact that inheritance occurs on a molecular level means that the behavior of complex living creatures, which Darwin had already reduced to the biological mandate for survival, can be further reduced to the level of chemical interactions. From there these chemical interactions can be reduced further, to blind physical processes.

Daniel Dennett likens Darwinian theory to a "universal acid" that eats through any container you try to keep it in; once it is out in the world, it inevitably becomes the explanation for *everything*: "In a single stroke, the idea of evolution by natural selection unifies the realm of life, meaning, and purpose with the realm of space and time, cause and effect, mechanism and physical law."

One of the theory's most important features is that it allows us teleological thinking within a purely mechanical system. Concepts like agency, will, desire, and need have no place in a truly materialist account of reality, but with Darwinism we can speak *as though* things had final causes while keeping always in mind that this appearance of teleology emerges from "the mere purposeless, mindless, pointless regularity of physics."

With the neo-Darwinist synthesis in hand, we are well on our way to the complete picture of physical reality that will for all intents and purposes prove materialism. In *The Selfish Gene*, Dawkins quotes approvingly the contention that all human efforts before Darwin came along to answer the question "What is the meaning of life?" were "worthless." Now another mystery can be solved. "If superior creatures from space ever visit earth," he writes, "the first question they will ask, in order to assess the level of our civilization, is: 'Have they discovered evolution yet?'"

Ten

SOME HARD PROBLEMS

My historical account is now essentially done. In telling it, I've tried to show that scientific materialism is one worldview among many, rather than a neutral description of the reality that inevitably emerges when we look the world frankly in the face. But showing a worldview to be a worldview is not itself an argument against it.

An obvious next step would be attempting to demonstrate that this particular worldview is untrue. But this attempt would immediately run into the foundation-building problems we've already discussed: One of the most important things a worldview determines is how its inhabitants evaluate truth claims and indeed whether truth can be demonstrated at all, and thus criticizing one worldview from the standpoint of another will always beg the question. I want instead to stay within scientific materialism's own bounds, to consider whether this worldview succeeds on its own terms, whether it provides a reasonably complete and coherent picture of reality as the worldview itself defines it, and whether this picture has a compelling claim to our allegiance according to the worldview's own ethical standards.

Let's start with completeness. Once scientific materialism has done its work, are there any mysteries left that seem likely to remain mysteries?

One obvious candidate is the origin of everything. Every human culture has asked some version of the question *Where did it all begin?* Aristotle understood the heavens to be eternal and unchanging, one of the few areas where medieval Christians differed with him. While the Copernican revolution shattered the Aristotelian picture of the unchanging heavens, it suggested that Aristotle was right about eternity. Beginning with Hume, secular philosophers rejected first-cause arguments on the grounds that the universe need not have had a start. "There is no reason to suppose that the world had a beginning at all," Bertrand Russell wrote in his own critique of the argument. The idea of time itself coming into being seems to require the existence of some timeless eternity out of which it might emerge, and this clearly smacks of metaphysics.

Einstein changed all this. Relativity tells us that time is not a universally experienced linear unfolding in which physical reality takes place but a part of that reality's fabric, a dimension that can be traversed at different rates. Einstein's understanding of mass and energy also suggests that this space-time fabric has to be expanding; otherwise it would collapse on the weight of itself. Einstein initially rejected this possibility, and he added a "cosmological constant" to his equations, which made them come out right without assuming expansion.

Soon after publishing the papers that made him famous, Einstein received a letter from a Belgian priest and physicist, Georges Lemaître, urging him to do without the constant. Lemaître speculated that our universe had exploded out from a point of infinitesimal compression (a "primordial atom," he called it) from which it had been expanding ever since. Astronomical evidence eventually confirmed this expansion, and Lemaître's version of the universe's origins gained wide acceptance.

The big bang theory fits the observable evidence but raises the question of where this infinitely compressed point of energy came from and why it got that way. Scientific materialism reframes every "why" as a "how," and every "how" as a "that," so we want to know something like: What was the prior state that gave rise to these conditions? But in this case, there can't *be* a prior state. "Before" and "after" are temporal concepts, and time is one of the things brought into existence at that moment.

Some scientific materialists respond with a shrug: *Everything that exists must have started somewhere.* (Note the neat reversal of the earlier shrug: *What makes you think that everything that exists must have started somewhere?*) Granting that this is true, the point where everything actually did start was an incredibly improbable state, and not just in an intuitive, commonsensical way: Physicists have come to understand entropy (the degeneration of systems from order to disorder, the diffusion of compressed energy) as the movement from low-probability to higher-probability conditions; in scientific terms, the very reason that the big bang was enough to get the universe going for billions of years is that it was an incredibly low-probability state. If we take seriously what the mathematical models tell us—that the universe was compressed into an *infinitely* small, *infinitely* dense point—we might even call the state impossible.

It is even more improbable that the particular conditions of the big bang should have been exactly those that would allow for the development of atoms, stars, planets, and, eventually, self-replicating chemical structures set out on the evolutionary path toward intelligent life. When it comes to the improbability of the emergence of the last of these, materialists can legitimately fall back on the cosmological scale of time and space, in which vanishingly improbable things become nearly inevitable. All that's needed are the initial conditions that make them possible. But such an argument can't be made about the initial conditions themselves.

A number of current cosmological theories attempt to address these issues. One proposes that space-time is engaged in an eternal oscillation from maximally compressed to maximally extended: The big bang was part of an endless series of big bounces. At the moment of this bounce, everything is up for grabs, physically speaking, and one of these oscillations simply wound up producing the conditions that allowed for life. Another popular option is multiverse theory, which holds that our universe is one of a potentially infinite number, again making the existence of a universe with the physical constants of our own a matter of statistical probability.

Physicist Sabine Hossenfelder describes our various theories of the universe's origins as "modern creation myths written in the language of mathematics." No evidence gathered within our own universe could differentiate a big bang reality from a big bounce one. While it is conceivable that we might find evidence of a neighboring universe, that could never tell us that there were infinitely many of them. "Not only is there no evidence" for these differing theories, Hossenfelder writes, "but it's also hard to conceive of *any* evidence that could settle the debate regarding which one was correct, because they are all so flexible they can plausibly be made to accommodate any data thrown at them." From a truly positivist standpoint, that makes them all nonsense claims.

Furthermore, these theories all suffer from the problem of infinite regress, which plagues any origin story. In the same passage in which he questions whether the universe had to have a beginning, Russell argues that all "First Cause" arguments are "exactly of the same nature as the Hindu's view, that the world rested upon an elephant and the elephant rested upon a tortoise; and when they said, 'How about the tortoise?' the Indian said, 'Suppose we change the subject.'"

Atheist lore has handed this story down in the form of an obstinate lecture-hall audience member (for some reason always an older woman) who glibly assures Russell that it's "turtles all the way down." This popular retelling implies that mythological creation stories suffer especially acutely from this problem, but there is something distinctly turtles-all-the-way-down about both the big bounce and multiverse theories. Russell understood that *any* explanation of origins falls into this trap, which is why he preferred to believe that the universe was eternal.

The problem for scientific materialists is that their own standards for truth suggest otherwise. And it does seem that the question *Where did it all begin?*—which, again, has likely occurred to every human culture that ever existed—remains a profound mystery rather than merely a technical problem yet to be mastered. To reply that any conceivable solution to the problem is bound to be unsatisfactory is simply to acknowledge the point.

CAN WE AT LEAST say that once things get going, once this expanding space-time of ours is underway, we have left the land of mystery?

Staying for a moment on the grand cosmological scale, there is in fact a sharp limit on how far our knowledge can extend. Because the speed of light sets an upper boundary on how quickly information can travel, because the universe is vast enough and expanding quickly enough for that limit to be meaningful, and because a finite amount of time has passed since the universe began, there exists what astronomers call a "cosmic horizon"—a point from beyond which information has simply not had time to reach us.

For obvious reasons, we can't ever know how much territory lies beyond this point, what portion of the whole it represents. We can't know whether or not the universe is infinite, whether it's open or closed.* If what we can know is only a tiny part of what exists—and, in the case of an infinite universe, this is certainly so—we can't know how representative it is of the whole.

Meanwhile, everything that we do know comes to us out of date. The information we gather at any moment is not about that moment but about

* I.e., whether something traveling in one direction would ever come back to where it started, as on a globe.

the moment when the information left its source. We have become inured to the romantic cliché that we gaze into the distant past when we look up at the night sky, that the stars whose light now reaches us might have burned out millions of years ago, but it remains an astonishing fact when considered anew. Closer to home the time lapse becomes negligible, but the fact remains that everywhere you look you see the past: What appears to us as a singular instant that we occupy simultaneously with all that surrounds us is countless different pasts arriving to us at once. This may be Einstein's most revolutionary insight: There is no such thing as a universally applicable "right now."

Yet life seems to each of us a succession of such nows. It's quite obvious and unproblematic that everything in the world occupies a slightly different portion of space, but we don't sense everything around us as occupying different times. Einstein himself was deeply troubled by what he called the "problem of the Now." It didn't seem right to him that subjective experience should conflict in such a radical way with the reality science reveals to us.

A lot of post-Newtonian physics troubled Einstein in this way. Quantum mechanics tells us that subatomic particles behave in a manner utterly inconsistent with our commonsense understanding of the physical world. Electrons "leap" from one orbital location to another without passing through the space in between. These quantum leaps "constitute their way of being real," as the quantum gravity theorist Carlo Rovelli puts it. What brings them into a determined position is their interaction with another entity: "An electron is a combination of leaps from one interaction to another."

Because studying electrons requires interacting with them, we can never know what state they inhabit between interactions. At larger scales, we can use information about an object at two different points to determine the path it took between them, but this method does not work for electrons, which exhibit a built-in randomness such that their previous position can't account for where they wind up. Instead we must treat them as taking every possible route between the two points, within a statistical matrix. This idea provoked Einstein's famous insistence that God does not play dice.

Subatomic particles also take on different characteristics depending on how they are studied, and two subatomic particles can become "entangled," such that observing one—and in so doing, determining certain qualities about it—makes the other take on corresponding qualities. This effect happens instantaneously—that is, faster than the information could possibly pass between them. Einstein memorably called this phenomenon "spooky action at a distance."

Because quantum mechanics defies logic in so many ways, Einstein felt confident that it would ultimately be proved mistaken, but every experimental and technological breakthrough of the last century has confirmed the theory's basic contours. Some new framework may well overturn it one day, but for now it remains as solid as any scientific theory can be.

Which doesn't mean that it makes any sense. Richard Feynman—a giant of twentieth-century physics who, unlike Einstein, specialized in the area—insisted that "nobody understands quantum mechanics." Of course, lots and lots of people understand the math behind it. (Not me.) They understand what experimental results its formulas predict, and they recognize when these results have occurred. But the results themselves suggest a reality that is not just counterintuitive but truly beyond comprehension.

Physicists use metaphorical language to approximate the significance of their mathematical results. They speak of antimatter as matter going backward in time. They say that photons are particles that have no mass. They refer to electrons dissolving into a "cloud of probability." But they do not, Feynman suggests, have any more idea than the rest of what any of it actually means.

Most scientific materialists aren't as troubled by that fact as Einstein was. Evolution equipped us to comprehend reality at a certain level—the level necessary to act as good survival machines for our genetic drivers. The propagation of our genes does not depend on our understanding of photons or black holes, so it's little wonder that they don't make much sense to us. A classical empiricism spiced with a tincture of skepticism tell us that there is a radical limit on what we can ever know. That is all fair enough, but it is a very different situation from the one that scientific materialism promised us. If we acknowledge that reality surpasses our comprehension—which it seems, as an empirical matter, to do—then we are back to mystery.

THE GREATEST MYSTERY of all is not any particular conflict between external reality and human experience but the problem that had struck me from my earliest encounter with materialism: the fact of human experience itself.

Materialism is resolutely antidualist. The doctrine's central contention is that there does not exist any other kind of "stuff" apart from matter. This means that any mental phenomena must be capable of being wholly redescribed as physical. Any remotely comprehensive materialist worldview needs to account for subjective mental experiences in objective material terms.

Over the past fifty years, the primary scientific-materialist effort in this direction has been a multidisciplinary approach called cognitive science, grounded in the belief that "information processing is the fundamental activity in the brain," as the prominent psychologist Steven Pinker puts it in *How the Mind Works*. What we call the mind is a function of this processing. This view is generally termed the "computational theory."

This is not meant as a metaphor. Strictly speaking, a computer is any machine that has been programmed to process information, and this is precisely what the theory holds the brain to be. The programmer in question here is natural selection. The evolutionary challenges of genetic propagation led a certain number of survival machines to develop "the ability to attain goals in the face of obstacles by means of decisions based on rational (truth-obeying) rules." ("The biologist Richard Dawkins called natural selection the Blind Watchmaker," Pinker writes; "in the case of the mind we can call it the Blind Programmer.")

The cognitive scientific approach's greatest practical achievements have been in the area of artificial intelligence rather than human psychology, but Pinker considers that work to be a clear sign that "the computational theory of mind is on the right track." If we can design a computer program that exhibits something like human-level intelligence, the theory goes, we can be fairly sure that it achieves this effect in something like the way that humans do.

"To the extent that thought consists of applying *any* set of well-specified rules," Pinker notes, "a machine can be built that, in some sense, thinks." Well, sure. And to the extent that thought consists of sitting on a head, a hat can be built that thinks. The cognitive-scientific definition of thought as the application of rules has allowed for a great deal of progress in the development of "thinking" machines, but it clearly leaves out a great deal—specifically, all the aspects of human thought that create a "mind-body problem" in the first place.

The Australian philosopher David Chalmers has drawn a now famous distinction between various "easy" problems of consciousness—"How does the brain process environmental stimulation? How does it integrate information? How do we produce reports on internal states?"—and the one "hard" problem—"Why is all this processing accompanied by an experienced inner life?" The hard problem is hard for several reasons. One is subjectivity: Consciousness involves—indeed, it consists in—a first-person point of view, while scientific materialism is grounded in third-person objectivity. Another is intentionality: Conscious thoughts are states in the brain that represent or refer to entities outside the brain. But how can one bit of physical matter be *about* another bit of physical matter? Finally there is what philosophers call "qualia": the ineffable qualitative features of being conscious that are so clearly missing from functionalist accounts of the mind. No matter how hard we try to convey to another person our experience of a given moment, there seems to be something left out—left out not just because of our lack of eloquence but because words can't possibly contain it.

Thomas Nagel captures the phenomenal quality of consciousness very well with this formulation: "An organism has conscious mental states if and only if there is something that it is *like* to be that organism, something it is like *for* the organism." Nagel's classic essay "What Is It Like to Be a Bat?" comes up in virtually every extended consideration of this topic because the thought problem in its title so clearly articulates what makes the hard problem hard. Bats are higher-order mammals of the sort we intuitively imagine to have conscious experiences, but because of their unique sensory apparatus, their experiences must be radically different from our own. The answer to the question "What is it like to be a rock?" is probably that it's not like anything at all. The answer to the question "What is it like to be a dog?" may well be that it's like being a hairy quadruped human of extremely low intelligence. But the question "What is it like to be a bat?" seems at once perfectly reasonable and radically unanswerable by us.

While a bat offers a particularly vivid demonstration of this lacuna, the same point ultimately holds for other human minds. Pinker's brand of functional cognitive analysis leaves out the subjective features of experience, which is precisely what the "what is it like" question is after. If we did not have firsthand experience of the qualitative feel of being a conscious human agent, cognitive science could not tell us anything about it, not even the mere fact that such a feeling accompanies all this information processing. It is not just that current theories are incomplete in this way but that it's difficult to see how *any* materialist account could be otherwise.

Chalmers gets at a similar point from the opposite direction with his discussion of "philosophical zombies," theoretical creatures that are objectively indistinguishable from humans—they have identical physical properties and exhibit the same behavior—but lack conscious experience. There is nothing that it is like to be a zombie, although zombies act to all appearances as though there were. If such creatures existed, Chalmers tells us, we would have no way of distinguishing them from conscious humans. Their existence is entirely consistent with the computational theory, which claims that all other cognitive functioning can be explained without recourse to experience. Indeed, the computational theory essentially treats us all as zombies as a matter of course.

Surprisingly enough, Pinker agrees with Chalmers about almost all of this. While he believes that some features of consciousness—specifically, self-knowledge and access to information—can be described in computational terms, he admits that "the computational theory of mind offers no insight" about subjective experience. Cognitive science does not have any answers to the hard problem. Nor does any other materialist account of the mind: "As far as scientific explanation goes, [sentience] might as well not exist."

In *How the Mind Works*, Pinker lists a number of rhetorical questions posed by philosophers of mind—including "How do I know you're not a zombie?" and "What is it like to be a bat?"—and sums up his answers to them thusly: "Beats the heck out of me!" He even throws in his own rhetorical question: "How can a book called *How the Mind Works* evade the responsibility of explaining where sentience comes from?" This actually seems like a pretty good question, but Pinker is entirely comfortable leaving it unanswered. When it comes to consciousness, "the mystery remains a mystery, a topic not for science but for ethics, for late-night dorm room bull sessions, and for [episodes of] the Twilight Zone."

One reason Pinker isn't troubled by this failure is that he doesn't think it matters all that much, because he believes the computational theory can still account for subjective motivations like beliefs and desires. His explanation for how this is possible starts with the insight that digital electronic computers are entirely physical in nature—they don't have experiences—and yet we speak of them all the time as though they were conscious agents: "The program doesn't *know* you replaced your dot-matrix printer with a laser printer. It still *thinks* it is *talking to* the dot-matrix and is *trying* to print the document by *asking* the printer to *acknowledge* its *message*." A philosopher of mind might call this "fuzzy thinking," Pinker allows, but we don't need to trouble ourselves with this accusation until it's "the befuddled computer scientists who call a philosopher when their computer stops working rather than the other way around." Failing that, we should recognize that "computation has finally demystified mentalistic terms."

Even a quarter of a century after the retirement of the last dot-matrix printer, I have a hard time believing that any computer scientists think of themselves as using "mentalistic terms" when ascribing motivation to machines. There is robust debate about whether a computer might one day achieve consciousness, but none of us think the top of a jam jar is conscious when we ask why it doesn't "want" to come off. Pinker is simply describing what Daniel Dennett calls the "intentional stance": Just as it can be useful from an explanatory standpoint to take the "design stance" toward evolutionary adaptations, imagining them to be the result of conscious engineering rather than blind natural selection, we can "decide to treat [an] object whose behavior is to be predicted as a rational agent" rather than brute matter.

When it comes to our *own* beliefs and desires, however, we define them by the experience of having them, rather than by their explanatory power. We may have beliefs (or believe ourselves to have beliefs) that remain unacted upon, that seem very real to us despite having no explanatory value whatsoever for another party analyzing our behavior, and we may find ourselves consistently acting in ways that work against what we want (or at least what we want to want). Furthermore, when we speak of the beliefs and desires of other human beings, we presume ourselves to be describing subjective experiences in some way equivalent to our own. We simply don't mean the same thing when we say on the one hand that our laptop insists on connecting to the wrong network and on the other that our girlfriend insists on seeing other people.

BECAUSE HE ACKNOWLEDGES the reality of subjective states that can't be captured by empirical means, Pinker is sometimes dismissively lumped alongside Nagel and other "New Mysterians," despite his materialist bona fides. To insist that the mystery of consciousness—or any mystery—is bound to stay a mystery amounts to an unforgivable sin among scientific materialists, as Daniel Dennett makes explicit in his own effort to tackle the mind-body problem.

As I've already noted, the book in your hand is not about the New Atheist movement that made Dennett famous. But long before he became a bestselling bomb thrower, Dennett was a philosopher who recognized the intellectual challenges faced by scientific materialism. Perhaps more than any other major philosopher of the last fifty years, he dedicated himself to resolving these challenges. It is that effort, rather than his polemics against religious faith, that matter here. I'm going to spend a decent amount of time on Dennett in the following pages, but I will be entirely concerned with his earlier academic work.

"Some people are tempted by the defeatist thesis that science couldn't 'in principle' explain the various 'mysteries' of the mind," Dennett writes in *Consciousness Explained.* The view that the mind exists but can't be studied by science is "actually dualism," he tells us—which is, of course, just about the worst thing any view could be. Dennett's own theory shows that "the paradoxes that beset traditional philosophical debates" on the mind are actually the product of "failures of the imagination, not insight." With Dennett's help, "we will be able to dissolve the mysteries."

His first target is the idea that consciousness can't even be approached from an objective standpoint. He believed that he had discovered the "neutral path leading from objective physical science and its insistence on the third-person point of view, to a method of phenomenological description that can (in principle) do justice to the most private and ineffable subjective experiences, while never abandoning the methodological scruples of science." This path involves something he calls "heterophenomenology," a fancy word that simply means asking other people to give verbal reports on their mental states.

Right off the bat, this approach seems to run up against precisely the hard problems we've already discussed. Granting that scientific inquiry sometimes deals with things that can't be observed directly, its indirect studies still involve objective facts like the cosmic microwave background or the fossil record. Verbal descriptions of mental states are not just indirect but inherently subjective.

Then there is intentionality. These verbal reports *refer* to our mental states. It is the fact of being conscious that allows the subject to make such verbal representations, and the fact of being conscious that allows the observer to make sense of them. The whole process depends upon one of the primary features it is supposed to explain.

Finally, there is the problem of qualia. We have already said that one of the signature features of qualitative experience is that there is something ineffable about it. If this is right, verbal reports of conscious states will always be insufficient.

All of this is not even to mention that heterophenomenology can be applied only to creatures with a capacity for language. Given how much language shapes our experience, the interior lives of entities that don't have language is apt to be radically different from our own, and it can't be studied in this way. Heterophenomenology can't tell us what it's like to be a bat.

These problems simply disappear, Dennett tells us, once we treat these verbal reports themselves, rather than the states they claim to describe, as the object of our study. We can adopt the intentional stance toward human subjects, remaining studiously agnostic on whether the mental states they are describing actually exist. The subjects could be zombies, or Turing-tested AI bots, or just pathological liars. It doesn't matter; the existence of the claims themselves is an objective, third-person-verifiable fact. We can further combine these claims to create a "heterophenomenal world" that we can study and interpret in the way we might a self-contained text, with only passing consideration of how the text relates to any reality outside its pages.

None of this seems to be getting us any closer to "the most private and ineffable subjective experiences," but Dennett assures us that this objection will dissolve once we understand the true nature of consciousness. He gets at this nature by addressing a related question: What is the evolutionary basis of consciousness?

Beginning with the now familiar progression of self-replicating chemicals, we arrive at early *Homo sapiens*, who had brains much larger than those of their closest primate relatives but still lacked language and the most basic forms of human culture. These early humans, Dennett writes, "were bipedal omnivores, living in smallish kin groups, and probably they developed special-purpose vocalization habits rather like those of chimpanzees and gorillas." One of the uses of this habit, Dennett proposes, would be to "ask for information" when stuck on some kind of undertaking: "Sometimes the audience present would respond by 'communicating' something that had just the right effects on the inquirer, breaking it out of its rut, or causing it to 'see' a solution to its problem."

Asking for help has both a benefit and a cost, because it gives out information to competitors at the same time that it solicits information from them. But suppose that one of these hominids once spontaneously asked for information "when there was no helpful audience within earshot—except itself!" If this prompting provoked a useful internal response, effectively soliciting the right answer without the cost of giving out information to others, it would have an obvious advantage over talking to the group.

We tend to assume that language developed as a means for communicating private thoughts to others, but Dennett suggests that language precedes thought, that thought begins when we use language to communicate to ourselves. In Dennett's telling, some early humans learned the trick of asking for help when no one else was around, which eventually became the trick of asking in a crowd but quietly enough that no one else could hear, and finally became the trick of asking without even vocalizing.

Human brains are not just larger than those of our nearest relatives; they also have a much higher degree of plasticity: They are capable of rewiring themselves on the basis of experience. This means that we can learn behavior—like the "trick" of asking ourselves for help—that isn't genetically hardwired into us. From the standpoint of the gene, there is an obvious advantage to having survival machines with the ability to learn in this way, but the learned behaviors are never encoded in the genes, and thus they can't be selected for on the genetic level. Yet they can be widely propagated by being observed or actively taught—through enculturation.

In *The Selfish Gene*, Richard Dawkins* sought to explain why certain elements of human culture thrive despite seeming directly contrary to genetic interests. Dawkins noted that bits of culture are themselves subject to both replication with variation and competition for survival, which are the two major ingredients for a process of evolutionary selection. He speculated that the basic units of culture might be subject to such a process, and he coined the term *meme* to describe the cultural equivalent of the gene. Dawkins was rather tentative about the whole thing, but Dennett makes cultural evolution central to his theory: "Human consciousness is to a very great degree a product not just of natural selection, but of cultural evolution as well."

The moment early humans started "talking" to themselves, their brains became hosts for memes, and an entirely new evolutionary arms race began. In order to live, memes need human brains with the rare capacity for rewiring. They compete for space in our brains and use us to replicate themselves. Because memes can be spread without their hosts living long enough to reproduce, they can take far less interest in our well-being than genes do. Thus a meme for suicide can do very well despite being catastrophic for its hosts, and a meme for monastic celibacy can thrive despite working against the interests of the genes that built us up in the first place. Memes have hijacked the survival machine.

A meme can go through countless variations in a few days, and it can be reproduced in the minds of millions of people at once. The result is that cultural evolution happens far more rapidly than the biological sort. As Dennett tells it, the early hominids needed several million years to develop brains with the level of neuroplasticity ours have. Humans that were

* Dawkins is another prominent New Atheist whose previous academic work contributed to the construction of the scientific materialist worldview. As with Dennett, I'm concerned with that earlier work, not with his New Atheist polemics.

essentially genetically identical to us needed about a hundred thousand years to develop the most rudimentary language; seven thousand years later, we had the *Iliad*; three thousand years after that, we have the riot of culture that surrounds us today.

It's a fascinating theory, but how does Dennett get from here to all the ineffable features of consciousness we've been discussing? The simple answer is that he does not. Instead he attempts the tried-and-true analytic solution of revealing an enduring human problem not to have been a problem at all but rather a conceptual confusion created by other philosophers. In this case, the problem is the very existence of qualitative experience, about which Dennett concludes: "Some messes are best walked away from."

Take the old Lockean notion of "secondary qualities." Because we understand these qualities as not inhering in the objects themselves, we imagine that they must "exist" somehow in our minds. Some light out in the world moves at a wavelength that we process as blue, we say, but the qualitative experience of *seeing blue* is an internal mental state. To Dennett, this is incoherent. If all the information that makes us see the light this way is contained in the wavelengths, the color *is* out there in the world. Seeing blue and processing this information are the same act. There is all of the cognitive functioning of the computational model, and then there is this endless swirl of language describing these functions, various parts of the brain telling various other parts what they're doing. There is no additional event going on that we need a concept like "qualia" to capture.

In other words, the one element of consciousness that Dennett believes can be studied objectively (i.e., the totality of our verbal reports on our mental states) turns out just to *be* consciousness, while the elements that seem obviously outside the reach of objective study (the inherent features of the states themselves) turn out not to exist at all.

An astonishing number of problems get solved by this move. How do we account for qualia in material terms? We don't have to, because there's no such thing as qualia. There can't be, because if there were, we'd be able to account for them in material terms. What is it like to be a bat? It's not like anything. Nor is it like anything to be a rock or a dog or a human infant or an adult human with severe aphasia or any other entity that can't report what it's like to be itself. How do we know? Because otherwise they would be able to tell us what it's like. How can we distinguish philosophical zombies from conscious human agents? Philosophical zombies are theoretically impossible: Any entity with the cognitive functioning and linguistic capacities of a human being would by definition be conscious. How can we know that two different people using the same language aren't describing different conscious states? Because the descriptive language is all there is to the states themselves.

The trouble here is common to many such analytic solutions: What Dennett is attempting to dissolve is not in fact a mere philosophical confusion but a persistent feature of our experience. Showing us that there is something contradictory or incoherent about the way philosophers have talked about certain problems doesn't make those problems go away. In this case, the mind-body problem stems from our feeling of occupying at once a private mental world and a shared physical one, knowing that these worlds relate to each other in important ways, and not understanding what to make of the obvious qualitative difference between them. It doesn't just *seem* to us that we have experiences; we do have them. How can we be sure? Because the seeming *is* the experience.

Well, Dennett would say, prove it. Any effort to do so renders our experiences into precisely the kind of reports Dennett insists they were all along. But in this case we don't *need* to prove it, because we simply know it to be so. If Dennett wants to deny the fact, we must leave him to it, as Locke would say. If he wants to convince *us* to deny it with him, however, the burden rests on him. Dennett believed that he had met that burden by providing an alternate explanation that allows us to transcend how consciousness "seems" and understand how it really is. The surest sign that he was wrong is that his fellow materialists are still working away at the problem some thirty years later.

The philosopher John Searle—an atheist committed to what he called the "scientific worldview" and yet a tenacious critic of the computational theory—took very seriously the question of why "so many philosophers and cognitive scientists can say so many things that, to me at least, seem obviously false." He suspected that it had to do with what they took to be the obvious other options. "The unstated assumptions behind the current batch of views," he wrote, "is that they represent the only scientifically acceptable alternatives to the anti-scientism that went with traditional dualism, the belief in the immortality of the soul, spiritualism, and so on." Ultimately the views were supported "by a terror of what are apparently the only alternatives."*

Dennett more or less acknowledges this motivation. From the beginning of *Consciousness Explained*, he makes clear that any satisfying account of consciousness simply must be a materialist one: "Settling for anything less in the way of an explanation would be just giving up." This approach is legitimate, so far as it goes. Dennett limits himself to explanations that count (for him) as explanations. Once faced with the inadequacy of his results, however, he tells us that this is simply the best we can do within the given constraints. But they aren't *our* constraints; they are his. If the thing we want explained can't be explained within them, the constraints themselves must be put into question.

I think Dennett understood that mind is its own kind of "universal acid." Once we allow for the existence of subjective experiences, they can't be contained in the way that Pinker and many other cognitive scientists want to believe. Pretty soon they eat through the whole materialist edifice.

---

* "Fear is the basis of the whole thing."

Eleven

A SATISFIED PIG

The reason that mind can't be contained, that its existence threatens materialism so much, is the very thing that makes the mind-body problem such a *problem* in the first place: not the mere fact that both mental and physical phenomena seem to exist, but the fact that they seem to interact. A central feature of consciousness is our sense of ourselves as *agents*—not just physical creatures who happen to have mental experiences but creatures capable of acting *in the physical world* on the basis of our own thoughts. In other words, we understand ourselves as having free will.

As with consciousness itself, a major complication in discussing free will concerns what we even mean by the term. Of course, we all want to do various things that we simply aren't free to do. None of us chooses the basic facts of our own existence, the time and place and conditions into which we are born, the extent of our capabilities and resources. We are often at the mercy of other people or of large impersonal forces. But all these limitations are consistent with a sense of ourselves as conscious decision-makers acting in the world to further our ends.

On the other hand, some forces—social, cultural, psychological, and biological—seem not just to limit our range of choices but to determine what choices we make within this range. We find ourselves doing in all apparent freedom things we nonetheless feel that we are doing against our will. Sometimes we do these things unconsciously (reaching for a buzzing phone moments after committing to a screen break); at other times we make quite conscious choices that still feel contrary to our deeper desires (going for a drink with colleagues at the end of a day that started with a commitment to exercise after work).

Where we once spoke of such behaviors in the morally charged language of "willpower" and "self-control," we increasingly understand them in the morally neutral terms of evolutionary psychology. We respond to sugary food and social media provocations because the conditions on the savanna programmed our brains to do so; we are subject to various cognitive biases because certain heuristic shortcuts conferred advantages on our hunter-gatherer ancestors. Over the years, researchers have announced the discovery of genes for reckless driving, credit-card debt, and infidelity.

When people hear that "science" has put the reality of free will into doubt, they generally think of such "discoveries." But this kind of soft determinism is compatible with a fairly robust sense of human volition. Materialism is deterministic in a far more severe sense. Materialist determinism is not the soft determinism of culture, psychology, or biology but the hard determinism of physics, which tells us that the current state of the universe was wholly determined by the physical state that preceded it, and that it in turn wholly determines the physical state to follow. In a physically determined world, you can no more choose to put down your phone than the phone can choose to be put down.

Many of our central intuitions about reality—particularly our moral intuitions—depend on our conception of ourselves and others as deliberative agents capable of choosing between different courses of action and thus responsible for these choices. We might abandon these intuitions, but as with consciousness, there is the deeper problem of experience. Critics of free will invariably dismiss it not as a "myth" or a "fallacy" but as an "illusion"—suggesting that they experience themselves as free just like the rest of us do. Indeed, it is not clear how they could do otherwise. What would it mean to embrace on the basis of rational argumentation the belief that even our beliefs are wholly determined? When free will's critics tell us to get over the illusion, they are counseling us to do something we couldn't possibly *choose* to do, according to their own reasoning.

The alternative left open to materialists is somehow to reconcile free will and physical determinism. Among scientific materialists, the most prominent compatibilist* is, again, Daniel Dennett, who wrote two books and many papers on the subject and suggested that his better-known writing on consciousness was initially undertaken as groundwork for his theory of human freedom.

In fine analytic tradition, Dennett begins his work on the subject by questioning whether the whole problem of free will is even real. He claims that the topic is "an almost exclusively Western preoccupation" and asks whether it even has significance for us "outside the lecture hall, outside our professional activities or midnight bull sessions." (These are presumably the same "late-night . . . bull sessions" to which Pinker consigns conversations about consciousness. They sound like a good time to me.) Dennett acknowledges that humans naturally "act under the idea of freedom," as he puts it, but he resists the suggestion that this idea requires treating humans as capable of bringing otherwise uncaused events into the world through mental volition. Such an expansive version of free will obviously can't be squared with materialism, but Dennett believes that it far

* The field of free will is littered with terminology, not always used consistently. *Compatibilist* is the prevailing term for those who believe that determinism and free will are compatible. Those who don't believe determinism and free will are compatible can be divided into "determinists"—who believe in physical determinism and (thus) not in free will—and "libertarians"—who believe in free will and (thus) not in physical determinism.

exceeds what he calls the free will "worth wanting," a rather limited sort with which determinism can easily be reconciled.

Like his version of consciousness, Dennett's free will worth wanting is a physical phenomenon that evolved gradually over millions of years. A key component of most concepts of free will is the ability to act according to the dictates of reason, and Dennett tells us that reasons themselves developed through natural selection. Once you have life, you have what might be called aims or interests or ends or goods. First and foremost, you have the aim of sustaining and propagating this life. Evolution will naturally favor those creatures that behave in ways that serve that aim—ones that successfully exploit their environment for energy; ones that successfully defend themselves from being exploited for energy by others; ones that pass down their successful strategies to their offspring. From our standpoint, we can understand these aims as the "reason" for this behavior—the now familiar move of adopting the "intentional stance." Of course we know that the vast, vast majority of organisms aren't capable of conceiving of their own behavior as furthering these aims. In this sense there are reasons for the behavior, but those reasons don't *belong* to the creatures themselves. They are, in Dennett's term, "free-floating rationale."

Over time, the evolutionary arms race dictates that organisms and their behavior—and with them the reasons that justify the behavior—become more and more sophisticated. As we just saw, a major turning point in evolutionary history occurs when the brains of certain hominids become complex enough to serve as the host for memes, especially the most powerful set of memes—language. At this point, brains become minds, and the animals that possess these brains become persons.

As memes compete with genes for control over us, we are driven toward a variety of interests or ends. Some of our behavior is dictated by the biological imperative to pass along our genes, but some is likewise dictated by a cultural imperative to pass along a bit of language or music or tradition or a funny way of cutting our hair. At the same time, the emergence of consciousness allows us to internalize previously free-floating rationale. What had simply been reasons for our behavior now become *our* reasons for our behavior.

It is essentially this combination—the fact that we are driven to behave in ways that serve a variety of sometimes conflicting ends and the fact that we understand the reasons for this behavior as fundamentally *our* reasons—that Dennett calls free will. We have this free will despite the fact that all our behavior remains thoroughly determined, not just biologically or culturally but physically.

Is this enough? Is this, indeed, all the free will that's really "worth wanting"? Before answering, we might fairly ask, Enough for what? Worth wanting in what sense? If Dennett believes that the free will "problem" is really just another example of Western philosophical "problem posing," why does he feel compelled to defend any notion of free will at all? Because he thinks the idea is good for us. Human beings have thrived by entering into mutually beneficial bargains with each other. Doing so requires us to be capable of acting in our own self-interest and capable of trusting others to do the same. There are always risks of freeloading, deception, gaming the system, but we can live with these risks, provided we know that the countervailing risk of being caught and punished will serve as an effective deterrent. From an evolutionary game-theory perspective, Dennett tells us, "holding people responsible is the best game in town."

What's more, humanity could easily lose the capability of acting "under the idea of freedom." As a product of cultural evolution, this idea has existed for a vanishingly small stretch of biological history, and there is no reason it must survive. Entire human cultures could abandon the idea and, in the process, lose freedom itself. To Dennett, this is the great risk of materialist determinism. The materialism meme is so well engineered for survival that it's bound to chase out its competitors. If determinists insist on spreading the meme that materialism and freedom can't live together, materialism will kill off the freedom meme along the way. If the freedom meme could instead evolve into something capable of living alongside materialism, it might continue to thrive in our brains.

Dennett doesn't put it exactly this way. He tells us that memes allow (or compel) human beings to have goals other than strictly biological ones, that they present to us an array of possible goods or ends, an array of possible behaviors, and thus create the context in which it would make sense to say that we have the freedom to choose among them. Memes make it possible for us to "transcend" our selfish genes, to become something more than survival machines (or, at least, to become survival machines for something other than our genes). But he never quite gets around to making the point that free will *itself* is a meme, though this seems to follow from the rest.

Presumably Dennett recognized that a picture of free will as a parasite that has invaded our brain and determines our behavior for the purposes of its own survival is fairly uninspiring, even if we take it to be a symbiotic or mutualist parasite whose survival ultimately benefits us. It certainly sounds far less like a kind of free will worth wanting. So he says instead that it is dangerous to insist on determinism because it will become a kind of self-fulfilling prophecy. We ought to believe in free will because it's good for us, and believing in it makes it so.

The parallels to certain rationalist defenses of religious belief are too obvious to ignore, and they are presumably what led his fellow "horseman" Sam Harris to say that Dennett's compatibilism is a form of "theology"—perhaps the worst insult that one New Atheist can hurl at another's beliefs. Finally, Dennett's version of free will, like his version of consciousness, appears obviously ersatz to virtually everyone but Dennett himself. In the absence of a more compelling compatibilist argument, we are left to choose between materialism and freedom—assuming we are free to make the choice.

A SATISFIED PIG

WHEN I SET OUT on this intellectual journey, I wanted to know how to live. I wanted a *way*. I've been sketching out scientific materialism's metaphysics and epistemology, but ethics may be the area where the worldview's failings are most evident.

Almost everyone agrees that reasoning about the subject of right and wrong is pointless without some belief in human agency, so let's assume for a moment the success of materialist efforts to reconcile physical determinism with a free will worthy of the name. Speaking about human behavior in terms of intentionally motivated actions still means dealing in final causes, which materialism doesn't allow us to do.

It isn't enough to adopt the "intentional stance" toward human beings, as we might toward our printer. We don't actually hold our printer responsible for a paper jam, because we know on some level that the intentional stance is a useful fiction. Moral evaluation involves taking the intentional stance and *meaning it.*

Dennett argues that memes make true intentionality possible. With their emergence, brains become minds, and intentions become real. Indeed, moral values *are* memes, and particularly successful ones. Some of them—the social virtues—happen to be symbiotic; others—the ascetic virtues championed by most religious traditions—are parasitic. In either case they ultimately thrive on the basis of their own fitness, not their benefits to us. But there is a small problem with memetic theory that we haven't yet addressed: From a materialist perspective, memes simply don't exist.

This is not to say that they aren't likewise useful fictions. We can take the intentional stance toward the memorable first four notes of Beethoven's Fifth Symphony, imagining that once this string of sounds was put together, it took on a life of its own, replicating itself by getting written down, played, listened to, hummed, recorded. This stance might have its (limited) uses for understanding how culture spreads and evolves. But the idea that the information contained in those notes is a self-replicating creature is just as fanciful as the idea that my printer has wants and needs.

Of course, the sheet music on which the symphony is written actually exists, as do the instruments on which it is played, the sound waves that carry that playing to my ear, the bit of neurological matter by which the tune is retained in my memory, and the lips with which I whistle it on the bus, passing it along to its next host. But the only thing that ties these disparate physical objects and events together, that makes ink on a page and a sound coming from my mouth "copies" of each other, is their shared content. The concept of a meme is senseless without intentionality, which is what we've enlisted memes to explain. To the extent that it makes any sense at all, meme theory requires its own kind of dualism.

Let's again set the objection aside, and assume that the materialist picture of reality might include motivated action. Scientistic epistemology is still limited in what it can say about these motivations. The human or social sciences take as one of their subjects the various things that human cultures and individuals have tended to value. These sciences can even provide evolutionary accounts of why certain human cultures and individuals value some things over others. But this is a wholly descriptive project, and it isn't what most people understand to be morality's task. It certainly isn't what I was after.

The most commonly proposed objective empirical standard has involved treating "good" and "evil" as synonymous with physical pleasure and pain. At the risk of belaboring an earlier point, these are subjective states of just the kind that materialism won't allow. Hobbes suggested that certain "inner motions" are naturally pleasurable or painful, and that we seek them out or avoid them on this basis. A good materialist will have to ask: Pleasurable or painful for *whom*? If there is no interior self that is experiencing these motions, only the motions themselves, what sense could such qualitative judgments about the motions possibly hold?

The best we can do is observe human behavior and assume that whatever experiences humans naturally seek out must be pleasant for them while whatever experiences they naturally avoid must cause them pain. But this invites a circularity. The qualitative features of experience were meant to explain motivated behavior; now we are using the behavior to identify the qualitative features. In that case the qualitative description adds nothing to the picture. We simply have experiences that humans seek out and experiences they avoid. Then what has been achieved when we describe the first as "good" and the second as "evil"?

Would it not be better to treat such value judgments as nonsense terms, more examples of the "absurd speech" that philosophers must clear out from the fields of knowledge? Many analytic philosophers actually do take this approach, but in practice most atheists—even thoroughgoing materialists—treat moral terms as meaningful. In fact, they consider it a slander against atheism to suggest that it can't meaningfully distinguish good from evil.

IF WE ASSUME THAT humans are conscious agents capable of choosing actions on the basis of subjective experiences of pleasure and pain, and that these experiences (their intensity, their duration, and various other characteristics) can be studied and even to some degree quantified, a science of morality grounded in these assumptions has obvious practical purposes. But achieving the good for ourselves is not what most of us take to be the point of morality. Modern utilitarians take for granted that we ought to consider the pleasure and pain of *others* when choosing our actions. Yet we have no obvious rational basis for doing this, a fact that early empiricists understood very well. They believed that it was the job of informal norms and formal laws—essentially, the job of other people—to create that rational basis by making it painful for us to cause others pain.

For Locke, this incentive system required a divine legislator capable of doling out infinite punishment and reward. It's common now to mistake Locke's scheme of divine justice for conventional theistic morality. Thus atheists often remark that we all know right from wrong, and that only theists need the threat of hell to do the right thing.

In fact Locke's view is hardly the standard monotheistic understanding. Granted, many medieval Christians had a morbid obsession with eternal damnation, but they took these punishments to be the repercussion of a sinful turning away from the Good, which they understood to exist in and of itself, much as Plato did. The Jewish and Catholic ideals of repentance—which insist that superficial acts of atonement motivated by self-interest won't bring forgiveness—are irreconcilable with Locke's morality. For the empiricist, to repent of an action simply *is* to recognize that it was not conducive to your ultimate self-interest.

The effort to ground morality in our own feelings of pleasure and pain rather than in the metaphysical reality of certain values is precisely what requires a system of punishment and reward to underwrite the good. The system does not exist to encourage "good" behavior but to *determine* what kind of behavior will ultimately be to our good. If the only coherent empirical good is our own pleasure, such a system is necessary to make otherwise selfless behavior into a moral good. But there is no sense in which selflessness can itself be construed as an inherent good. This is why Hobbes and Locke agreed that there is no such thing as "right" or "wrong" in the state of nature. Bentham shared this view, which is why he thought we needed a legal code relentlessly concerned with encouraging sociable behavior.

Mill thought we could do away with an overbearing state in favor of an education that made people take the suffering of others as seriously as their own, even without the threat of punishment. Such education can't actually make people selfless—in the empirical view, true selflessness is simply impossible. Rather, education can condition people such that acting for the greatest happiness of the greatest number becomes the source of their own happiness while causing pain to others causes them pain.

If the empiricist understanding of human nature as wholly malleable is correct, however, this kind of education can be done on behalf of any values at all. Young people can be taught to take pleasure in helping strangers, but they can equally be taught to take pleasure in running strangers out of town. History shows that people can be made to internalize a huge variety of moral codes. This tells us almost nothing about the merit of the codes themselves.

Even as a science of personal decision-making, the stuff of life hacks and productivity gurus, utilitarianism has its limits. It can tell me that a small expenditure of pain at the dentist's office today will likely save me far more pain from a root canal next year. It can tell me that the cigarette that gives me momentary pleasure now will lead to a painful and untimely death in the future. But suppose I just *want* the cigarette now. If forced to defend the choice, I might even say that a life without these little pleasures isn't worth having, that I would rather live a shorter life with a more painful end that includes the occasional smoke. If a utilitarian were able to "prove" that this choice was the irrational product of some cognitive bias, I might answer, "Who says I have to be rational?" And utilitarianism is hopeless in the face of such questions.

A relatively common modern view holds that reasoning about good and evil is unnecessary, because moral truths are self-evident. The vast majority of us have a shared intuitive sense of right and wrong, even if we don't always act on it, and this consensus is enough to get us through.

The few people who lack this sense are sociopaths, and we don't need any rational basis for condemning them—again, it's just self-evident that they're wrong. This view sometimes goes further and suggests (as David Hume did) that the main cause of moral confusion is religious superstition, which attempts to convince people to live their lives according to various life-denying values that fly in the face of our common moral sense.

In reality, common sense has a fairly spotty moral record. For a nineteenth-century liberal like J. S. Mill, it was common sense that white Europeans should rule over the people of the Southern Hemisphere. Mill stated repeatedly that the kind of liberty he advocated was not appropriately extended to "backward states of society in which the race itself may be considered as in its nonage." This belief was not religiously motivated; it was explicitly grounded in an Enlightenment faith in reason. For many Darwinists of the early twentieth century, it was similarly obvious that poor, disabled, or "mentally enfeebled" women ought to be sterilized. Failing this, their children ought to be left to starve to death before living to have children of their own. Again, this belief was grounded in reason, not faith. In both cases, the forces of enlightenment complained that religious believers put their own race at risk with their acts of charity toward these subrational populations.

The point here is not to demonstrate that atheists have been responsible for their share of moral outrages. It is simply to show that there are no enduring moral principles even among the partisans of reason, and that legitimate disagreements exist not just about the proper means toward our moral ends but about the ends themselves.

Finally, one could say that it is all to the good that scientific materialism doesn't have the wherewithal to settle such disputes. Perhaps the kind of totalizing worldview that seeks to define ultimate goods is part of the problem. Empiricism has gone hand in hand with political and economic liberalism, and these systems have made a virtue of remaining agnostic about ultimate goods. The marketplace does not impose answers to these questions; it serves instead as a venue for working them out.

Many critics of liberalism and capitalism—theist or not—will tell you that this is a kind of subterfuge. To quantify relative goods in a way that makes them essentially fungible just *is* the expression of a particular conception of the ultimate good. In particular, it expresses the idea that there are no truly ultimate goods, that everything is up for negotiation and every man has his price. But let's take liberalism at its word and presume that it creates a neutral space in which people with widely varying conceptions of the good can live happily together without being coerced into agreement. To say that we are each free to answer the question of the good in our own way still leaves the question itself unanswered. Where are we each supposed to get our personal answers, if not from our view of reality?

The problem is how to live our lives. What does flourishing look like for us? It is all well and good to celebrate the fact that liberalism won't force an answer on us, but many of us manifestly don't have a satisfactory answer to hand, and we are looking for some help. This is the question of meaning that led Mill to his mental collapse.

Mill saw that a strictly quantitative Benthamite utilitarianism was helpless in the face of this question. For a certain kind of person, a life lived in pursuit of happiness is an empty one. It is, paradoxically, an unhappy one. Eventually Mill concluded that we needed to recognize the qualitative difference between goods, in addition to the quantitative ones. But how could we possibly make this distinction? Doesn't it require some criterion for value beyond utility? Mill's answer was that those humans with sufficient education and cultivation to appreciate the qualitative difference between goods ought to be the arbiters of such things:

> It is better to be a human being dissatisfied than a pig satisfied; better to be Socrates dissatisfied than a fool satisfied.

> And if the fool, or the pig, is of a different opinion, it is because they only know their own side of the question. The other party to the comparison knows both sides.

This view is bizarre on many levels. For starters, no human being knows what it's like to be a pig, any more than Socrates knew what it was like to be a fool. And it isn't at all clear that Socrates (who in any case was quite famously someone not given to dissatisfaction) would have opted against being a satisfied fool. In fact, this is basically what he claimed to be. Mill's view that those with education and cultivation ought to decide things for those without it drove his support of colonialism, and it drives today many of the uglier aspects of paternalistic technocratic liberalism.

James Mill worked most of his life for the British East India Company and wrote a three-volume history of British India without ever traveling to India or learning any South Asian languages. He did not know both sides, even in the limited way he believed himself to. But having done these things would still not have entitled Mill to manage the lives of millions of people who had never consented to his authority. In reality, we cannot ever experience the goods of others in the way that they experience them, least of all when we are engaged in the comparative act of weighing them against our own. For that is precisely not how we treat goods when we are actually living them.

I'VE BEEN ASSUMING that scientific materialism must come with a moral system grounded in reason and the facts of human nature, because reasoning about matters of fact is the form of knowledge that scientific materialism recognizes. But maybe I'm wrong to think a worldview has to hold together in this way. Maybe one can accept the scientific materialist account of moral values as mere sentiments or even memetic parasites while still embracing those values as one's own and attempting to live by them. In the same way, one can accept that consciousness and free will don't "actually" exist while going about one's life as a freely acting conscious agent. One can even recognize love as a neurochemical process driven by the genetic pilot whose survival we exist to secure while still loving one's spouse and children with all one's heart.

But to say all this is simply to say that scientific materialism can't possibly serve as a *way*. It can't, after all, be lived in, even by those who find its claims about the world convincing. It isn't just that scientific materialism does a poor job of answering the question of meaning but that it can't make sense of the question at all. It treats meaning as one of those pseudo-problems best left to the proverbial late-night dorm room bull session. Since meaning doesn't concern matters of fact or matters of logic, it must be consigned to the fire.

One of the defining features of the New Atheists—the thing that made them so appealing to some and so smugly unappealing to others—was their self-satisfied Epicureanism. They knew how to enjoy life, and they knew that they knew it, and they found something frankly neurotic about the religious morbidity of those who weren't sharing in the fun. Dawkins quotes approvingly a remark made to him by the biologist James Watson, the codiscoverer of DNA: "Well, I don't think we're *for* anything. We're just products of evolution. You can say, 'Gee, your life must be pretty bleak if you don't think there's a purpose.' But I'm anticipating having a nice lunch." ("We did have a good lunch, too," Dawkins adds.)

But not everyone has the wherewithal to spend their life eating nice lunches with famous friends, and even some of those who do will find it an insufficient basis for flourishing. Dismissing certain problems as nonsensical doesn't actually make them go away, if they were felt as real in the first place. G. E. Moore once said that life would never have presented him a philosophical problem, but once philosophy presented the problems, he happened to find them interesting. This fact made it easy enough for him to be "guided by intellectual curiosity alone," as Bertrand Russell thought philosophers should be, and may have accounted for why Russell found himself so in thrall to Moore.

For Russell, the problems were felt, which raises the great paradox of his career. If Russell had stuck to logical analysis, he would have been a figure like Moore—widely respected among professional philosophers but mostly unknown to general readers. He would not have written the work that was collected into *Why I Am Not a Christian*, and he would not have wound up on my grandparents' shelves. Russell became world-famous because he remained throughout his life deeply engaged by the kinds of questions that philosophers had historically thought it their job to answer, precisely the kind he had removed from the philosophical agenda.

Russell was the last major English-language philosopher with a mass readership, and this readership has consisted almost entirely of people for whom the *Principia Mathematica* is literally unreadable.* They read instead his work on ethics and religion and politics. The general understanding that he was among the world's most important academic philosophers contributed enormously to his authority as a commentator on subjects like contraception, pacifism, and nuclear disarmament, but Russell insisted that the two roles bore no relation to each other.

Ironically, the analytic-philosophical insistence that these sorts of human issues are not philosophy's real subject is the primary reason that English-language philosophers after Russell stopped having a mass readership. It turns out that people *care* about these problems a lot more than they care about philosophy as the analytic school defines it.

But what exactly *was* Russell doing when he wrote about these questions, if it wasn't philosophy? Was it all just sophistry and illusion? Per-

* I count myself among them.

haps one could say, following his Apostles lecture, that Russell was "merely" doing poetry. (Hence his Nobel Prize in Literature.) But he was clearly aiming for something other than "aesthetic satisfaction." He meant to convince people that his views were correct.

If Russell really believed that he had drawn a kind of limit to what could be said without falling into meaninglessness, why did he spend so much of his life—probably more of it, finally, than he spent philosophizing—crossing that limit? And what would it mean actually to live within those lines?

Twelve

HOW LITTLE HAS BEEN DONE

In the spring of 1912, an odd young man arrived at Bertrand Russell's room in Cambridge. The visitor explained in heavily accented English that he worked at an airplane factory in Manchester. Though he had no formal training in philosophy, he'd taken an interest in the discipline, and he wanted to study with Russell.

"My German friend threatens to be an infliction," Russell wrote in a letter the next day. "He came back with me after my lecture & argued till dinner time—obstinate & perverse, but I think not stupid." For the next several months, according to Russell's biographer, Ray Monk, the young man "remained only a figure of curiosity, fun and slight condescension, referred to, not by his name, but only as 'my German,' 'my German engineer,' and even, on occasion, 'my ferocious German.'" It was November before Russell discovered that his German was actually Austrian, by which time he had concluded that talking to him was "really rather a waste of time."

The ferocious German's name was Ludwig Wittgenstein. He was the youngest of eight children born to one of Europe's richest men, all of them seemingly brilliant and most of them troubled. Three of his four brothers died by suicide. (The fourth lost his right arm in World War I and became perhaps the greatest one-handed piano player who ever lived.) The family was highly musical and highly cultured in general, among fin de siècle Vienna's greatest patrons of the arts. Brahms and Mahler attended the Wittgenstein's salons. Music and literature would have a profound influence on Ludwig's life, but his early interest was engineering. Of all the children, he seemed the most likely to follow his father into industrial manufacturing, and he was sent to England to study aeronautics.

His studies in Manchester led Wittgenstein to an interest in pure mathematics, which in turn led him to Russell. After their initial encounter, Wittgenstein attended all of Russell's lectures, but Russell remained uncertain whether he was fit to study philosophy, so he gave Wittgenstein an essay assignment. The result has not survived, but it was enough to prove Wittgenstein's brilliance; Russell came to believe that his young protégé would solve the remaining problems of mathematical logic that Russell felt too old and tired to attack. (Russell was not yet forty at the time and had almost sixty years of life left.)

The two men's roles now switched, with Russell holding Wittgenstein in fearful awe. "His disposition is that of an artist," Russell wrote, "intuitive and moody." He would later remember Wittgenstein as "the most perfect example I have ever known of genius as traditionally conceived." For his part, Wittgenstein remained worshipful about the *Principia* but spoke frankly of his disdain for Russell's popular work, especially the writings on ethics and religion that would be collected in *Why I Am Not a Christian*. He had a similarly difficult relationship with G. E. Moore, who likewise recognized Wittgenstein's genius and took great steps to further his Cambridge career and get his ideas into writing. (Wittgenstein remarked that Moore "shows you how far a man can go who has absolutely no intelligence whatever.")

Russell, Moore, and others who spoke with Wittgenstein became convinced that he had profound truths to give philosophy, but they worried that he would never set them down. He had no interest in publication or professional advancement. Russell thought it likely that he would go mad or take his own life before completing his work. This fear became more acute when Wittgenstein announced his intention to move to Norway, live in isolation for several years, and put his interior life in some order. "Perhaps you regard this thinking about myself as a waste of time," he wrote to Russell, "but how can I be a logician before I am a human being!"

AT THE START of World War I, Wittgenstein enlisted on the Austrian side. He was eager to put himself in harm's way, and he expressed deep frustration at spending the war's first years safely stationed in Kraków. During this time, he finally began writing his thoughts on logic into a manuscript. His writing took a dramatic turn when he was sent to the Eastern Front. He spent two years fighting in the Romanian trenches, during which Russell and others in Cambridge had no contact with him, no idea whether he was alive or dead. By the time they heard from him again, Wittgenstein was in an Italian POW camp, and he had completed the only book he would live to see published.

The *Tractatus Logico-Philosophicus* is arguably the greatest philosophical work of the twentieth century, and certainly one of the most challenging, but it is also a rare work whose point can be summed up in a few lines. Wittgenstein himself gives this summary in the book's preface and again in its final pages: "What can be said at all can be said clearly; and whereof we cannot speak, thereof one must be silent."

That a book that aims to prove the clear simplicity of expressible truth should prove so difficult to comprehend was an irony Wittgenstein recognized and regretted. The fact that his work was not easily understood frustrated and puzzled him. Having spent years arriving at his insights and putting them into literary form, he believed the results ought to be self-evidently true. In fact, a major part of his argument was that all real truth is self-evident.

The book sets out to address two problems raised by the logical analytic view that all meaningful statements concern either matters of empirical fact or matters of logical relationship. The first sort of statements raise the first problem: How do statements and facts relate to each other such that one can take the former to describe or contain the latter? In other words, what is it about a factual statement that allows us to "check" it against an experience or a state of affairs and thus to classify it as empirically "true" or "false"?

Philosophers have always been alive to the risk that the words we use to describe possible experiences might be describing something else—or nothing at all. But clarifying the matter requires the use of other words (or some other means of representing experiences), and how do we know that those are doing the job we want them to do? So long as an object is present in front of us, we can simply point to it, and it is tempting to say that words point to objects in this way. But even pointing out an object is not so straightforward. What feature of the object do we want to invoke? If I point at a red chair and make a sound, do you take that sound to indicate "chair" or "red" or "sit!"?

The second class of statements produces a second kind of problem. The idea behind formal logic is that empirical data that have been properly checked against reality can then be plugged into logical equations and that the results will have validity, provided that the equations were properly formulated. But what does it mean for such logical statements to be "properly" formulated? The truth of a logical statement is a different kind from the truth of an empirical statement, for there is really nothing to "check" it against.

The general understanding is that the truths of mathematics and other systems of logic emerge from the fact that these systems are self-contained and internally consistent. So long as one follows a system's rules, the results will be legitimate. If the system produces results that are contradictory or absurd, either the rules are not being applied properly or the rules themselves need to be clarified or adjusted in some way.

But logical systems are notoriously bad at talking about themselves, so they must take for granted certain rules that they cannot prove.* What makes the rules true? And how can we be sure we are applying them properly? How could we ever recognize the results of an otherwise legitimate application of the rules as contradictory or absurd (and thus as calling the rules themselves into question) if the system itself is the guarantor of logical coherence? These are the subjects of metalogic, and they require stepping outside of a given system to posit certain basic axioms and definitions.

The need for such axioms had sent the young Russell toward philosophy in the first place, but even he had not found a way to do without them. To get the whole of logic from just a handful of posited truths seems like a fair deal, but the moment we step outside the system in this way, we've entered an infinite regress. If the rules of a system aren't logically formulated and consistent with each other, the whole system is useless. But how can we know that our metalogical assertions take a logical form? Do we need a meta-metalogic, and a meta-meta-metalogic, and so on? Ultimately, we are forced to take some things on faith—just what we're trying to avoid.

You may have noticed that these two problems have a similar form. In both cases we want to be able to define certain basic terms, but to do so requires making use of other terms, which will inevitably need their own definitions. At some point we simply have to let things mean what they mean. Wittgenstein's breakthrough was to understand these problems as

* A decade after Wittgenstein published the *Tractatus*, Kurt Gödel published his famous incompleteness theorems, proving that it was impossible to design a system of axioms that was both complete and consistent, as Russell hoped to do. Gödel did this precisely by showing that any system could inevitably express certain statements about the system itself that were both true and unprovable.

the same problem and to solve them at one go, by way of his famous picture theory of language.

How does a picture of a house represent a house? Well, it just *does*. It represents a house by looking like a house. A picture is a "model of reality," as Wittgenstein puts it. It stands outside its object and represents it. But a picture "cannot place itself outside its form of representation" in order also to represent the relationship between itself and its object. For that we need another picture, with another form. If you don't know what a house is—perhaps because you are from some nomadic culture that lives only in tents—the picture can't tell you what it shows. But if one tries to solve this problem by adding a title that reads, "This is a picture of a house," you aren't in any better shape, since that word has no meaning for you. You already, as it were, *know* that it's a picture of a house; what you don't know is what a house is. Meanwhile, those of us who do know what a house is don't need in addition to the picture the information that the picture is a picture of a house. Either the information is right there in the picture itself or else the picture is not, in fact, a picture of a house.

Whether or not the picture corresponds to some actually existing house—whether we might call the picture empirically true—is, on the other hand, a fact that rests completely outside the picture itself. To learn that, we would have to "check" the picture against the world. But this checking requires only two things—the picture and the house. We don't need in addition some guide to tell us how the picture and the house correspond.

In the *Tractatus*, Wittgenstein contends that language works like this. Propositions resemble the states of affairs they describe—not pictorially but logically. In a basic language-learning book, we might find a drawing of a house with the word *HOUSE* written underneath it. The point of the word is not to tell us what is shown in the drawing. Rather, the point of the drawing is to tell us what is shown in the word. But how do we know what features of the drawing are meant to be captured in the word? How do we know, for example, that the word isn't meant to describe buildings in general as opposed to the specific type of building in which people live? After all, any picture of a building must be a picture of a *kind* of building—there is no way to draw a picture of "buildings in general."

Suppose that beside the house is a drawing of a store with the word *STORE* written underneath, and beside that a church with *CHURCH* written underneath and beside that an office tower with *OFFICE TOWER* written underneath, and then at the top of the page, in slightly larger font, the word *BUILDING* appears. Then suppose the following page had a similar arrangement of different kinds of vehicles and the page after that had different kinds of foods. One could well imagine in addition a little descriptive note at the beginning of the book: *The following pages contain pictures of different types, arranged by category. The English word closest to the picture names the type itself; the English word at the top of each page names the category to which all of that page's types belong.* But this note is clearly pointless. Anyone with remotely enough English to comprehend it will not have any need of such explanation, and for anyone else the explanation will be useless. The pages themselves must just show us what they're doing.

In Wittgenstein's view, the metalogical rules and definitions of a logical system are like that additional explanatory note. Take, for example, one of the most common metalogical axioms, the so-called law of identity. This takes the form of the tautological statement that A = A. We need this statement to be true for any statement of equality to do its work, but no proof can be provided without the statement already in hand, which is why nearly every logical system simply begins by positing it.

But a person who needs to be told that A equals A either doesn't understand what A is or doesn't understand what equality is. It's useless to tell that person that it is a law that A = A. It is transparently incorrect to say that two things that are different are exactly the same, but it is equally useless to say that two things that are exactly the same are exactly the same. Of course they are. Indeed, if they are *exactly* the same, they are not even two things; they are one and the same. The statement "A = A" does not really *say* anything, insofar as it doesn't tell us more than the statement "A" already does.

"The identity of the meaning of two expressions cannot be *asserted*," Wittgenstein tells us. "For in order to be able to assert anything about their meaning, I must know their meaning, and if I know their meaning, I know whether they mean the same or something different." He believed this to be equally true of all the other rules of logic. We don't need to be given rules for using propositions whose sense we already grasp; part of grasping their sense is understanding how they can and can't be used.

All logical proofs essentially work by way of equation—that is, by asserting that one entity or proposition is equivalent to another. Of course, there are true statements in logic that are not immediately self-evidently true. But each *step* in a logical proof is meant to be self-evidently true; otherwise there would need to be some intermediate step in which the step was shown to be legitimate. This is the intuitive chain by which we arrive at demonstrative truth. The way that you "prove" a logical truth is by *making* it self-evident. Once that work has been done, the proof becomes redundant. It shows us something that was there all along. Something that, in theory at least, we could have "seen" from the very start. If we had been sufficiently perspicacious, we generally feel at the end of a good proof, the truth *would* have been immediately self-evident. This means that logic itself is essentially superfluous: "The propositions of logic are tautologies," Wittgenstein writes bluntly. They "say nothing."

Once we understand this, he believes, it "becomes clear why we often feel as though 'logical truths' must be '*postulated*' by us." But it also becomes clear that "the laws of logic cannot themselves obey further logical laws." We can't make any assertions about a system of meaning that the system can't itself demonstrate, but if the system properly demonstrates its meanings, the assertions are unnecessary. Metalogic is a pointless exercise: "Logic must look after itself."

Here another irony arises, for the *Tractatus* is in large part a work of metalogic. It consists in assertions about the way that logical systems mean the things they mean, which by its own reckoning makes it superfluous. Wittgenstein begins his preface by suggesting as much, speculating that the book "will perhaps only be understood by those who have themselves already thought the thoughts which are expressed in it." Near the end of the book, he describes the work as a ladder that can be tossed away once someone has climbed up it. "My propositions are elucidatory in this way," he concludes: "He who understands me finally recognizes them as senseless."

THE PART OF the *Tractatus* that deals with the picture theory—which is to say, most of it—seems to have been completed before Wittgenstein was sent to the front lines, and he considered it preliminary to the rest of the work, which is dedicated to applying these points to various perennial philosophical questions, particularly questions of ethics and the meaning of life. In one sense, Wittgenstein's view on these subjects is wholly consistent with the larger analytic tradition. For it clearly follows from Wittgenstein's other theories that we can't say anything meaningful about the significance of the world as such from within the world. That includes any value statements but also more generally any statements about what things mean. "In the world everything is as it is and happens as it does happen," Wittgenstein tells us. "*In* it there is no value—and if there were, it would be of no value."

Very near the end of the *Tractatus*, Wittgenstein suggests what he takes to be the "right method of philosophy": "to say nothing except what can be said, i.e., the propositions of natural science, i.e., something that has nothing to do with philosophy: and then always, when someone else wished to say something metaphysical, to demonstrate to him that he had given no meaning to certain signs in his propositions."

But Wittgenstein understands the consequences of this approach very differently from the average scientific materialist. He truly believed that his work had solved all the problems of philosophy, but he also believed that in doing so it had shown "how little had been done when these problems have been solved." What is there still left to do? Wittgenstein speaks at several points in the book's last pages of the "riddle of life." What is this riddle? He doesn't say. Indeed, he insists that he could not say: To be able to frame the question would mean being able to say what form the answer would take. From the standpoint of his own philosophy, "the riddle does not exist." Yet he makes it fairly clear that the riddle *does* in fact exist. It's tempting to speculate that the riddle is some version of the question "What value does life have?" In other words, why go on living? Why not just give it up—as Wittgenstein often considered doing, and as three of his brothers ultimately did?

The kinds of scientific statements that his own philosophy allows as meaningful will not answer that question. "We feel that even if *all possible* scientific questions be answered, the problems of life have still not been touched at all." The answers to scientific questions can't tell us the meaning of life. They can't even tell us the meaning of the natural world. "At the basis of the whole modern view of the world," Wittgenstein writes, "lies the illusion that the so-called laws of nature are the explanations of natural phenomena." We think that the laws of nature explain why things happen in the way that they do. But they simply tell us *that* things happen in this way. Natural laws are logical propositions under which the empirical facts all "fit." But logical propositions don't add anything to the picture.

Modern people treat the laws of nature just as the ancients treated God or Fate, Wittgenstein writes. But at least the ancients understood that they were invoking a mysterious force outside the world as the world's explanation. And this is the only place that such an explanation could ever be found: "The solution of the riddle of life in space and time lies *outside* space and time. (It is not the problems of natural science which have to be solved.)"

But what outside could there be?

What does a painting of a house *mean*? We know the painting depicts a house, but what is the depiction's significance? The painting did not need to be a painting of a house—it could have depicted anything. Why a house? Why *this* house, and not another? Why these colors, in this style? These questions may well have answers, but the painting itself cannot clarify those answers beyond simply showing us this house with these colors in this style. At a certain point the picture must just be taken as it is.

To one of the propositions in the book's last pages Wittgenstein adds a parenthetical: "(Ethics and aesthetics are one.)" You could say that the proper answer to the question of why to go on living could be shown to us by someone who lives an exemplary life. But these people can never tell us their answer, because their answer is their life. "There is indeed the inexpressible," Wittgenstein says. "This *shows* itself; it is the mystical."

To the *Tractatus*'s earliest readers, the concluding references to a mystical "whereof we cannot speak" seemed a form of intellectual fastidiousness. A good positivist would not insist that there is simply nothing beyond the bounds of language and sense experience; it is enough to say that whatever lies out there is beyond our reach. But when Russell was finally able to meet with Wittgenstein again after the war, he was shocked to find him turned into a full-blown mystic. Russell expected Wittgenstein to return to Cambridge and take up a professorship. After all, he was the greatest philosophical mind of his generation, and he now had a finished work that could earn him a proper degree and a position. But Wittgenstein took seriously the idea that he had solved (for himself at least) philosophy's outstanding problems. In the process, he had convinced himself that the problems of philosophy were not actually the problems of life—that is, not the problems that had sent him in this direction in the first place. For Wittgenstein, the last pages of the *Tractatus* had become the point of the whole project. Why would he go on doing philosophy? He had not gotten into it for a job or even to enjoy a stimulating intellectual activity. He had questions that needed to be answered, and he'd thought that philosophy might answer them. Now he knew that it would not.

Soon after the armistice, Wittgenstein renounced his inheritance, leaving his share of the family's enormous fortune to his surviving siblings. He took jobs as a schoolteacher in several small Austrian villages. By all accounts he was a terrible teacher, severe and ill-tempered, frustrated by the slowness of his students. (This is hardly surprising, as he had already shown himself frustrated by the slowness of some of the smartest men alive.) This career ended in 1926, when he struck one student until he collapsed, and the student's father tried to have him arrested. Wittgenstein resigned his position and presented himself at a nearby Benedictine monastery, where he inquired about joining the order. The abbot turned him down, but Wittgenstein stayed for several months, working instead as a gardener.

INTERLUDE

The Refuge of Art

By the time I read the *Tractatus*, I had already given up on scientific materialism as a solution to the riddle of my life, but I hadn't given up on the riddle itself, and I hadn't given up on the possibility that some solution might somehow be found. Two of Wittgenstein's ideas struck me with particular force. First, that any possible solution would have to take the form of a way of life rather than a piece of knowledge, that it would have to show itself rather than being stated explicitly. Second, that art had an essential role to play in situating me on that way.

Having long before decided to dedicate myself to becoming a great novelist, drawn to the goal by the simple love of reading and writing, I now saw this calling as the one thing that might somehow justify my life. I began obsessively reading writers who shared this elevated view of literature, particularly the great modernists who explicitly treated art as a kind of faith and the artist as the high priest of a godless church.

I have always been a completist by nature. If I really love a work, I seek out everything by that artist—even the most minor forgotten juvenilia found only in out-of-print editions ordered from rare-books shops. When I decided to tackle James Joyce, for example, I read not just the stories in *Dubliners* and his three published novels, but his poems and his play and the posthumously published variants of his work. I read Richard Ellmann's classic biography, noting Joyce's own lifelong struggle with the Catholic faith, his refusal to kneel and pray at his mother's deathbed, his desire to "forge in the smithy of the soul the consciousness of a new race," as he puts it in *A Portrait of the Artist as a Young Man.* I had graduated from college the year before, and I worked that winter as a ski instructor in the Catskills. I lived alone and spent each night drinking and reading *Finnegans Wake* out loud. I intoned every word—if they can all be called "words"—into the empty silence of the night, and it felt something like a mystical experience, in Wittgenstein's sense: I was engaging in thought beyond the reach of language.

In a similar spirit I read my way through Virginia Woolf, Marcel Proust, Thomas Mann—seeking out the major works as well as the minor ones, reading textual variations that were of interest only to scholars. I read all of Beckett and Nabokov and Borges. After returning from the mountains, I entered a graduate writing program. Most of my fellow students were learning the craft by way of short stories, often ones with strongly autobiographical subject matter. They hoped to develop their skills at a manageable scale, perhaps getting one or two bylines in respectable journals while they did, laying the groundwork for the novels they would tackle when they were ready. I understood this to be the sensible approach, but I didn't think I had the time for it. I was in a rush for greatness. I needed my very first work to be the kind of thing for which a person could be remembered; I was after immortality, and I wasn't sure how long I would live to achieve it.

I began a baroque fantasy about the inhabitants of a fallen empire. Everything about the book—not just its characters and setting but the days of the week and the units of measurement—was my own invention. I wasn't interested in self-expression; I wanted to create a space for the inexpressible. One of my great heroes was Gustave Flaubert, who had aimed to make a novel about nothing at all, a pure expression of style without content. I called my own effort in this line *The Secret of Durable Pigments*, an allusion to *Lolita*'s closing words: "I am thinking of aurochs and angels, the secret of durable pigments, prophetic sonnets, the refuge of art. And this is the only immortality you and I may share, my Lolita."

When I brought pages from this work into the classroom, the other students were frankly baffled by it. A few professors politely advised me to try something less ambitious. They acknowledged that I might have some talent but thought that I had not yet found the proper direction in which to take it. This only made me push further in the direction I was already headed. The thing I was attempting to do—whatever that was—might have been too ambitious for most twenty-four-year-olds, I told myself, but I was more dedicated than they were. It meant more to me. I would just have to read more and think more and write more than others did.

But it wasn't enough. *I* wasn't enough. By the program's end, other students were submitting their half dozen carefully polished stories as their thesis projects, and I had not even completed a full first draft of anything. I got a job as a grant writer in a college development office. Each evening I came home from work, took a short nap, and stayed up all night working on the book. This schedule didn't leave time for much else of a life, but I didn't want much else of a life. I was going to die soon enough, and whatever living I had done would simply disappear. This at least would last—if I could somehow get it finished and get it right.

I lived in fear that I would be taken before my task was done. My few romantic relationships were unhappy and short-lived. I didn't have much to offer another person. When I did go out, I drank heavily and smoked and took drugs, not especially rational behavior for someone obsessively concerned with his health and terrified of his mortality. Plenty of people I knew were doing the same, but I did it with a sense of mission. I had the notion that this derangement of the senses was helping me to stare down the ineffable. Some part of me wanted to face my fear of death by bringing it close to me.

Passing your days alone, telling yourself stories about an imagined world, can be a wonderful way to spend your life, if the work gives you pleasure, but at a certain point it stopped doing that. I was constantly writing at the limits of my own ability—pushing past those limits, really—which was exhausting and dispiriting. I felt inept. I also felt isolated and misunderstood. I was living near my family, surrounded by people who loved me, but their love felt like a trap meant to distract me from this work. At the same time, some part of me knew that the results were just not good enough. Certainly not good enough to justify my outsize ambitions or the pains I was taking; likely not even good enough to be published as respectable apprentice work.

Through all this, reading remained the one thing that consistently made me happy. As I moved from the novels of the great writers I loved to their essays and their letters and their journals, I found that many of them had been influenced by the same handful of philosophers. One of these was Friedrich Nietzsche, whom I'd read in college like any self-respecting atheist-in-training. At the time, I had read him superficially—a way of reading that Nietzsche's work tends for various reasons to encourage. By now I had more experience reading philosophy, and I approached him with attention and care.

Another name that came up repeatedly was that of Arthur Schopenhauer, whom I knew mostly as Nietzsche's great influence. Schopenhauer himself insisted that his work was a kind of footnote to the philosophy of Immanuel Kant, whom I had read in very small doses in undergraduate classes. Now I attacked the main body of his work. This led me to writers Kant discussed, including Jean-Jacques Rousseau. My reading of Russell and Wittgenstein had already brought me to Baruch Spinoza, who influenced Rousseau. Working backward in this way, I returned eventually to the writers with whom I started the previous section, particularly Montaigne and Descartes.

For many contemporary atheists, materialism and atheism are synonymous, but my reading showed me that scientific materialism and its relations are not, in fact, the only atheist worldviews. Indeed, I learned that the atheist intellectual tradition is much richer than most contemporary atheists will allow. Like scientific materialism, the competing atheist tradition came into its own (at least in the West) in the post-Enlightenment era. It was initiated by figures like Schopenhauer and Nietzsche, and it runs from the phenomenology of Edmund Husserl and Martin Heidegger to the existentialism of Jean-Paul Sartre and Albert Camus.

These are among the most famous names in the history of atheism, but their intellectual influence has been largely written out of the picture by modern-day materialists. Bertrand Russell's nine-hundred-page *History of Western Philosophy* includes just a dozen pages on Schopenhauer and Nietzsche, two of the most important philosophers of the nineteenth century, and none at all on Heidegger, already recognized by the time of the book's publication among the most important of the twentieth. Christopher Hitchens's anthology of atheist thought, *The Portable Atheist*, features more contributions by the illusionist Penn Jillette (one) than by Schopenhauer, Nietzsche, and Heidegger combined (zero). One of the last things Hitchens wrote before his death from esophageal cancer was a critique of Nietzsche.

One obvious explanation for this hostility is historical: Russell was writing (and Hitchens was raised) in a postwar England that was understandably wary of a German philosophical tradition that seemed to have provided Nazism's intellectual underpinnings. There's probably also a more general Anglo-American suspicion of European airiness at play. Many of the writers I've named above are part of the philosophical school that has come simply to be called "Continental," because it has dominated French and German philosophy in the same way that analytic philosophy has dominated the English-speaking world.

But I suspect that the most significant reason scientific materialists have sought to downplay the nonmaterialist atheist tradition is that this tradition has been in turn deeply hostile to materialism. In fact, the most devastating philosophical attacks on materialism have come from this parallel tradition of post-Enlightenment atheists. The thinkers in this alternate tradition differ in many ways, but they all ground their work in precisely those features of human experience that materialism can't accommodate: subjectivity, consciousness, and agency. They take seriously, in a way that materialism does not, the question of what it means to view ourselves as the originators of whatever value and meaning exist in the world. This meaning-making project is the starting point of their work. They treat the nonexistence of God as a premise rather than a conclusion, as I was trying to do.

Perhaps what distinguishes these two traditions most dramatically is their view of human reason. Scientific materialists insist that evolution has given humans the power to understand (and thus to control) our environment. This is the greatest power we have, the one that separates us from the other animals who are otherwise our near relations, but it is constantly being threatened by the powers of irrationality, especially religious superstition. Romantic idealists suspect that reason has alienated us from ourselves, precisely by separating us from our animal relations. For all its power, reason is a kind of curse. I found this view appealing, for I felt that I had come to the limit of what reason could provide, and what I saw at those limits haunted me.

Another feature that joins many of these writers is their honesty about the bleakness of the atheist vision. They express in their public writings the kind of profound pessimism about reality that Russell saved for his private letters. Some seek to overcome this bleak reality, others resign themselves to it, but none look upon it with the glib complacency of Dawkins and Watson enjoying a good lunch. This atheistic pessimism is memorably presented in Philip Larkin's poem "This Be the Verse": "Man hands on misery to man / It deepens like a coastal shelf / Get out as early as you can / And don't have any kids yourself." This vision spoke powerfully to my own sense of despair.

Finally, all of these thinkers place artistic creation at the center of their systems. If human beings are truly responsible for making whatever meaning exists in an otherwise meaningless world, then life can be justified only—to the extent that it can be justified at all—on aesthetic grounds. Perhaps for this reason above all, I found in these writers an atheist tradition that made sense to me as scientific materialism did not. I didn't see my philosophical project as a sideline to my literary efforts. They were part of the same project, and that project was my life.

PART II

Absolute Reality

Thirteen

THE INTELLECTUAL LOVE OF GOD

The romantic idealist tradition is suspicious of reason, but its roots lie in a very different spirit. Just as empiricism travels from the severe skepticism of David Hume to its mirror image in the epistemological certainty of modern-day scientism, modern-day irrationalism develops from a great faith in reason's ability to deliver us the truth of reality. It begins with Descartes, whose speculative skepticism was really a starting point from which to demonstrate just how much knowledge reason could give us.

As I've already noted, Cartesian rationalism was the main alternative to Baconian empiricism in early modern philosophy. The greatest philosopher to follow Descartes in the rationalist tradition was also one of the first modern thinkers to be widely accused of atheism (like Hobbes, he denied the charge). Baruch Spinoza was born in 1632, just a few months after John Locke, into a family of Sephardic Jews in Amsterdam. He received a traditional Jewish education centered around Torah readings and Talmudic study, until an older brother died and he left off his studies to work in his father's trading firm.

After his father's death, Spinoza briefly set up shop with another brother. He began to pursue secular study, learning Latin from a local radical who had been expelled from the Jesuits. This allowed him to read Descartes and Hobbes, both of whom had spent long periods in Amsterdam and had extensive followings there. (The Dutch Republic was the most tolerant place in Europe at the time, which is what had brought the Sephardic Jews expelled from Spain and Portugal to Amsterdam in the first place.)

The local Jewish community banished Spinoza at the age of twenty-three. Excommunication—the declaration of herem—was relatively common at the time; without any civil authority, religious leaders had few substantive punishments at their disposal. It sometimes lasted only days. Spinoza was given a lifetime ban, expressed in a scathing judgment. Other Jews were instructed not to have any contact with him, "do him any favor," or read anything that he wrote. "Cursed be he by day and cursed be he by night," the verdict read. "Cursed be he when he lies down and cursed be he when he rises up."

Scholars have long argued over which particular heretical views earned this punishment; Spinoza's later work suggests plenty of possibilities. Among other things, he denied that Moses wrote the Torah, that the Jews had a special covenant with God, that humans were endowed with immortal souls, and that miracles occurred. Whatever its cause, the punishment did not strike a fatal blow. "All the better," Spinoza supposedly said. "They do not force me to do anything that I would not have done of my own accord if I did not dread scandal." (He might at least have regretted the separation from his surviving family, but he would later argue that intellectual freedom is a far greater good than any human affection.)

FOLLOWING HIS EXCOMMUNICATION, Spinoza took up his own version of that quintessential Enlightenment project, a theory of human knowledge. He begins his *Treatise on the Emendation of the Intellect* as Descartes had begun his *Discourse on the Method* and Locke would begin his

Essay Concerning Human Understanding, with an autobiographical account of how he came to the subject:

> After experience had taught me that all the usual surroundings of social life are vain and futile; seeing that none of the objects of my fears contained in themselves anything either good or bad, except insofar as the mind is affected by them, I finally resolved to inquire whether there might be some real good having power to communicate itself, which would affect the mind singly, to the exclusion of all else: whether, in fact, there might be anything of which the discovery and attainment would enable me to enjoy continuous, supreme, and unending happiness.

When commencing his own search for certain knowledge, Descartes had decided to "obey the laws and customs of my country," adhere to the faith in which he'd been raised, and generally behave to all outward appearances like one who accepts the commonly held opinions of his neighbors. Spinoza seems to have been on a similar course at the time of his banishment, after which it was obviously no longer tenable. Having come to believe that the "ordinary objects of desire would be obstacles in the way of a search for something different and new—nay that they were so opposed thereto, that either they or it would have to be abandoned," he left his commercial business in Amsterdam for the Hague, where he worked as a lens grinder (optics being among his intellectual interests) and otherwise dedicated himself to study.

As Spinoza saw it, you couldn't simply develop an intellectual method and follow its steps while otherwise living according to the status quo, because the truth is not a collection of isolated facts that experience delivers through the senses, formed into simple ideas that we combine in our cognitive workroom. Once fully apprehended, the real truth is singular and unified. It involves our whole selves. Furthermore, it is *good*—the source of "continuous, supreme, and unending happiness."

We have returned to a now familiar point: Questions about knowledge, truth, and the good can't be easily separated. Spinoza soon abandoned his epistemological treatise and set out to write a statement of his whole philosophy. He called that statement—widely considered the greatest metaphysical work of the modern age—the *Ethics*. Completing it would occupy the remainder of his (short) life, apart from brief periods when he set it aside to write the two books he would publish in his lifetime.

THE FIRST OF these other works was a study of Descartes, written at the urging of Spinoza's correspondents and admirers, who thought him an unusually powerful explicator of Cartesian thought. Using Euclid as a model, the book proceeds in the "geometric style" that would later mark the *Ethics*: Rather than advancing an argument with conventional rhetoric, it builds out from a series of definitions and axioms through demonstrations to propositions that are meant to have the certainty of mathematical truth. *The Principles of Cartesian Philosophy* would be the only work Spinoza published under his own name, and he tried to make clear that it was an explication rather than an endorsement of Cartesianism.

This seems to have been largely a defense against legal repercussions: Spinoza's watchword, engraved in the ring he wore every day, was *Caute*: "caution." In fact Spinoza's own philosophy does differ from that of Descartes, but generally on points that make it more rather than less radical. As this Spinozistic philosophy made its way through European intellectual circles, Spinoza himself gained a reputation as an atheist—or, more commonly, "that atheist Jew."

He considered this accusation wrong on both counts. By his own lights, he had ceased to be a Jew at the time of his excommunication. In the Hague, he had many friends among a society of nonconforming Christians—mostly Anabaptists and Quakers—but he lived the rest of his life as a member of no religious community or sect, a vanishingly rare experience for any European of that time. Circumstance made him a living embodiment of the great Cartesian thought experiment: a person with no tradition or authority to fall back on, seeking to answer life's fundamental questions entirely from scratch. But he was equally insistent that he was no atheist. Indeed, he claimed to have a love of God to rival that of any believer.

Even in the Dutch Republic, atheism was not a safe position to hold, and it was in part to rebut the charge—and in part to create a more hospitable reception for his actual thought—that Spinoza set aside a completed draft of the *Ethics* to write his other major work, the *Theological-Political Treatise* (*Tractatus Theologico-Politicus*). The *Treatise* would become a foundational work in the history of political liberalism on the basis of its concluding thesis—that freedom of thought "can be granted without detriment to public peace, to piety, and to the right of the sovereign." But before arriving at it, Spinoza conducted an attack on religious convention that was entirely unprecedented. ("I durst not write so boldly," Hobbes remarked upon reading it.)

Like Hume and many who followed him, Spinoza believed that fear and human vulnerability were the primary causes of religious superstition: "If men were able to exercise complete control over all their circumstances, or if continuous good fortune were always their lot, they would never be prey to superstition." This premise leads to a point that echoes the opening of the *Treatise on the Emendation of the Intellect*: "It is particularly those who greedily covet fortune's favours who are the readiest victims of superstition of every kind."

Those who derive their happiness from worldly pleasures are in a continuously precarious state, because such pleasures are fleeting and not within our power. Reason is little help in securing them, so such people will reject reason, though it is the source of true and lasting happiness. Having put their fate in fortune's hands, these people naturally fall into superstition in a misguided attempt to regain control—hence Spinoza's earlier conclusion that he could pursue truth or worldly goods, but not both.

From Hume to Mill to Russell to Dawkins, the mainline atheist tradition teaches that life's everyday pleasures—food and drink and sex, conviviality and companionship—are the only real human goods. The great evil of religion is to place our hopes in some imaginary world, teaching us to deny ourselves (and others) the very real pleasures available to us here and now. To the extent that our dependence on external goods puts us at the mercy of fortune, the Baconian tradition tells us that we can master fortune through instrumental reason. The ultimate cures for superstition are empirical knowledge and the world-mastering work to which such knowledge can be put. By comparison, Spinoza sounds more like a medieval ascetic or a classical Stoic, arguing that the supposed pleasures of daily life are fleeting and precarious and that a good life consists in the search for enduring truth.

Spinoza insists that knowledge of this enduring truth can be had directly, through the "natural light of reason," without the mediation of religious authority. Natural knowledge, he says, "has as much right as any other kind of knowledge to be called divine, since it is dictated to us, as it were, by God's nature." When we rely on the word of prophets or the authority of scripture for our knowledge of God, that knowledge comes secondhand and is always susceptible to doubt, unlike the immediate, clear, and certain knowledge of reason.

It would be one thing if the biblical prophets had been men with unusual powers of rational thinking whose works taught us to know God through reason. In that case, they would be like teachers leading us through the steps of a proof, at the end of which we would possess our knowledge of God directly. We could, to borrow Wittgenstein's later formulation, kick the ladder out from under us. Instead, religious prophets claim to have access to truths that can be had only through their mediating power.

What's more, the prophets' own knowledge of God is indirect, as any empirical knowledge must be. They experience signs—a messenger angel, a flaming bush, a rainbow in the sky—but never God itself. Philosophers know God directly, through reason rather than experience. It's therefore not just unfair but absurd that philosophers are accused of atheism by "those who openly declare that they do not possess the idea of God and that they know God only through created things."

The central metaphysical claim of all "true" religion, as Spinoza sees it, is that a singular, supreme, and omnipresent God exists. Their central moral claim is that we are called to love that God and love our neighbor. Both these claims, he says, can be arrived at through pure reason, and Spinoza shares Locke's view that faith is superfluous where reason does the job. There remains one function for scripture and ritual and the other trappings of traditional religion: to encourage "obedience and piety."

What actually distinguishes the great biblical prophets is their moral authority. They are exemplary instances of obedience to God's will, and their function has always been to call others to this obedience. Reason, too, dictates obedience and piety, and the truly free and rational person will act in accord with reason's dictates. So for the truly rational man, traditional religion is wholly superfluous. But most human beings are neither rational nor free. Scripture is "adapted to the understanding of the masses," and it has a purpose for anyone who "feels that this will enable him to obey God with heartier will in those matters that pertain to justice and charity."

Properly speaking, the Bible is a call to the very same action—love of

God and love of neighbor—that reason dictates. It does not especially matter that many claims made by the prophets are counter to reason because, again, "scripture teaches only piety, not philosophy," and piety is ultimately demonstrated by our actions rather than adherence to dogma: "Only by works can we judge anyone to be a believer or an unbeliever."

On one hand, this means that the partisans of religious tradition have nothing to fear from freethinkers. On the other hand, it means that any authority—religious or otherwise—that acts to constrain the free use of reason is acting against the interests of piety. Those who denigrate the use of reason are guilty of a far greater impiety than those who denigrate the authority of scripture.

This discussion naturally leads to the question of legitimate political authority. Spinoza's answer to the question owes a great deal to Hobbes, whose works were printed in the Netherlands at a time when they were still suppressed in his home country. "In order to achieve a secure and good life," rational people will "unite in one body," transferring their natural rights to a sovereign in whom all power is invested. But for Spinoza the ongoing legitimacy of the sovereign—the thing that makes individuals living under its power willing subjects rather than slaves—is the fact that it makes "the welfare of the whole people, not the ruler" its supreme law.

A key feature of this form of government, as Spinoza sees it, is that its laws are "based on sound reason," which in turn will make it the freest form of government, for where "everybody can be free as he wills," everybody can "live whole-heartedly under the guidance of reason." The public practice of religion "must accord with the peace and welfare of the commonwealth, and consequently must be determined only by sovereigns," but individuals should (and by necessity do) have freedom of conscience—"inward worship of God and piety itself belong to the sphere of individual right."

This is the *Treatise*'s ultimate argument: that the very purpose of the state is to guarantee for each of us this inward freedom—the freedom to think what we please, and the freedom to say what we think.

UNSURPRISINGLY, THIS ARGUMENT would not have the desired effect of creating a more hospitable reception for Spinoza's *Ethics*. Spinoza probably understood as much by the time he finished the *Treatise*, which he published not only under a pseudonym but under the imprint of a pseudonymous publishing house. The book was a scandalous bestseller, and for a time its author (soon enough revealed as the already notorious "atheist Jew") became Europe's most hated man.

Spinoza responded to this development with his usual equanimity, though he gave up any hope that the *Ethics* would appear in his lifetime. He began preparing his complete works in the original Latin and a Dutch translation for posthumous publication. This didn't amount to much of a delay: He died at age forty-four, just a few years after completing the *Ethics*, from a lung ailment exacerbated by breathing glass shards in his optical workshop.

Throughout the *Treatise*, Spinoza takes for granted that the foundational tenets of "true" religion can be established rationally, without the aid of revelation or tradition. In the *Ethics*, he attempts to prove as much. "Prove" here is meant in the mathematical sense—as already mentioned, his argument is made in the "geometric form" of a Euclidean proof.

I first picked up Spinoza's *Ethics* in my early years as an atheist, after learning that Spinoza was a great inspiration for Wittgenstein (whose own *Tractatus* was named in tribute to him). I've read it several times since, and I can't say that I have mastered it. It's a difficult book, but an oddly moving one, given the form it takes. The reader who attends carefully to it is granted moments of what feels like sublime access to rare truth—truth that can't easily be conveyed to another person precisely because of the manner in which Spinoza expresses it. The caveat that has undergirded this entire book—that I am neither a trained philosopher nor an intellectual historian, that I am simply trying to convey what these books meant to me in my search, rather than offering a definitive reading of them—is perhaps most relevant in this case.

With that settled, the first thing to say about the *Ethics* has already been suggested above: It attempts to offer its reader at once a complete metaphysics, a complete epistemology, and a complete ethics. Along the way, it anticipates and attempts to solve all of the major problems with the empirical tradition raised in the previous section: the mind-body problem; the problem of free will and determinism; the is/ought problem; and, finally, the problem of finding meaning in a naturalistic worldview, particularly in the face of death. It also does all of this in under two hundred pages, with very little of what one would recognize as philosophical argument.

The *Ethics* begins by defining its terms, including the term *God*, which Spinoza defines as a "being absolutely infinite." To say that God is "absolutely infinite," as Spinoza sees it, is to say that God is not just infinitely wise or infinitely powerful but infinite in every possible way, "a substance consisting of an infinity of attributes." This absolute infinitude differs from infinitude "in kind." If something is infinite in size, for example, then anything that has extension must be a part of it; there is simply no place for anything else to be that this infinitely large thing doesn't include. But one could imagine a thing without extension (e.g., a thought), and this thing would not necessarily be part of the infinitely large thing. By contrast, the fact that God is infinite in all ways means that anything that exists in any way is part of God: "Whatever is, is in God, and nothing can be or be conceived without God."

Spinoza's God is not the biblical God of Abraham. To begin with, Spinoza's God is not a being analogous to humans, "consisting of a body and a mind, and subject to passions," as he occasionally appears to be in the

Hebrew Scripture. Most theologians in Spinoza's time and our own would agree on this point. It was a central tenet of the Judaism in which Spinoza was educated that God does not have a body, a voice, a face, or any other such physical attribute, despite rare scriptural suggestions to the contrary. (This is precisely why empirical knowledge of God is bound to be indirect.) But Spinoza's God isn't even the more abstracted God of these theologians. Spinoza's God is not transcendent; it does not exist outside or beyond the natural order. Spinoza's God *is* the natural order—*Deus, sive Natura*, in his famous formulation: God, *or* Nature.

It follows from this that God did not create the universe, and he certainly did not create the universe for some reason. "Nature has no end set before it," Spinoza tells us, and "all final causes are nothing but human fictions." In fact, the very idea that God created things for some end "takes away from God's perfection": Any God that could bring the universe into existence to achieve some end might just as easily bring the end into immediate existence. Everything that exists, exists *necessarily*, just as God exists necessarily: "All things have been predetermined by God, not from freedom of the will or absolute good pleasure, but from God's absolute nature, or infinite power."

Because thinking things and extended bodies both exist in nature, thought and extension must be among God's infinite attributes. But God is also a unified thing, which means that these attributes can't be radically separated in the way Descartes believed: "The thinking substance and the extended substance are one and the same substance, which is now comprehended under this attribute, now under that." In place of Cartesian dualism, Spinoza proposes a form of what is these days called "dual aspect" theory: Thought and extension are the same substance looked at in different ways.

All matter is also mind. In the case of human individuals comprehended under the attribute of extension, our bodies are composites of a great many extended things—all of our body parts—which are in turn composites, continuing downward almost infinitely. And in the case of human individuals comprehended under the attribute of thought, we are likewise a composite of a great many thinking things. Every bit of extended matter in our bodies is also a bit of thinking stuff. No singular, unified Cartesian thinking thing controls each human being; there is instead a riot of thinking things that somehow act in a coordinated manner, just as the riot of individual cells somehow act as a singular body.

But of course for Spinoza there *is* a singular unified thinking thing—that is, God: "The whole of nature is one individual, whose parts, that is, all bodies, vary in infinite ways, without any change of the whole individual." We are all like cells in the body of God. And what is true about us as extension is also true about us as thought: "The human mind is a part of the infinite intellect of God."

We can understand more clearly now why it is such a mistake to understand God as a transcendent creator with a personal relationship to us. We do not grant the cells in our body free will and then bestow our favor on the ones that obey our commands, finding our happiness in their obedience. We can also understand why Spinoza's worldview is profoundly deterministic. The parts of our body act as nature dictates; if they all had free will, we could not exist as unified selves. This is just our relationship with God, *or* Nature.

SO WHY DO we believe ourselves to have free will? How can we be so profoundly mistaken about such a prominent feature of experience?

Think of a person attempting to determine the distance from the earth to the sun. Strictly on the basis of sense perception, Spinoza says, the sun appears to be a few hundred feet above us. Our perceptions are not "wrong," exactly, but they are inadequate to answer the question. A person who knows the actual distance to the sun and also knows why it appears so much closer than it really is will not have a different sense perception, but that person will have adequate knowledge to form a valid picture of reality. Similarly, humans believe in free will because they "are conscious of their actions and ignorant of the causes by which they are determined." A person with knowledge of the chain of efficient causes that have led to their actions will still experience those actions as consciously willed but will simultaneously understand that they were ultimately caused by something outside of themselves.

In Spinoza's epistemology, there are three sources from which we form "universal notions"—that is, notions about God or human freedom or the distance to the sun or anything else that extends beyond our immediate subjective experience. The first is "opinion or imagination," which consists primarily of our knowledge "of singular things which have been represented to us through the senses in a way which is mutilated, confused, and without order for the intellect." This is the kind of knowledge delivered by looking up at the sun. The second source of universal notions is reason—that is, "common notions and adequate ideas of things." Our knowledge of the true distance of the sun is a common notion, and our knowledge of why the sun appears as it does despite being so far away is an adequate idea of the sun's distance.

Almost by definition, we can see that the first source of knowledge is the cause of our false beliefs. Again, our sense experiences are not in themselves wrong—there is no Cartesian demon systematically tricking us—but they are inadequate sources of knowledge. Reason can make use of experience while delivering us valid notions, but it also depends on transcending our own experience. Reason is about the objective reality of things rather than our subjective perceptions; it's about the necessary and universal rather than the contingent and particular. Reason's tendency, as Spinoza says in perhaps his most famous line, is to see things "under a certain aspect of eternity" (*sub specie aeternitatis*).

This point is essential for the tradition that we're starting to describe. The empirical tradition tends toward analysis—breaking things up into the smallest possible parts; this competing tradition tends toward synthesis—treating things as much as possible as unified wholes. In this view, we can never really understand an individual parcel of reality outside the context of some totalizing view of reality as such.

Spinoza identifies a third source of knowledge beyond imagination and reason, which will be even more important for the romantic idealist tradition—that is intuitive knowledge. Because we are not atomized individuals but essential pieces of the whole, our minds by their very nature have "adequate knowledge of God's eternal and infinite essence" without needing to use reason to get "outside" themselves. This intuitive knowledge is the greatest kind of all, since "all things are in God and are conceived through God." In fact, it's ultimately the only one we ought to be after: "Our greatest happiness, or blessedness, consists . . . in the knowledge of God alone, by which we are led to do only those things which love and morality advise."

INTUITION IS NOT OBJECTIVE like reason, yet it isn't susceptible to the confusions of imagination. This might raise the question of why imagination—by which we essentially mean here sense perception—is susceptible to such confusions in the first place. What leads us away from those things that love and morality advise?

We experience sense perceptions when some extended body outside of us affects our own in some way. The mind—which, again, just *is* the body under a different aspect—perceives "the idea of the affection of the body," but this happens in a confused way, because it is not in the mind's nature to have an adequate idea of itself *as body*. In the third part of the *Ethics*, Spinoza takes up "the origin and nature of the affects." In so doing, he seeks to "consider human actions and appetites just as if it were a question of lines, planes, and bodies."

The starting point for the geometry of human appetites is this: "Each thing, as far as it can by its own power, strives to persevere in its being." This striving is not just a feature of all existing things; it is their essence. To strive to persevere in being is what it means to be. Because this striving is our essence, we express it under the aspect of body *and* mind: We strive as extension and we strive as thought. And since the mind has consciousness of itself as body, we both strive as mind and are conscious of ourselves as striving. This combination—"appetite together with the consciousness of appetite"—Spinoza calls "desire."

The human body interacts with other bodies in ways that can either increase or diminish our powers of striving. The passion that accompanies the increase of power Spinoza calls "joy," and the passion that accompanies the decrease in power Spinoza calls "sadness." From these three "primary affects"—desire, joy, and sadness—Spinoza develops a taxonomy of human passions. Love, for example, is "a joy accompanied by the idea of an external cause," while hatred is a sadness so accompanied. Hope is "an inconstant joy, born of the idea of a future or past thing whose outcome we to some extent doubt," while fear is "an inconstant sadness" similarly born.

Like most philosophers, Spinoza uses *passion* in its root sense, derived from the Latin *patios*, "to suffer" (an etymology it shares with the term *passive*). The passions are not just strong emotions but things that we *undergo*. The mind suffers passively because it has inadequate ideas of reality. Spinoza gives the name *bondage* to "man's lack of power to modify and restrain the affects." In other words, the great source of human unfreedom is not the fact that we live in a physically determined reality but our imperfect understanding of that reality.

A central cause of this bondage is that familiar Aristotelian culprit, belief in final causation. We understand nature as working toward some end determined by God, but if God *is* nature, this is clearly a mistake. We similarly understand ourselves as acting to fulfill some ends, whether determined by God or by ourselves. Another mistake. Our striving is the efficient cause that explains our behavior, but this striving is not a striving toward some greater end.

By recognizing the fact that we are necessary and determined parts of nature—by seeing reality and our place within it *sub specie aeternitatis*—we gain adequate ideas and become truly free. This sort of freedom is the ultimate goal of Spinoza's philosophy. The free man is blessed—meaning both happy and virtuous. Needless to say, being "virtuous" doesn't mean conforming your actions toward God-given ends or obeying God's commandments. It means more perfectly expressing your striving to be: "Virtue is human power itself."

This doesn't mean that the free and virtuous man will dominate others or impose his will. Those who live according to reason are bound to live in agreement with each other, because they all share adequate ideas of their interacting parts in nature. The free man will not feel hate toward others, even those who hate him, since hate is an evil, i.e., a weakening of one's own power. Nor will he feel pity toward others. He will seek to free himself equally from hope and fear, to conquer fortune and direct his actions "by the certain counsel of reason." He will not care for the esteem of the multitude, and he will not be "made anxious . . . in order to preserve his reputation."

Finally, there is this: "A free man thinks of nothing less than death, and his wisdom is a meditation on life, not death."

A FREE MAN thinks of nothing less than death: This was the moment of the *Ethics* that spoke most directly to me the first time I read the book. I was perhaps twenty-five at the time, a couple of years removed from my last radiation treatment, still checking in with the oncologist every three months. The fact that I would die—that all of my hopes and dreams and efforts would ultimately come to nothing but dust, along with everyone I ever loved—was my first thought upon waking up each morning and my last before going to bed. None of my philosophical reading to that point had offered any help with this problem, so I'd found a more mundane solution: I developed the habit of drinking while I wrote, so that by the time I was done with my night's work I was ready to pass out.

As a similarly death-haunted young man, Bertrand Russell briefly found inspiration in Spinoza's example. Spinoza has been a hero to many intellectual atheists, and with good reason. He dedicated himself to the search for truth, lived by his ideas, and seems to have found genuine peace and happiness in doing so. He was not forced to drink hemlock by his Jewish community or the Dutch authorities, but one can well imagine him accepting this fate in the same spirit as Socrates.

There is only one problem with Spinoza as a model for an atheist looking to live a meaningful life: the absolute centrality of God to his worldview. Because Spinoza's God does not transcend nature, does not care for human beings, does not demand our worship, many consider it a God in name only. By this reading, Spinoza is a naturalist, and when he speaks of "God, *or* Nature," one can just skip over the first two words. But Spinoza considered himself a greater theist than orthodox believers. Given the level of his intellectual honesty, given how far he was willing to go in criticizing traditional religious practice, and given the fact that he published the *Ethics* posthumously, there can be little doubt that he was sincere in this view.

If Spinoza had believed in only two types of knowledge—the imagination and reason—he would not be so far off from a run-of-the-mill empiricist. Even his desire to see things under the species of eternity might be understood as a version of the inductive movement from the particular to the general. One might then be able to argue that his worldview did not require the concept of God. But Spinoza believes in the third kind of knowledge, our intuitive knowledge as parts of a unified whole. Not only that, but he believes it is the knowledge that ultimately matters in the end. This is the subject of the *Ethics*' final section, "Of Human Freedom."

For Spinoza, the reason that allows us to view reality *sub specie aeternitatis* is a mere stepping stone toward true freedom, while intuitive knowledge is what ultimately sets us free. "From the third kind of knowledge," he writes, "there necessarily arises an intellectual love of God." This intellectual love of God is everlasting, and so when we participate in it, we participate in eternity: "The human mind cannot be absolutely destroyed with the body, but something of it remains which is eternal."

Spinoza's "intellectual love of God" is not another name for the scientific materialist wonder at the sublime cosmos that stands in for religious feeling. The third kind of knowledge—intuition of the essence of God born of the fact that we share in this essence, that we partake in God—simply does not make sense if one swaps in *nature* for *God*, as many people suggest we can do throughout Spinoza's work. It relies on the idea that all of nature is not just matter but is at the same time mind, that we are connected to a world of thought in the same way that we are connected to a physical world. It also requires us to understand the totality of nature as a coherent whole, not as a collection of random, contingent facts.

Russell often said that Spinoza's God is the God in which he *wanted* to believe. But this belief ultimately became impossible. When it did, the idea that reality could be apprehended through pure reason became equally impossible. If there is not "God, *or* Nature" but just "Nature," then there can be no metaphysics. When the idea that we can have truth through intuition—that something deep within ourselves can reveal to us the workings of outer reality—gets stripped of even the minimal Spinozistic God, some very strange notions follow.

Fourteen

CONSULT THE INNER LIGHT

The roots of romantic irrationalism are already present in the hyperrational Spinoza and his belief in an intuitive knowledge that ultimately surpasses reason. But Spinoza did not actually denigrate reason as such, which is what the tradition came to do within a few generations of his death.

In 1749, the Academy of Dijon in France solicited entries for its annual essay competition, seeking responses to the question of "whether the restoration of the sciences and the arts has contributed to purifying morals." Published the following year, the prize-winning essay answered definitively in the negative, but it was not written by a counter-Enlightenment reactionary. Its thirty-eight-year-old author was a friend of the great French philosophes, and he shared their critical assumptions about biblical revelation, religious tradition, and political authority. But he drew from these assumptions radically different conclusions, ones that would make him the age's most revolutionary thinker.

Jean-Jacques Rousseau was born in Geneva in 1712. His mother died in childbirth, and his father soon abandoned him to the care of aunts and uncles. At sixteen, he ran away from home, and he soon arrived destitute in the Italian city of Turin, where he converted to Catholicism in order to receive charity from the church, in the process losing his Genevan citizenship. He briefly trained for the priesthood but found himself unable to submit to the authority of this education. Instead he picked up his learning here and there over the following decade, most of it spent living with an older noblewoman, herself a devout Catholic convert, who began as his benefactor and became his mistress. (He called her "Momma," and she called him "my little one.") He eventually made his way to Paris, where he attempted to make a living writing music and dramas. He befriended several major French intellectual figures, including Jean-Baptiste d'Alembert and Denis Diderot, who invited him to write an entry in their *Encyclopédie*.

Around the time he finished that work, Rousseau came across a newspaper advertisement for the Dijon academy's contest. The question gave him a flash of insight that he would continue tracing out for the rest of his life. "The moment I read this," he'd later write, "I beheld another universe and became another man." Encouraged by Diderot, he put his thoughts into an essay and submitted it.

Before setting out his argument, Rousseau announces that he has taken the side in this debate that "suits a decent man who knows nothing and who does not think any less of himself for it." In other words, his ignorance makes him a living embodiment of the principle that virtue does not depend upon learning. Whatever facts will eventually be marshaled for his case, he tells us frankly, it remains a subjective truth grounded in his own nature. This sets an enduring pattern for Rousseau, who consistently elevates psychological authenticity above rational argumentation.

Having established this starting point, he acknowledges the "grand and beautiful spectacle" of the modern man, "dissipating by the light of his reason the shadows in which nature has enveloped him; rising above himself; soaring by his mind to the celestial regions; traversing with the steps of a giant, like the sun, the vast expanse of the universe." But right away he notes the cost that comes with these developments.

Rather than liberating us, advances in "the sciences, the letters, and the arts" serve to "spread garlands of flowers over the iron chains with which men are burdened, stifle in them the feeling of that original freedom for which they seemed to have been born, make them love their slavery and fashion them into what are called civilized people." Human achievements have inspired in individuals "the desire to please one another with works worthy of their mutual approbation." This might not seem like such a problem, but the desire for admiration divides us from ourselves: "Incessantly it is customs that are followed, never one's own genius." It also divides us from one another, as a "procession of vices" follows from the social convention in which "our passions . . . speak a borrowed language": "Suspicions, offenses, fears, coolness, reserve, hatred, betrayal continually conceal themselves behind that uniform and deceitful veil of civility, behind that much lauded urbanity we owe to the enlightenment of our age." Among many other consequences, Rousseau notes that people would rather adopt a "dangerous Pyrrhonism" than be scorned for their ignorance.

So it is not simply that our advances in arts and sciences have failed to bring about an equivalent moral progress but that "our souls have been corrupted in proportion as our sciences and arts have advanced towards perfection." This tension is not peculiar to the modern age. Ancient Egypt, Athens, and Rome fell successively into decadence and decline after taking on the mantle of civilization. Even the most advanced arts and sciences can't tell us how to live, which is the only bit of wisdom ultimately worth having.

Rousseau does not say this as a religious conservative arguing that material and intellectual progress turn us away from the moral authority of scripture or the church. In the version of the story that he is telling, institutions like the church and cultural artifacts like the scriptures are part of this corrupting civilization, which leads us to ignore our own inner sense of right and wrong. Virtue is the "science of simple souls" whose principles are "engraved in all hearts." To learn her laws, one need only "listen to the voice of one's conscience in the silence of the passions."

EVENTUALLY PUBLISHED AS the *Discourse on the Arts and Sciences*, the prize-winning essay made its author a celebrity throughout Europe—an ironic outcome, given the negative role that seeking the good opinion of others plays in the essay's moral landscape. With Rousseau such ironies abound: He was an enlightened critic of enlightenment, a great literary artist who deprecated both literature and artistry, an intellectual with a thoroughgoing suspicion of the intellect. The first *Discourse* was the beginning of a sustained attack on modern civilization made from within that civilization's own walls.

Four years later, Rousseau submitted a second essay to the academy, this time in response to the question "What is the origin of inequality among people, and is it authorized by natural law?" Rousseau opens what is now called the *Discourse on Inequality* as he did the earlier *Discourse*, with an expression of basic Enlightenment assumptions, in this case the assumption that the civil order was not given to man by God at the time of creation, that humanity began in a state closer to the condition of "savage" or "primitive" peoples still seen in other parts of the world—or even to the condition of nonhuman animals. Indeed, Rousseau tells us that his predecessors in this Enlightenment line did not go far enough: "The philosophers who have examined the foundations of society have all felt the necessity of going back to the state of nature, but none of them have reached it." Their mistake was imagining the condition of civilized man *dropped into* the state of nature, without understanding how much about civilized man is determined by civilization itself.

In his truly natural state, Rousseau insists, man was entirely self-sufficient: "The productions of the earth provided him with all the necessary support, instinct led him to make use of it." Eventually humans become victims of their own easy flourishing. Populations grow, and resources become less immediately available. The species occupies larger swaths of the globe, arriving in climates less perfectly suited to human needs. Under these conditions, survival requires ingenuity. Competition rewards "reflection of a sort," bringing out humanity's unique capacity for self-awareness and abstract thought.

Like many thinkers before and after, Rousseau recognizes the capacity for reflection as the signature difference between humans and other animals, but he differs from others in the view he takes of this difference. "I almost dare affirm that the state of reflection is a state contrary to nature," he writes, "and that the man who meditates is a depraved animal."

Reflection is contrary to nature first and foremost because it leads us to *act* contrary to nature, something creatures without reasoning power can't possibly do. Humans are the only animals that seek to improve upon nature by acting according to reason rather than instinct. Before Rousseau, modern thinkers tended to treat what he dubs "perfectibility"—the conscious ability to improve our condition in the world—as our greatest power, the one that allows us to rule over the rest of the natural order (and, not incidentally, allows more civilized humans to rule over "savages"). Rousseau turns this view on its head, suggesting that "this distinctive and almost unlimited faculty is the source of all men's misfortunes."

Reflection produces in man the "first movement of pride," a central concept for Rousseau. He carefully distinguishes pride (*amour-propre* in French) from love of self (*amour-de-soi*). A healthy care for one's own survival and well-being in absolute terms is the driver of all natural behavior. By contrast, pride is a care for how you are viewed in the eyes of others and where you stand in a relative hierarchy. *Amour-de-soi* seeks flourishing through the fulfillment of naturally occurring needs. *Amour-propre* seeks the appearance of flourishing through the fulfillment of an endlessly multiplying array of artificial needs.

Mankind's very first reflections (Rousseau tells us) concern relative differences. The most basic abstract concepts that the struggle for survival suggests to us are comparative qualities: large/small, strong/weak, fast/slow. From these come our earliest sense of hierarchy and inequality. We understand ourselves as superior to most other animals. We also recognize some animals—namely, other human beings—as approximate equals who share our basic needs and impulses. This sense of shared interest leads to a sense of community. Humans become less solitary; they build fixed shelters and occupy them in groups; they develop family bonds. Rousseau calls these bonds "the sweetest feelings known to man," but even this blessing is mixed: "Jealousy awakens along with love; discord triumphs, and the gentlest of the passions receives sacrifices of human blood."

So it is with Rousseau, for whom every step toward civilization is a step toward ruin. A generation's development of "conveniences unknown to their fathers" becomes "the first yoke they imposed on themselves without thinking about it and the first source of the evils they prepared for their descendants." The invention of song and dance and other amusements—essentially, the emergence of human culture as such—gives rise to "vanity and contempt, on the one hand, and shame and envy, on the other."

Eventually this poisoned progress brings us property and the division of labor. We get the exchange of goods and services. All of this works to the advantage of the stronger and the smarter, and natural inequalities become exacerbated, their effects made permanent. This kick-starts civilization as we know it—"the successive development of the other arts, the progress of languages, the testing and application of talents, the inequality of fortunes, the use or abuse of wealth." The rich come to dominate the poor, and they come to enjoy this domination for its own sake, "like those ravenous wolves which having once tasted human flesh refuse all other food."

Among its many other problems, this state is incredibly unstable. The rich are themselves vulnerable to domination, since their place in the hierarchy is no longer proportional to any natural advantage. The result is a "perpetual conflict . . . between the right of the stronger and the right of the first occupant which ended only in fights and murders."

Here we are quite far along in the journey toward civilization, but we only now arrive at the "war of all against all" that Hobbes mistook for the state of nature. Rousseau agrees with Hobbes that the political state and the rule of law emerge as a solution to this grim condition, but he doesn't think they emerge because citizens choose for rational reasons to give over their natural rights to a sovereign. Instead they come when the rich recognize "how disadvantageous to them was a perpetual war in which they alone paid all the costs and in which the risk to life was common to all, while the risk of goods was theirs alone." In response, the rich man developed "the most carefully considered project that ever entered the human mind." He set out to make his adversaries into his defenders by instilling in them maxims and institutions "that were as favorable to him as natural right was adverse to him."

The claim that the modern state's broad array of rights and protections—the "rules of justice and peace" that apply equally to all citizens—are in fact a con perpetrated by the rich and powerful against the poor and the weak is one of Rousseau's most influential ideas. Among those who believe in the liberal values espoused by the likes of Locke and Mill, it still has the power to shock. And it continues to raise the same question it raised at the time: What is the alternative?

"MAN IS BORN FREE, and everywhere he is in chains." These are probably Rousseau's most famous words, from the first chapter of his essay *On the Social Contract*, published in 1762. This observation is found throughout his work, but here he tries to discover some form in which this state of affairs might be justified. It's worth spending a moment on Rousseau's answer because, like the social-contract theories of Hobbes and Locke, it establishes certain principles essential to the moral and ethical traditions that follow.

In the second *Discourse*, Rousseau had identified the formation of the family as man's first step away from his naturally solitary state. Here he calls the family "the first model of political societies." This is obviously a very different kind of collective from the sort of political regime envisioned by Rousseau's contractarian predecessors. Where Hobbes had claimed that individuals in the state of nature would give over their rights absolutely to a sovereign who could keep order, the commitment of a family's members are to each other and to the family as a whole. It is true that the family—as conceived at this time—has a "head" (the father), but he is constrained as much as the family's other members to act for the good of the collective.

The creation of a family leads to the development of familial love, which in turn becomes the determining feature of family life. Sentiment, rather than reason, keeps a family together. The kind of rational self-interest that Hobbes and Locke take as the prime motivation for social organization is not sufficient to make a true family. A properly constituted state—one initiated by the social contract in Rousseau's form—will be similarly governed by what he calls the "general will," rather than by a collection of individuals each pursuing his or her own interest.

Rousseau's general will is not simply the "will of the people" as discerned through a democratic process. Nor is it some aggregation or balancing of conflicting individual interests through the strategic compromises we associate with properly functioning modern states. The collective body created by the social contract has a metaphysical unity, and the general will is whatever this unity wills. A body would no more harm one of its members than we would harm a part of our own body; at the same time, the parts of the body naturally want the good of the other members and of the body as a whole. For this reason, Rousseau assures us, "the general will is always right."

The idea of humans as parts of a body recalls Spinoza's metaphysics, in which the truly enlightened individual understands himself as part of the greater whole. Just as empiricism tends toward philosophical analysis, liberalism tends toward a focus on personal autonomy, and Rousseau is pushing back on the latter tendency as Spinoza did on the former one. (One could say that the general will is what an individual wills once he learns to view his own condition *sub specie aeternitatis.*) Recognizing yourself as part of a whole rather than as an atomized individual means recognizing limits on your actions, but Rousseau follows Spinoza in understanding this recognition as the definition of true freedom, because it is freedom from individual passions.

Rousseau has a name for those unfree people who follow their particular will rather than the general will, people who pursue their narrow interests, victims of the false consciousness of *amour-propre*, which makes them acquisitive and materialistic beyond any natural need. These people are *bourgeois*. Though the word had existed in French since the Middle Ages as a neutral term for the emerging urban mercantile middle class, Rousseau was the first to use it with the political and moral valence it carries today. At the same time that Adam Smith was arguing that the acquisitive self-interest of this class was the great driver of a flourishing society, Rousseau named it the enemy of the common good.

A family whose members are constantly asking themselves whether remaining in the family still serves their self-interest is not a family at all. Similarly, a political society whose members are concerned only with rational self-interest might be a country (*pays*) but it will never be a fatherland (*patrie*). So the social contract carries with it the commitment that whoever does refuse to obey the general will "be constrained to do so by the whole body, which means nothing else but that he be forced to be free."

Rousseau was writing before the rise of European nationalism. He was consciously calling for something new—or at least something that had been mostly lost since the age of the Greek city-states. In the prerevolutionary France where most of his audience lived, for example, people could think of themselves as subjects of the king without thinking of themselves as especially French. (Many spoke mutually incomprehensible regional dialects.) Much of the rest of Europe was composed of fragmented principalities on the one hand and the multinational Ottoman and Holy Roman Empires on the other. Around this time, Rousseau formally disavowed Catholicism so he could once again identify as a citizen of the Republic of Geneva, which he saw as one model for his proposed fatherland, and he expressed openly his belief that the monarchies of Europe were destined for collapse.

The states that replaced these monarchies would have to be founded on radical equality—not just political but material equality, as each citizen stayed within the limits of man's natural needs. But this would not be a loss for those who would otherwise have more, because they would abandon the artificial needs imposed by *amour-propre*. They would not see themselves in competition with their fellow citizens but rather as part of one whole whose flourishing concerned them as the family's flourishing concerns each of its members.

One obvious objection to this alternative is that humans aren't naturally inclined to feel familial love toward strangers who just happen to share their national borders. But Rousseau does not think that familial love itself is "natural." It is an artifact of human culture, a learned behavior. The fact of human perfectibility—a fact that has had so many lamentable consequences—means that humans can be made to feel a patriotism that will drive them to join the metaphysical unity of the fatherland, provided they are educated to do so.

IN THE SAME YEAR that the *Social Contract* appeared, Rousseau published an account of the stages of development that turn natural man into a properly free citizen instead of the bourgeois that civilization tends to produce. *Emile, or On Education*, which Rousseau considered his greatest work, is not a conventional philosophical tract but a fictional depiction of the upbringing given to a boy of average capabilities and intelligence whose wise parents put him in Rousseau's care.

I won't go through all the steps of this education, but its result is that Emile comes into adulthood as a man whose "power and will [are] in perfect equality." His strength comes not from the technical mastery of his surroundings, not from a Baconian ability to dominate nature, but from a willingness to live within nature's bounds: "Man is very strong when he is contented with what he is; he is very weak when he wants to raise himself above humanity." Like Spinoza's free man, Emile finds a paradoxical liberation in "yield[ing] to necessity."

The book also includes Rousseau's most extensive consideration of spiritual questions. Rather than describing Emile's religious education, he offers a "paper" he has transcribed, based on the report of another young man. It tells the story of a born Calvinist who finds himself destitute in an Italian city, where he converts to Catholicism for practical purposes. Caught up in doctrinal disagreements, he becomes equally alienated from his adopted faith and the faith of his fathers. With no faith at all, his life is utterly without moral direction. In desperation, he seeks out a "decent ecclesiastic" who had earlier visited him in the almshouse. (Rousseau later revealed this character to be a composite of two priests he knew around this time in his life.)

Originally from Savoy—the region surrounding Geneva—this priest himself fled to Italy after getting a young woman pregnant. Though the taint of scandal follows him, he lives a devout life with an outward commitment to Catholic practice. The young man finds in him "virtue without hypocrisy, humanity without weakness, speech always plain and straightforward, and conduct in accordance with this speech." The priest takes up this young man much as Jean-Jacques takes up Emile: He serves as an example without ever forcing religious doctrine or any other abstract ideas on his pupil. Morally at sea and struck by the priest's happiness in the face of exile, poverty, and persecution, the young man asks for his secret. Only then does the priest offer an account of his own beliefs.

Sent off by his peasant parents to attain a living in the church, the priest relates, he dutifully studied "what had to be known in order to be ordained": "I learned what I was supposed to learn; I said what I was supposed to say." But this progress was disrupted by the realization that "in obliging [himself] not to be a man"—i.e., making a vow of chastity—he "had promised more than [he] could keep." Because his sexual urges seemed entirely natural to him, and because "conscience persists in following the order of nature against all the laws of man," he could only conclude that the church's laws were wrong in this area. But because he had been raised in "a church which decides everything and permits no doubt," he found that "the rejection of a single point made [him] reject all the rest," bringing him to the point of Pyrrhonian skepticism. Like Descartes and many before him, however, he determined that he could not remain in the extremes of "uncertainty and doubt," so he set out to answer life's fundamental questions.

Consulting the works of the great philosophers, he found that they all disagreed with one another; three thousand years of speculation had delivered no progress on metaphysical matters. He concluded that the human mind was simply not up to the task: "We do not have the measurement of this inner machine." So he set aside metaphysics and attempted to answer only those questions that were relevant to his life. He likewise set aside philosophical works, opting instead to "consult the inner light."

This inner light may not be able to answer the most profound metaphysical questions, but in those areas we can remain in skeptical uncertainty, since they aren't relevant to our conduct. What the young man wants to learn from the priest—and what Jean-Jacques wants to impress upon Emile—is not the art of metaphysical speculation but an answer to the question of how to live.

When we consult our "inner light," we find ourselves oddly divided. There is a part of us—our bodily part—subject to the passions and the "empire of the senses," but there is another part—what one can only call our spiritual part—inclined "to the study of eternal truths, to the love of justice and moral beauty." This suggests that our body and our spirit are distinct in some way, that they are not simply the same thing viewed under different "aspects," as Spinoza would have it. It also suggests that we already know the answers to the moral quandaries facing us. Moral truth is "written by nature with ineffaceable characters in the depth of my heart," the priest explains. "Everything I sense to be good is good; everything I sense to be bad is bad."

Rousseau understands that this contradicts the prevailing empiricist view that "nothing exists in the mind other than what is introduced by experience, and [that] we judge a thing on no ground other than that of acquired ideas." It also contradicts the empiricist view that we can reason our way to moral laws grounded in rational self-interest. For the priest (and for Rousseau) the fact that reason inevitably deals in self-interest is precisely why it can't be an arbiter of moral truth. It is just as apt to give us casuistic justifications for giving in to our passions as it is to guide us in the right direction. "Too often reason deceives us," the priest says. "But conscience never deceives; it is man's true guide."

So ends the defense of natural religion that makes up the first half of the priest's profession. The second half—which proved far more consequential for Rousseau—contains his rejection of revealed religion. If we are meant to reject philosophy because great thinkers could not agree with one another, how can we not notice the disagreements among the great religions? If we are meant to reject the authority of books and other men in favor of the truth in our own hearts, how can we put our faith in scripture and prophecy?

On this matter, the priest ultimately arrives at Spinoza's view that all the world's great revealed religions share a core of truth that happens likewise to be the truth of natural religion. Beside this truth, the details in which they differ hardly matter. This doesn't mean that the priest has given up on religion; to do so would likely lead him back into the extreme doubt of Pyrrhonism. He practices with devotion the faith in which he was raised, and he ends by suggesting that the young man do the same, for "in the uncertainty in which we dwell, it is an inexcusable presumption to profess a religion other than that in which we were born, and a falseness not to practice sincerely the religion which we profess."

THE PROFESSION OF FAITH of a Savoyard Vicar is often published as a stand-alone volume, which is how I initially came to read it, the first work by Rousseau that I encountered outside of undergraduate politics courses. How could it not have a profound effect on me? It told the story of someone raised in the Catholic Church, suffering a crisis of faith, who turns to the great philosophers for answers and finds them wanting. I could not mistake the fact that Rousseau's vicar would have advised me to return to the church and stop asking questions that can't be answered.

This raises a tension that becomes more acute as we move through the romantic idealist tradition. Rousseau tells us not to seek the truth in books or secondhand knowledge, but Rousseau's own advice can come to us only in these forms. There is something inherently paradoxical about an authoritative case against authority or a carefully reasoned argument against the primacy of reason. Rousseau may have had this problem in mind when he presented the vicar's profession as itself a secondhand report. "I do not want to argue with you or even attempt to convince you," the vicar assures us. "It is enough for me to reveal to you what I think in the simplicity of my heart." Rousseau makes the same claim in his own words before presenting the vicar's profession: "I am not propounding to you the sentiment of another or my own as a rule. I am offering it to you for examination."

There is another possible reason for Rousseau's careful caveats, which is his own protection. If this was their purpose, however, they failed utterly. The combination of the *Profession* and the *Social Contract*'s attacks on the monarchy led to Rousseau's expulsion from Paris. No longer welcome in Calvinist Geneva, he spent the rest of his life wandering Europe. He traveled briefly to England to stay with David Hume, but he soon fell out with the easygoing empiricist and published an attack against him. He turned increasingly to the isolation he considered man's natural state, and he died nearly destitute in 1778.

His last major work was his *Confessions*, a remarkably frank book that is generally considered the first modern autobiography. It is utterly fitting that he capped his career with an extended examination of his self. In it he complains bitterly of his fate. At one point he writes in despair about his decision to submit his first entry to the Academy of Dijon: "I did so and from that moment I was lost. All the rest of my life and of my misfortunes followed inevitably as a result of that moment's madness."

Fifteen

DENYING KNOWLEDGE TO MAKE ROOM FOR FAITH

A decade after Rousseau's death, his strange posthumous life began. After the French Revolution, the Jacobins exhumed his body and entombed it at the Pantheon. Robespierre explicitly invoked Rousseau's ideas as a justification for the reign of terror that followed.

In the revolution's wake, the grand feelings of national identity that Rousseau had championed became a major feature of European political life. ("We have created Italy," one statesman remarked after that country achieved political unification. "Now we must create Italians.") So too did Rousseau's ideas that politics should be driven more by emotion than by reason, that individual rights were a form of bourgeois decadence, and that those who defied the general will could be "forced to be free." Rousseau became a wellspring of the Romantic movement, with all the danger and excitement it entailed. In one mark of this influence, the German philosopher Immanuel Kant ranked the publication of *Emile* alongside the revolution in its historical importance.

Kant doesn't look at first glance like the most promising Rousseauian disciple. For much of his career, he was an avatar of precisely the self-confident rationalism that Rousseau targeted so poisonously, and his biography is a study in contrasts to Rousseau's unstable and peripatetic existence.

Born in 1724—about a decade after both Rousseau and Hume—Kant was raised in a strict Pietist household. His entire life was marked by discipline and regularity. He never left the immediate surroundings of his Prussian hometown, Königsberg, and it is often reported that his neighbors could set their watches by his daily walk. The only occasion that broke the habit, the story goes, was his reading of *Emile.**

After coming of intellectual age squarely within the post-Cartesian rationalist tradition, Kant dedicated his early career to reconciling this tradition with Locke's empirical attack on innate ideas. His encounter with Hume's work—which began making its way into German translation when Kant was in his forties—exploded this effort. Reading Hume, Kant later said, awoke him from his "dogmatic slumber."

As a rationalist, Kant could not accept that the entire project of the natural sciences rested on the shoddy foundations of habit or the related claim that moral laws were simply prudential tools for getting along in life. Yet he couldn't see an easy way to refute either claim. Hume had provoked in him the question that occupied so many Renaissance and Enlightenment philosophers: How do we steer a middle course between dogmatism and skepticism? He struggled over the problem for more than a decade before producing his greatest work, *The Critique of Pure Reason*, the first of three "critiques" that make up the centerpiece of his mature philosophical system.

KANT WAS AMONG the first modern philosophers to earn his living as a professor, and also among the first to write in what we would now disparage as an "academic" style. Though capable of striking metaphors and

* Another version of this story substitutes Hume's *Treatise* as the book that disturbed Kant's routine, which suggests both the importance of the pair to Kant's thought and the fact that the story is likely apocryphal.

even stylistic beauty, Kant was no literary artist in the manner of Rousseau or Hume.

Very few people today read his work outside of academic settings, but that is just what I did in my late twenties and early thirties. As with Spinoza, I often struggled with this project, but I also found it surprisingly moving and powerful, despite its occasional obscurity. This made me better able to understand another historical paradox—that such a dry and systematic writer could inspire the wild and emotional responses that I'm going to try to capture in the pages ahead. All of this is meant as a caveat. There is no way to appreciate the rest of this story without appreciating Kant's contribution to it, but there is likewise no way to grasp Kant's contribution that doesn't involve some heavy lifting.

It will give some sense of what's ahead if we start by noting that Kant finally answered the question of skepticism by finding a new and remarkably ungainly way to ask it: "How are a priori synthetic judgments possible?"

Kant is here invoking two binaries we've already discussed. The first is that between a priori and a posteriori truth; the second is that between analysis and synthesis. Kant agrees with Locke that no knowledge *truly* precedes experience. As he uses the term, a priori knowledge is knowledge that does not depend on experience of particular cases, i.e., knowledge that is certain, universal, and necessary. The modern empirical tradition tells us that analytic truths can be had prior to experience, because they are already contained within concepts themselves. When we learn that all bachelors are unmarried men, we don't gain any new knowledge about bachelors; we have simply clarified what the concept entailed in the first place. Synthetic judgments bring additional information to the picture, and they must be had empirically. When we learn that some bachelors are happy to remain bachelors while others wish to get married, we have gained knowledge that was not contained in the original concept. This is an a posteriori truth, not just in the sense that it must come from experience but in the sense that it is uncertain and contingent. Further research could very easily reveal that those bachelors who claimed to be happy were secretly pining to pair off. And even if the original claim were true, it might well stop being so in the future. We could certainly imagine a world in which it was false.

So we have two sorts of judgments: a priori analytic and a posteriori synthetic. But the judgment that all effects must have causes is something else entirely. Assuming that Hume is wrong and such a truth could be known, it would have to be certain, necessary, and universal knowledge, but it is synthetic in the sense that it is not simply revealed through an analysis of the concept of causality. If we want to establish a rational basis for the judgment—and with it a rational basis for the empirical sciences in general—we'll have to show how a judgment could be at once a priori and synthetic.

Kant does this by way of what he calls his "Copernican revolution": Instead of assuming that "our cognition must conform to objects," he asks whether we might make better sense of things by assuming "that objects must conform to our cognition."

The empiricists are justified in their fundamental claim that "all our cognition begins with experience." But even the most basic experience, Kant adds, combines "what we receive through impressions and what our own cognitive power supplies from itself (sense impressions merely prompting it to do so)." The empiricists acknowledge this point when they classify certain features of experience as "secondary" qualities produced by the combination of reality and sensory processing while insisting that others are "primary" qualities inherent to objects themselves. But distinguishing the "raw material" of reality from our own cognitive contribution to it is not a simple matter. Can extension and duration be so clearly ascribed to objects apart from our experiences of them in a way that color or taste or texture cannot?

Time and space can't be empirical concepts that we have generalized from experience, Kant insists, because we could never have experience as such without already cognizing them. We can't experience things happening simultaneously or in succession and then abstract from this experience the concept of time; our minds must have already temporally arranged events for us to experience them as simultaneous or successive. Similarly, our minds must have already spatially arranged objects for us to experience them as near or far, adjacent or separate, or in any other relationship that might suggest the abstract concept of space. Space and time are "necessary a priori principle[s] that underlie all our intuitions": They are our way of having experiences rather than features of whatever we're experiencing.

Kant explicitly rejects the Berkeleian possibility that reality might be *entirely* mental in nature. According to Kant, that mistaken belief—which he calls "empirical idealism"—is a natural consequence of "transcendental realism," i.e., the belief that the transcendental features of experience are intrinsic parts of reality. People arrive at the (correct) view that time and space must be mental constructs while still holding on to the (incorrect) view that they are inherent qualities of reality, and so they conclude that reality must itself be a mental construct. Kant argues that there is a certain reality independent of our mental processes. Setting aside the details of this argument—which many have found extremely persuasive—it follows from it that empirical idealism must be wrong, just as surely as transcendental realism is. In place of these views, Kant gives us transcendental idealism—roughly, the view that the *material* of reality exists independently of our minds but that its *form* comes entirely from us.

But then, what is the matter to which we are giving this form? Kant gives the object of our experience the evocatively vague name *Ding an sich*—"thing in itself." If Kant is right, this thing must be radically different from our experience of it, beginning with the fact that it does not exist in space or time. "All our intuition is nothing but the presentation of appearance," Kant tells us. "The things that we intuit are not in themselves what we intuit them as being." Yet we have no other way of experiencing outside these forms, which means we can never know them as things-in-themselves.

The idea that the world of sense experience is a world of appearance is familiar enough; we are back in Plato's cave, watching shadows on the wall. But Kant breaks with his rationalist predecessors in his insistence that reason can never move beyond these appearances to arrive at the underlying reality. The world of appearance—the "phenomenal" world—is all reason can ever know. The world of things in themselves—the "noumenal" world—rests forever beyond its grasp.

MANY PEOPLE HAVE found this limitation a source of great anxiety, even horror. Kant is more hopeful about it. Precisely because appearances are all we can ever experience, they are not "mere" appearances to be distinguished from reality. They *are* reality—at least, our reality. If we keep within their bounds, we find a surprising benefit: We are delivered from the threat of skepticism.

Just as reason provides the formal elements of space and time, it orders reality within these forms through "categories of understanding" much like Aristotle's metaphysical categories—things like quantity, quality, relation, and causation. The categories are the broad ways we make sense of the objects of experience. Like the pure forms of intuition, they can't be derived empirically; they must already be present for experience to take the form it does. Without them, our experiences would lack even the most basic continuity; they would not really be experiences at all.

What Kant calls the "law-governed coherence" of reality—the fact that it isn't just a chaotic mess of unconnected inputs—is underappreciated.

Every temporal state continues on smoothly from the one that precedes it. Every bit of space connects up with the rest. That our own formal systems of thought should hold together this way is natural enough. What's strange is that "nature must conform to the categories"—that the external world lines up exactly with our powers of reasoning. This fact leads Spinoza to the belief that we are all parts of a rational whole. Kant argues instead that imagination joins the diverse elements of experience—what he calls "the manifold"—into a unified whole. *We* are nature's lawgivers.

Transcendental idealism has two great advantages over other systems. First, it establishes reason rather than custom, habit, or practical necessity as the proper basis for empirical science. If we take the pure concepts of understanding as our way of organizing and experiencing reality, then we can rise above Humean skepticism. We can know that the laws of nature are necessary and universally applicable, because nature is something that humans experience, and human cognition necessarily and universally imposes these laws. Second and equally important, transcendental idealism establishes once and for all that reason is useless when we move beyond these human experiences.

Attempts by pure reason to answer such metaphysical questions as whether we have real freedom, whether we have immortal souls, and whether God exists all require us to apply the formal categories of intuition and understanding outside the realm of experience. We simply can't answer such questions in this way. Kant is particularly devastating in his critique of the rational proofs of God's existence, which he leaves in even worse shape than Hume did.

In one of his rare literary flights, Kant describes the "land of pure understanding" as an island, "enclosed by nature itself within unchanging bounds." This island is "the land of truth," but it is "surrounded by a vast and stormy ocean, where illusion properly resides and many fog banks and much fast-melting ice feign new-found lands." Despite these hazards, humans are naturally drawn to leave our island: "This sea incessantly deludes the seafarer with empty hopes as he roves through his discoveries, and thus entangles him in adventure that he can never relinquish, nor ever bring to an end." The perplexities that arise when we depart the land of truth are not simply instances of faulty reasoning; they are "unavoidable illusion[s]" inherent to reason itself: "Even the wisest among all human beings cannot detach himself from them." Yet by subjecting pure reason to a proper critique, we can learn to recognize these illusions.

At this point it seems that he has left us in a familiar place: All efforts to "sound the depths" of reality are doomed to fail. We are inevitably confined to the world of experience, however much we might believe that some other world exists. But Kant does not entirely accept this conclusion. He tells us repeatedly throughout the first *Critique* that we simply can't help straying beyond the bounds of experience. Our minds can't be confined to the island of truth.

Kant's insistence that we subject reason to the discipline of critique sometimes resembles the positivist's effort to get us to stop asking metaphysical questions, or at least to stop expecting answers to them. But Kant suggests another reason that we can't give up these questions. After demonstrating the undecidability of the fundamental metaphysical questions, Kant adds this note: "Yet because of reason's honor and even security, neither withdrawing from the quarrel nor watching it indifferently as a mere mock combat is feasible, and even less feasible is simply commanding peace; for the object of the dispute is of great interest."

The first *Critique* ends on a note that confirmed everything I'd come to think on my journey to that point. Simply put, the answers to metaphysical questions *matter* for us. For some of us, it is not just difficult but impossible to put them aside, because this interest is not just abstract curiosity. The answers to these questions relate to the one question we can't ever stop asking: *How are we to live?*

ANSWERS TO THAT question are the domain not of theoretical or speculative reasoning but of practical or moral reasoning. At various points throughout the *Critique of Pure Reason*, Kant suggests that this latter sort of reasoning may provide working answers to metaphysical questions. He takes up the possibility at greater length in his *Critique of Practical Reason*.

Despite the contrasting titles, he doesn't mean to distinguish practical reasoning from pure reasoning. In fact, the second *Critique*'s central question—its equivalent to the first *Critique*'s famous query about a priori synthetic knowledge—is whether *pure* practical reasoning is possible.

Most practical reasoning is thoroughly empirical in nature. Only experience can tell us the likely outcome of our actions, which is our usual concern when deciding how to act. If we want to be liked by our peers, experience tells us to be kind and agreeable. If we want to lose weight, experience tells us to diet and exercise. These are what Kant calls "maxims"—guidelines for efficacious behavior.

Maxims are contingent and probable rather than necessary and certain: One could easily imagine a world where being well liked required commanding respect through a severe demeanor or one where human physiology worked in such a way that being sedentary encouraged weight loss. Furthermore, they are particular rather than universal, because they take the "if . . . then" form of what Kant calls "hypothetical imperatives." It's all well and good to have guidelines for popularity and weight loss, but if I'm perfectly content being solitary or overweight, these rules have no relevance for me. Hypothetical imperatives teach us how most effectively to pursue our own interests. They are, Kant says, "mere precepts of skill."

Empiricists put this kind of reasoning at the center of their moral theories. As we've seen, a science of morality can give us rules for achieving a given moral goal, but it can never tell us what our goals should be. At best, empirical study can tell us what actual humans have tended to hold as good, and it can show us what behavior or social order is most likely to secure those interests.

In the absence of a metaphysical order that could impose some *ought* upon our actions, is there an alternative to the utilitarian approach? What we want here is some rule for action that is universal rather than dependent on personal interests. Such an a priori rule—if one existed—would have to be generated not just by practical reason but by *pure* practical reason, which explains the import of Kant's initial question.

Pure reason can't provide maxims for practical action, since such maxims have a strong empirical element. But just as pure understanding determines by way of the categories the form that experience itself can take, pure practical reason might determine the form that any properly stated maxim could take. That form could obviously not be the "if . . . then" of a hypothetical imperative. It would instead be a *categorical* imperative, one that held in every case—not as a means to a particular end but as an end in itself. Furthermore, it would have to "qualify for universal legislation."

One can see this point by taking a contrary example such as the maxim "Endure no affront unavenged." An individual might rationally conclude that it served his own ends to adopt this maxim, but he could never rationally will that the maxim be universalized, because that would mean that his act of vengeance would be avenged in turn upon him.

The great achievement of the categories is synthetic unity of the manifold. The chaotic mass of sensory experience is made into a coherent whole. The categorical imperative would have to achieve a similar unity of manifold human actions, in which the chaotic mass of human interests is likewise made coherent and whole. Taking all these points together, Kant states the categorical imperative as follows: "So act that the maxim of your will could always hold at the same time as a principle of universal legislation." In other words, act in such a way that you would want to live in a world in which *everyone* acted that way.

For Kant, it isn't enough that one's actions should happen to meet this standard; true moral action must be taken *because* it meets the standard. The moral value of an action can't be determined by its consequences, because consequences can be known only empirically. Besides which, judging actions according to their consequences means applying a hypothetical imperative. We would always be left with the question of why certain consequences ought to be preferred over others. Bentham and other empiricists believed that society could be structured such that individuals maximizing their own self-interest could produce collective moral goods, but such actions could never be moral from Kant's perspective, so long as they were still being driven by the passions rather than moral choice. The moral value of an action must be judged by the standard of the categorical imperative.

Here we begin to see Rousseau's influence. For Rousseau, a morality based in self-interest is a bourgeois morality. True morality means willing the general will. This is the same law enshrined by the categorical imperative. Like Spinoza, Rousseau believed that the man who followed the general interest rather than his own was the truly free man. For many people, it seems paradoxical to locate freedom in constricting our behavior this way, acting for reasons other than our own interests, but so long as our actions are guided by hypothetical imperatives, they are determined by ends we have not ourselves legislated, and this is no freedom at all.

Kant follows both these thinkers in making autonomy—that is, the ability to live according to one's own laws—the central feature of his moral system. Living according to no laws at all, following one's impulse from moment to moment, means being governed by the passions, the very opposite of freedom. Acting rationally to choose our means but doing so in pursuit of ends dictated by nature or culture is similarly a kind of bondage.

True freedom entails rationally legislating not just our means but our ends, and only the categorical imperative can provide this sort of autonomy.

Utilitarianism is predicated on the idea that humans have natural preferences and desires; no matter how free we may be to pursue those desires, we could never be free to determine them. "We are free to do what we will," as Locke puts it, "but not to will what we will." Even those empiricists like Mill who place great store in the power of education to modify our desires see it as essentially a conditioning force, one that determines preferences for us. When Kant calls upon us to universalize our maxim, he is saying precisely that we ought to choose what to will. Do we have the freedom to do this? Given the constraints of physical determinism, do we have any freedom at all?

Certainly not in the material world—about that the empiricists are right, says Kant, for that world is causally fixed. But here we are saved once more by our recognition that the sensible world is a world of appearance. If it were a world of things in themselves, no freedom of any kind would be possible for us. As it is, the causal determinism of the sensible world applies only to "the acting subject as appearance." When we consider our own existence as things in themselves that do not "fall under the conditions of time," we are not determined by physical laws.

There's an obvious echo of Spinoza here: So long as we view our actions under the aspect of time, they are physically determined, but once we view them under the aspect of eternity, freedom becomes possible. The question of whether real freedom exists in the suprasensible world can't be answered through pure reason, but practical reason can't help presuming this freedom, and this presumption is legitimate, provided that we embrace metaphysical freedom as a "regulative principle" without claiming to have gained any substantive knowledge by doing so. Reason can accept metaphysical truth "as a foreign offering not grown on its own soil."

If such propositions are foreign offerings, where do they come from? In what soil have they been grown? Early in the first *Critique*, Kant tells us that philosophy seeks to answer three fundamental questions: *What can I know? What ought I do?* and *What may I hope?* The first question is the domain of speculative reason, the second of practical reason. But the third question is not the domain of reason at all; that's a point Kant has gone to great lengths to establish. Since reason can't weigh in on the world of things-in-themselves, we are free to invest our hopes there, and even obliged to do so when practical reason calls for it.

Over the course of the second *Critique*, Kant adds the existence of the immortal soul and the existence of God to the existence of human freedom among the metaphysical points that can be established as regulative principles. Kant does not argue that belief in God and in the immortality of the soul are necessary to make conforming to the moral law a rational obligation. In that case, the categorical imperative would be transformed into a hypothetical imperative of the form "If you want to enjoy eternal happiness, so act that . . ." The very form of the categorical imperative, not any eternal reward that might go with it, makes it a rational obligation. The true aim of morality, Kant writes in one striking passage, is not to make us happy but to make us "worthy of happiness." What a pure rational faith can add to duty is "the hope of someday coming to partake of happiness to the degree to which we have taken care not to be unworthy of it."

This pure rational faith finally gives us some access to the noumenal world, but it would never have done so had reason not raised these metaphysical quandaries. Here is another argument for why we should not aim to stop asking these questions, even if such a thing were possible. However much confusion it has caused, our wandering into this area is "the most beneficial straying into which human reason could ever have fallen, because it ultimately impels us to seek the key to get out of this labyrinth—the key which, when found, also uncovers what one did not seek and yet requires, namely an outlook into a higher, unchangeable order of things."

The long-standing assumption has been that our view of the ultimate nature of reality ought to condition our view of how we live our lives. Kant insists that we can't have meaningful knowledge about the ultimate nature of reality but that we must have some answer to the question of how to live, and so he tells us that our knowledge of the moral law ought to condition our metaphysical beliefs.

Of course, it would be irrational to hope for something that contradicted reason. This is why it is so important to Kant that reason has no purchase on the noumenal world. When it comes to things in themselves, Kant writes in one of his most famous lines, "I have found it necessary to deny knowledge in order to make room for faith."

KANT IS THE most influential modern philosopher, probably the most influential philosopher in history after Plato and Aristotle. But his followers prefer to take his influence in pieces. Some find his metaphysics frankly absurd but nonetheless embrace a Kantian ethics grounded in rational autonomy. Others accept transcendental idealism while treating his ethics with contempt. His aesthetic philosophy has influenced thinkers who have no interest in either his theoretical or his practical philosophy. Many atheists celebrate him for putting the final nail in the coffin of rational theology, and such people can only be embarrassed and dismayed by the fact that he ended by embracing the rational necessity of belief in a transcendent God.

What unifies all of these pieces is the idea that humans shape reality rather than passively receiving it through sense experience. Truth could never be a correspondence between our mental constructions and the unconditioned facts of the external world, because these mental constructions are all we can possibly know. The atheistic philosophers who follow in Kant's tradition all give creative imagination a central place in the meaning of life, and this fact goes a long way to explaining why I found their brand of atheism so much more appealing than the brute materialism that seemed their only real alternative.

From my earliest encounters with Kant's work, I admired the central role he gave to consciousness and freedom, those two undeniable features of human experience that materialism handles so poorly. I also appreciated the central role he gave to aesthetic experience. I was a young writer, a person who had decided to dedicate his life to artistic creation, and I believed that such work could be—ought to be—significant. I was even beginning to believe that it might hold the key to the thing I was seeking: a way to make a life lived without God a meaningful one.

Sixteen

THE ARTIST FORMING THE WORK

Unlike Rousseau, Kant was by no means an antirationalist; he sought to establish reason's limits so that it could confidently do its work within them—and so that it could avoid the confusion that inevitably arose when those limits were broken. He made the following of rules the foundation of his philosophy and on a personal level lived an almost comically well-ordered life. Yet his work had a radically disordering effect on others.

One admittedly extreme example was Heinrich von Kleist, who was a committed believer in the Enlightenment project of mapping the world through reason until he encountered Kant's philosophy in 1801 at the age of twenty-three. "The thought that here on earth we know nothing of the truth, absolutely nothing . . . has shaken me in the very sanctuary of my soul," he wrote to his sister. "My only purpose, my supreme purpose has collapsed; I have none left." Kleist quit his job at the Prussian Ministry of Finance and wandered Germany in search of a new "plan" by which he might live. He also wrote plays, poems, and stories that are among the most powerful works of German Romanticism. After a decade he found his plan in the form of a suicide pact with a terminally ill female friend. On November 21, 1811, he shot her and then himself to death.

On the other end of the spectrum of responses lay Georg Wilhelm Friedrich Hegel, who believed that Kant had pointed the way toward reason's total comprehension of reality. For Kant had shown reality to be a product of the mind, and he had likewise shown that the mind—even if it could not know objective truth—could know itself. The history of philosophy was best understood as the history of reason's unfolding self-knowledge. Hegel's view treats the world as a kind of spiritual intelligence, more or less explicitly returning God to the center of philosophical study. (Hegel's God is the same "Absolute" that Bertrand Russell briefly embraced.)

Hegel was the dominant force in Continental philosophy after Kant. But for those who took Kant's great legacy as the destruction of rational metaphysics, Hegelianism could only be considered a reactionary effort to make philosophy once again theology's handmaiden.* This was the view of Kant's greatest atheist disciple, Arthur Schopenhauer.

Born into a wealthy family in 1788, Schopenhauer spent his early years traveling with his parents, becoming fluent in English and French, and developing a cosmopolitanism that would mark the rest of his life. His father was a merchant and his mother was a popular novelist. (She was by far the more famous writer during their lifetimes.) When Schopenhauer was still a teenager, his father died, leaving him financially independent. He and his mother had a fairly loveless relationship, to which many attribute his work's persistent misogynistic streak, but she established a literary salon that exposed him to many of the era's most significant figures, including Goethe, his major influence besides Kant.

Schopenhauer developed his mature worldview at a remarkably young age. His earliest work, *On the Fourfold Root of the Principle of Sufficient Reason*, submitted as his doctoral thesis when he was twenty-six, contains

* The major German idealists—Fichte, Hegel, and Schelling—were all onetime seminary students; Hegel and Schelling were roommates at seminary.

his entire philosophical system, and his most complete expression of that system, *The World as Will and Representation*, appeared when he was barely thirty. He was a great literary stylist; today he is widely considered one of the finest writers of German prose who ever lived. He was also notably obstinate and difficult. When he briefly set up as a philosophy instructor, he intentionally scheduled his course at the same time as Hegel's. As a result, no one showed up. For the rest of his life, he sprinkled his work with vitriolic attacks on Hegel, German idealism, and academic philosophy in general.

Because he was independently wealthy, he was able to abandon his teaching career and continue writing despite a lack of audience. Over the following decades, he published a few short works that elaborated on the ideas laid out in his major early books. Finally he published a collection of essays and aphorisms that brought him the literary success he'd long believed himself due. At this point, he revised and expanded his earlier writing for new editions. This publication history turned his entire body of work into one network of thought, with the earliest making references to the latest, and each piece presuming knowledge of the others.

Something like this level of coherence would likely have been present in any case. By Schopenhauer's own admission, all of his works were an elaboration or extension of a single point. "My philosophy is like Thebes with a hundred gates," he wrote late in his life: "One can enter from all sides and through each gate arrive at the direct path to the center."

HIS INITIAL ENTRY gate was the same one that led Kant to transcendental philosophy: the nature of causation. The "principle of sufficient reason" is simply the principle that, as Schopenhauer puts it, "everything has a reason or ground which justifies us in everywhere asking why." This principle can't be proved, for one must already embrace it before seeking a proof for anything. Nonetheless it has been embraced, implicitly or explicitly, by nearly every philosopher. The "why," Schopenhauer writes, is "the mother of all sciences." But he believes that the nature of sufficient reason has been consistently misunderstood.

Kant's transcendental idealism saves us from skepticism about material causation by showing the inextricable relationship of subject and object—"that the world is just as dependent on us, as a whole, as we are on it in particular." There is no preexisting external world to which we are simply given access by way of our senses, no objects without subjects. Kant tells us that the understanding converts mere sense perception into experience by way of the categories. Schopenhauer clarifies that the "complicated clockwork of the twelve Kantian categories" can be reduced to one. All experience is experience of change, and all understanding "is an immediate, and therefore intuitive, apprehension of the causal connection."

The single rule of understanding is the law of causality, or "the principle of sufficient reason or ground of becoming": "If a new state of one or several real objects appears, another state must have preceded it upon which the new state follows regularly, in other words, as often as the first state exists." Without the application of this law, we would have sensory impressions but no experience as such. The understanding is "the artist forming the work, whereas the senses are merely the assistants who hand up the materials."

By way of his distinction between analytic and synthetic judgments, Kant also showed that the principle of sufficient reason had a second, very different application besides the law of causality. While the first application applies to "changes in real objects," the second applies to our judgments of concepts and abstract representations. In making judgments, we follow the principle of sufficient reason of knowledge: "If a judgment is to express a piece of knowledge, it must have a sufficient ground or reason; by virtue of this quality, it then receives the predicate *true.*" The conflation of these two applications had led to many philosophical mistakes, not least the various rational proofs for the existence of God, which generally involve answering questions about grounds of knowledge as though they were questions about material causation (and vice versa).

But Schopenhauer insists that there are still other cases in which we are justified in asking (and answering) the question "Why?" He gives as one example an equilateral triangle about which we ask why its sides are equal. There is a good answer to this question: because its angles are equal. Yet the equality of the angles does not "cause" the equality of the sides in the material sense—the one equality does not precede the other and bring it into existence—and the concept of equal angles does not logically contain the concept of equal sides.

This example illustrates a third form of sufficient cause, which arises when we take representations only in their formal aspect—that is, only considered as spatial or temporal. The definitive feature of space and time is that "all their parts stand in mutual relation." In its spatial aspect, this relation gives us geometry. In its temporal aspect, it gives us pure successiveness—i.e., arithmetic. Because of this interrelation, "every part [of space or time] is determined and conditioned by another." Thus the relationship of the angles and sides of our triangle. One does not materially cause or logically explain the other, yet the existence of one determines the other's existence. This determination occurs according to what Schopenhauer calls the "principle of sufficient reason of being."

A single remaining object of cognition has not been captured by these three types. Rather, a single one for each of us: our own selves. On one hand, we are conscious of ourselves as physical bodies, empirical representations in space and time who are subject to the principle of sufficient reason of becoming. But we are also conscious of ourselves *as* conscious selves, somehow apart from the succession of physical states that our body occupies.

All knowledge is a relation between a subject and an object. In this one case, the knower and the known are identical; they are both the subjective "I." The experience of consciousness can't be separated from the subject having that experience, for this subject would itself have to be conscious in order to have the experience, and we would have the same problem separating the subject from the experience of the experience. Yet it is still the case that we have knowledge of our own subjectivity as such, over and above our knowledge of the objects of consciousness. Without this, we could not have any sense of a unified self, no sense that the never-ending succession of conscious experiences is happening to a single "I."

Materialists may deny that unity by showing that we can't account for it in empirical terms, but for most of us that just goes to show that empirical terms are insufficient. Our sense of self is given to us immediately, and no rational proof can be made against it, for we are not in a realm where the ground of knowledge determines truth.

So what is it that we know, when we know ourselves *as selves*? For Schopenhauer, this knowledge is intimately related to our ability to act in ways that are internally motivated rather than simply physically determined. Again, many materialists would deny that we have such an ability, but for most of us it is inarguably the case.

It is possible to evaluate the motives of other conscious creatures from the outside, treating motivation as a special application of the law of causality. If a rock that was sitting still suddenly starts moving, we know that some external cause is at work, even if we can't identify it. If a person sitting across from us on the train suddenly stands up, and no external cause is apparent, we presume a more or less conscious internal motivation. But this gives us only indirect knowledge of motivation, and we would never arrive at this application of causality if we did not also know motivation in another way, "from within and quite directly, and thus in accordance with its whole mode of action."

What we come to know, when we know ourselves through self-consciousness, as the object for our subject, is not ourselves as knower but ourselves as *willer*, and the principle of sufficient reason as applied to this object is the "law of motivation": "With every decision that we observe in ourselves and also in others, we regard ourselves as justified in asking, why?" Without some motivation, the action of a conscious being is "just as inconceivable as is the movement of an inanimate body without a push or a pull."

Because this motivating will can't be made into either an empirical or an abstract representation, very little can be said about it, apart from the fact that it does exist: "Just because the subject of willing is immediately given in self-consciousness, it is impossible to further define or describe the nature of willing." But Schopenhauer clearly states something I had already felt while reading the scientific materialists: If our sense of ourselves as freely acting will is inconsistent with our picture of material reality, we should not assume that the former must yield to the latter. The inner sense "is the most immediate of all our knowledge [and] this immediacy must ultimately throw light on all the other branches of knowledge which are very mediate."

We do know one other thing about ourselves as willer. Although we can't know ourselves as knower, we recognize that the self that knows and the self that wills are indeed the same unified self. They are both *us*. Again, this is not a conclusion that can be defended rationally; it is something we know in the same immediate way we know that time can be experienced in only one direction.

But suppose we ask how we can know that immediate experience is reliable. There is no way to answer that question. Once we have outlined the fourfold root of sufficient reason, we have given all of the ways in which we might coherently ask "Why?" about any event, object, or state of affairs, and we have given all of the forms that a legitimate answer to the question can take. "The identity of the subject of willing with that of knowing," Schopenhauer tells us, "is the knot of the world, and hence inexplicable."

This knot—the relation between the will and representation—is the ultimate subject of all of Schopenhauer's philosophy, the central town square toward which every gate and every road ultimately leads.

SCHOPENHAUER CAME TO see *Fourfold Root* as a "preface" to *The World as Will and Representation*, and he insisted that the first had to be read for the second to be understood. The only other requirement, he added, was knowledge of Kant's philosophy, for the book was essentially a revision of Kant's thought on the basis of *Fourfold Root*'s clarifications.

From Kant, of course, we get the realization that what we take as the objective world is fundamentally a representation. This representation is constructed from the material of sense perception, given the form of space and time by our intuition, and transformed into a coherent objective reality by the understanding on the basis of a single governing principle, that of causality.

This way of putting matters lays bare a major inconsistency in Kant's philosophy. Kant treats the thing in itself as a kind of stimulus that brings about the sense perceptions from which sensibility and understanding produce the appearance of reality. Our sensory intuitions are prompted in some way by the thing in itself, or by that portion of it whose form makes it a suitable object for the forms of intuition. This obviously suggests that the thing in itself *causes* these perceptions, bringing about the appearance as its effect. But that is impossible. Just as we can't speak of the thing in itself as existing in time or space, we can't speak of it as caused by or causing anything, because causation is one of the formal elements that we provide ourselves.

Then what is "behind" our sense perceptions, if not the thing in itself? Nothing. Any other possible alternative would run into the same causality problem. The law of causality applies to objects; it can never be applied to a relationship between subject and object. Our sense perceptions provide the material for experience, but they don't "get" this material from some other source. They just are what they are—sensations. This doesn't mean that there is no objective reality; it means that our representations *are* objective reality. To seek after some object behind the object is the mistake of materialism. But it is similarly mistaken to say that the world is pure subjectivity. Instead Schopenhauer arrives at a version of Spinoza's conclusion: Subject and object must be the same thing, viewed under different aspects.

If the world viewed as object is representation, what is the world viewed as subject? Well, it says it right there on the tin: The world is *will*. We've been prepared for this conclusion by *Fourfold Root*, where the will was shown to be the fourth type of object available for our cognition, and the relationship between this type and the first type (empirical representations), particularly between ourselves as will and ourselves as body, is the "knot of the world." Now Schopenhauer proposes that this relationship is our one piece of insight into the relationship between appearance and thing in itself.

As we know from *Fourfold Root*, all empirical knowledge is a knowledge of changes of state. We are aware of something as representation when it changes, or when the things around it change and it does not. Our experience of our bodies as representation is an experience of bodily action, and our subjective experience of these actions is that they are willed by us. Our body is "the objectification of the will"; our will is "our being in itself."

Faced with this double knowledge, we have a theoretical dilemma. On the one hand, we can presume that we are unique among all objects in having this double reality, being at once representation and will. This leads to solipsism, or "theoretical egoism," in which one "regards as phantoms all phenomena outside its own will." Like many philosophers, Schopenhauer acknowledges that theoretical egoism can't actually be refuted but finds such refutation unnecessary: "As a serious conviction, [solipsism] could only be found in a madhouse; as such it would then need not so much a refutation as a cure."

The alternative is to presume that our double knowledge of ourselves reflects a profound truth about the world, that everything that has material reality for us as representation also has its own subjective reality as will. We naturally make this presumption when it comes to other human beings, and it isn't hard to extend it to nonhuman animals that we see engaged in what appears to be motivated action. But are we really prepared to ascribe will to chairs and rocks and books and, well, everything?

If we struggle with the idea, Schopenhauer says, it's only because we misunderstand the nature of our own will. We think of it as intimately related to our conscious thoughts. But we've already seen that our will is often not under our conscious control, and that the very possibility of its being so—the possibility that we might consciously "choose" what to will—raises all sorts of conceptual problems. Moreover, that possibility suggests that something in us causes our will, which in Schopenhauer's reading simply can't be the case.

Once we recognize this fact, Schopenhauer's idea becomes more plausible. We already recognize will in animals that can't be consciously aware of their own motives: "The one-year-old bird has no notion of the eggs for which it builds a nest; the young spider has no idea of the prey for which it spins a web; the ant-lion has no notion of the ant which it digs a cavity for the first time. . . . In the actions of such animals the will is obviously at work as in the rest of their activities, but is in blind activity."

Once we understand the will as pure activity, unguided by reason and uncaused by motive, we can see it everywhere. It is "the force that shoots and vegetates in the plant, the force by which crystal is formed, the force that turns the magnet to the North Pole . . . and finally even gravitation, which acts so powerfully in all matter, pulling the stone to the earth and the earth to the sun." The will on display in all of this is "the innermost essence, the kernel, of every particular thing and also of the whole."

Rather than assuming that we can best understand our own knowing and willing by referring them to "movement from causes through electricity, chemistry, and mechanism," we would do better to understand "the inscrutable forces that manifest themselves in all the bodies of nature" by reference to our experience of our own will. "Spinoza says that if a stone projected through the air had consciousness, it would imagine itself to be flying of its own will," Schopenhauer writes. "I add merely that the stone would be right."

THIS IS CHALLENGING STUFF, and I'm afraid I've made Schopenhauer sound like another obscure and difficult philosopher in the Kantian mode. I hope some of these quotes give a small sense of what a pleasure he is to read. More important, I want to give a sense of how urgently his work speaks to the most important human questions.

What does it mean to recognize the will as thing in itself? First of all, it means recognizing the ultimate unity of all existence. Plurality is a category of time and space, applicable only to phenomena, and if we ourselves are will—being in itself—then we are one with everything else. This sounds a bit like Spinoza's view, with one significant difference: Spinoza's world is ordered and rational, while Schopenhauer's will is neither of those things. It would never make sense to speak of "God, *or* Will" as Spinoza does of "God, *or* Nature."

Because the will is groundless, we likewise can't speak of its having a creator, let alone being created for some higher purpose. Once we know the noumena to be blind striving, we know there is no place there for God. The world as will is utterly incompatible with theistic belief of any kind. And Schopenhauer seems more than most of his atheist predecessors—and far more than most who have followed him—to recognize the full implications of this fact.

Seen as will, the world is a kind of thoughtless, meaningless pulsing. Seen as representation, meanwhile, it is an endless parade of suffering. The will manifests itself at different grades of objectivity, and these grades are in constant struggle. Each grade of objectification is analogous to a Platonic form or idea—thus the type "horse" is a particular level of objectification, while an individual horse is an instance of will exhibiting this grade.

The "universal forces of nature" represent the lowest grade of objectification. This includes gravity and the impenetrability of matter as well as "rigidity, fluidity, elasticity . . . and qualities of every kind." These qualities are the same wherever they appear, subject to the most consistent physical laws. At higher grades of objectivity, we see greater individuation, leading to differences in types and species, and finally to human beings, who show a marked difference even among different individuals of the species, and each of whose action seems determined by the law of its own individual character.

Will is constantly struggling to individuate itself, and "every grade of the will's objectification fights for the matter, the space, and the time of another." As a result, "everywhere in nature we see contest, struggle, and the fluctuation of victory." In practice, this means that "every phenomenon of the will, and even that which manifests itself in the human organism, keeps up a permanent struggle against the many chemical and physical forces that, as lower Ideas, have a prior right to that matter." This struggle is the source of "the burden of physical life, the necessity of sleep, and ultimately of death."

The war can never be won or lost, for it has no purpose or end. What that means for human beings specifically is this:

> Life itself is a sea full of rocks and whirlpools that man avoids with the greatest caution and care, although he knows that, even when he succeeds with all his efforts and ingenuity in struggling through, at every step he comes closer to the greatest, the total, the inevitable and irremediable shipwreck, indeed even steers right on to it, namely death. This is the final goal of the wearisome voyage, and is worse for him than all the rocks that he has avoided.

Even suicide is no solution. For Schopenhauer, there can never really be an ethical "ought," so one can't exactly say that it's "wrong" to take one's own life, but one can say with certainty that it is no way to escape the problem of the will. For suicide is a preeminent act of the will. The appropriate response to the reality of existence is instead a kind of stoic quietism. The will's "self-elimination" comes not by suicide but by resignation: "This is the ultimate goal, and indeed the innermost nature of all virtue and holiness, and is salvation from the world."

AS HUMAN BEINGS, we have a unique resource in pursuit of this goal. In their endless struggle for time and space, the higher orders of objectified will developed the tools of understanding and knowledge. In these cases, the law of causality that determines all representation takes a new form. Among animals, bare cause and effect becomes stimulus and response; among humans, motivation and conscious action.

"Originally and by its nature," Schopenhauer tells us, "knowledge is completely the servant of the will." It came into being so that certain orders of will might better impose themselves on others and win a temporary advantage in the endless war of existence. This "subjection of knowledge to the will" is inevitable for animals, but in rare cases among human beings "knowledge tears itself free from the service of the will." This happens in moments of "fixed contemplation," when we consider some object not "in accordance with the principle of sufficient reason" but "out of its connection with any other." In such moments, we can ourselves be separated from the ongoing struggle of life. "We lose ourselves entirely in this object," Schopenhauer writes, "so that it is as though the object alone existed, without anyone to perceive it."

We do not contemplate the object as pure will, for the will is the world as subject and we can never have objective knowledge of it. But nor are we simply recognizing the object as representation, which means subjecting it to the principle of sufficient reason. Instead, we recognize the object as Idea, in Schopenhauer's special use of the Platonic term. We recognize a type or grade of objectified will, but not an individual object caught up in the chain of causality.

This is very different from the kind of contemplation of nature done by scientists. The purpose of science is to seek the cause or ground of things, and so it is entirely absorbed by the principle of sufficient reason. Because of this, science "is with every end it attains again and again directed farther, and can never find an ultimate goal or complete satisfaction, any more than by running we can reach the point where the clouds touch the horizon." Furthermore, science is a form of instrumental reason that exists to serve the will, as most scientists themselves recognize. This is the meaning of Bacon's dictum that "knowledge is power." But power is exactly what we are *not* after here. We want contemplation as an end in itself, divorced from any larger worldly purpose, the kind Spinoza calls for when he tells us to see the world under the aspect of eternity.

There are extremely rare human beings—geniuses—with a particular talent for viewing objects in the world as Ideas. Genius is a very different talent from intelligence as we commonly understand that term. "Whereas to the ordinary man his knowledge is a lamp that lights his path," Schopenhauer writes, "to the man of genius it is the sun that reveals the world." The genius often lacks prudence and common sense: "A poet may know *man* profoundly and thoroughly, but *men* very badly; he is easily duped, and is a plaything in the hands of the cunning and the crafty." But the genius has a profound insight into the nature of things that compensates for these weaknesses.

Most of us are not lucky enough to be geniuses, but nearly all of us at least have some sense that can allow us to appreciate the mind of a genius when it is presented to us. For this reason, one of the highest forms of the genius is the artist, who makes this insight available to the rest of us, and one of the highest human activities is the contemplation of art, which for some brief period offers those of us with the capacity for it the opportunity for fixed contemplation and an escape from the will.

Art is "the way of considering things independently of the principle of sufficient reason, in contrast to the way of considering them which proceeds in exact accordance with this principle, and is the way of science and experience." The best art doesn't merely depict nature as nature is commonly experienced. Instead it "plucks the object of its contemplation from the stream of the world's course, and holds it isolated before it." In doing so it "pauses at this particular thing; it stops the wheel of time; for it the relations vanish; its object is only the essential, the Idea."

On the basis of this definition, we can appreciate the characteristics of true art. It is not conceptual or didactic. It deals in Ideas but not in ideas—that is, not in the abstract concepts of reason. It is not mannered or imitative of other works of art; it does not display the aesthetic fashions of its time and place. Mannered and fashionable works are given "loud and ready applause" in their time, but they are discarded as soon as the spirit of the times has changed. Genuine works of art "belong to no age, but to mankind."

The greatest of all the arts is poetry, and the greatest of all poetic achievements is tragedy. It is no accident that "the purpose of this highest poetical achievement is the description of the terrible side of life." In tragedy, "the unspeakable pain, the wretchedness and misery of mankind, the triumph of wickedness, the scornful mastery of chance, and the irretrievable fall of the just and the innocent are all here presented to us." For this very reason, tragedy gives us "a significant hint as to the nature of the world and of existence." We see there "the antagonism of the will" brought into "fearful prominence."

All of this puts the artist in an unusual position. Art provides the rest of us an opportunity for contemplation as an end in itself, and with it a brief escape from the endless struggle of the will. But the artist is precisely someone who has put his talent for contemplation to a further end, namely the creation of that work of art, and artistic creation is an act of enormous will. Perhaps no philosopher has granted more importance to art than Schopenhauer did, but he depicted the life of the artist as one of great suffering. Certain compensations come with it—"the pleasure of everything beautiful, the consolation afforded by art, the enthusiasm of the artist which enables him to forget the cares of life"—but they come at great cost. Art provides the rest of us with a great spectacle, but the artist "bears the cost of producing that play; in other words, he himself is the will objectifying itself and remaining in constant suffering."

For all of these reasons, there is a type of human being that is even higher than the artist, and this is the saint: the person who has achieved resignation, "that disposition of the mind which alone leads to true holiness and salvation from the world."

ON THE BASIS of what has come before, it may be surprising to hear Schopenhauer use terms like *saint* and *holiness* and *salvation.* In fact, it may be surprising to learn that his philosophy includes an ethical component at all. In a sense it does not. Schopenhauer utterly rejects the traditional distinction between theoretical and practical philosophy. The proper concern of all true philosophy is the nature of things as they are, not how we would like people to act. There is no theoretical basis for any kind of "ought," and even if there were, it could have no effect on the free and groundless will: "We are as little able to produce a virtuous person by ethical discourses or sermons as all the systems of aesthetics from Aristotle's downwards have ever been able to produce a poet."

At the same time, he believed that true insight into the nature of reality called us toward a certain path of action, one that has been universally recognized across cultures and traditions as the way of virtue. First and foremost, this path entails refusing to impose one's will on other people: "Cases of wrong can all be reduced to the fact that I, as the wrongdoer, compel the other individual to serve my will instead of his own, or to act according to my will instead of to his."

Schopenhauer seems to be advocating the approach of Spinoza, Rousseau, and Kant: Virtue consists in subsuming our individual will into the general will, acting in a way that brings all wills into harmony. But these thinkers assumed a rationally ordered world, one in which such harmony is possible. For Schopenhauer a harmony of wills is impossible, for the will just *is* struggle, combat, suffering. The truly virtuous person is not one who wills the general will but one who renounces the will entirely.

Given what we know about the will and suffering, it's tempting to advocate this path on the basis that it might lead to lasting happiness—what Spinoza called "blessedness." But happiness is just the temporary satisfaction that comes from a cessation of suffering or from briefly grabbing an advantage in the battle of wills. The person with the greatest capacity for happiness will likewise have the greatest capacity to suffer, for that is the person most attuned to the ups and downs of the struggle.

How is it, then, that certain people find themselves drawn to the virtuous life? It comes from the place that Rousseau advocated and Kant absolutely rejected as the proper source of morality: the emotions. Those who have a true understanding of the suffering of life will feel a natural sympathy toward other sufferers—not just family and friends (such limited sympathy is really a form of self-love) but all human beings and indeed all animal life.

This is not a position one can be argued into. Disinterested virtue is "a direct and intuitive knowledge that cannot be reasoned away or arrived at by reasoning." Such intuitive knowledge "cannot be communicated, but must dawn on each of us." For this reason, ethical discourse is always inadequate to its task. Goodness is expressed "simply and solely in deeds, in conduct, in the course of man's life."

In particular, this conduct shows itself as "denial of the will-to-live." Every religious tradition worthy of the name holds this truth near its core, Schopenhauer tells us, and nearly every tradition has among its avatars of virtue the ascetic mystic who recognizes the oneness of everything and chooses the path of resignation. It hardly matters whether these traditions are theistic or atheistic, or what metaphysical gloss this renunciation is given: "A saint may be full of the most absurd superstition, or, on the other hand, may be a philosopher; it is all the same. His conduct alone is evidence that he is a saint."

Schopenhauer recognized and embraced the clear connection between his philosophy and various traditions of Eastern thought. He was perhaps the first modern Western philosopher to take Eastern philosophy seriously, and he was just as likely to quote the Bhagavad Gita as he was Plato or Aristotle. At least as Schopenhauer understood them, the great Eastern religions—Hinduism and its Buddhist offshoot—are fundamentally atheistic. Of course, they speak about a whole pantheon of deities, but this is a very different matter from belief in a transcendent God: "For it will surely never occur to anyone to confuse Almighty God with, say, the *Brahma* of the Hindus, who lives and suffers in you and me, in my horse and in your dog." Furthermore, they recognize the unity of all things and the fundamentally illusory nature of the world as representation, and they call for renunciation as the only way out of the cycle of suffering.

Although the saint does not renounce life for the sake of happiness or satisfaction, to witness a saintly life is not just to admire but to envy it. We can't help telling ourselves, "How blessed must be the life of a man whose will is silenced not for a few moments, as in the enjoyment of the beautiful, but forever."

SCHOPENHAUER'S PHILOSOPHY ELICITS incredibly strong reactions. Many atheists—Bertrand Russell among them—have found his life-denying pessimism frankly repugnant. I loved it. Of all the thinkers I examine in this book, none, other than Wittgenstein, spoke to me so profoundly. (You may have already noticed some fairly obvious parallels in their thought.) Everything about Schopenhauer's work seems designed to appeal to an artistically inclined depressive, which is precisely what I was at the time I encountered him.

As I've already mentioned, he had an enormous influence on the modernist cult of the artist as expressed by Proust and Mann and Joyce. These writers brought me to Schopenhauer, with their call to live out a life of artistic suffering. When I read him, it began to seem that there was a real way for me to live as an atheist. Nor was it lost on me that his was a fundamentally *religious* atheism.

But one more thing about Schopenhauer's thought must be said explicitly.

He embraces Indian religion in part because it represents for him what "civilized" Europeans were before being corrupted. And he happens to have a very clear idea of what the corrupting force was. In Schopenhauer's view, all of the truly theistic religions have their roots in Judaism. Furthermore, it is from the Jewish story of creation that we get materialism, the idea that the objective world must have persistent existence apart from our experience of it. Even worse, we get the insistence that this creation is ultimately good, a view antithetical to Schopenhauer's pessimism.

Schopenhauer argues that Judaism is the only major religion that lacks the tradition of mystical renunciation. Even Christianity, which has its philosophical roots in Neoplatonism, carries the same fundamental truth as Eastern thought. It is in essence an Indian religion that had the misfortune to grow up in Jewish soil: "The sublime founder of Christianity has necessarily to adopt and accommodate himself, partly consciously, partly, it may be, unconsciously, to [Jewish] doctrine; and so Christianity is composed of two very heterogenous elements." Only the first of these—the "purely ethical element"—deserved the name of Christianity, while the other element was just "Jewish dogmatism." The Protestant Reformation, which did away with the Catholic monastic and ascetic traditions and valorized everyday life, denies precisely what is valuable in Christianity by attempting to bring it back to its biblical Jewish roots.

The upshot of all of this is that Schopenhauer's work is littered with expressions of anti-Semitism. Granted, it is a philosophical rather than racial or cultural anti-Semitism. There is nothing in it of animus toward actual Jewish people. (Schopenhauer was a great admirer of Spinoza.) In fact, it is generally not even directed at Jews. Mostly it is directed toward theism in general or the Protestant theology of the German idealists, which he tends to disparage by calling it "Judaic." It's possible while reading Schopenhauer to set these remarks aside, along with the rest of his vitriol toward Hegel and the masses who preferred Hegel's work to Schopenhauer's own. But you can't pretend they aren't there, especially given what was later made of them: Hitler quotes Schopenhauer extensively in *Mein Kampf*, and he claimed to have carried Schopenhauer's work with him on the front lines in World War I.

Of course, it's not fair to blame a thinker for his followers, particularly when those followers have badly misread him. The Nazi worship of force and power and struggle is the precise opposite of Schopenhauer's ethical philosophy. You can't blame Schopenhauer for Auschwitz any more than you can blame Rousseau for the guillotine. Yet it is a fact that the irrationalist philosophical tradition that both men advanced has been put to horrific ends. Indeed it has been put to such horrific ends, and put to them so frequently and consistently, that one can't help taking these fruits into consideration when judging the tradition as a whole.

Seventeen

MAN IS SOMETHING THAT SHOULD BE OVERCOME

Although Schopenhauer places tragedy at the top of his artistic hierarchy, he holds one art form entirely apart from the others. Music is the one truly nonrepresentational art, the one in which "we do not recognize the copy, the repetition, of any Idea of the inner nature of the world." All other art is a copy of the phenomenal world—a representation of a representation—but music is "a copy of the will itself." Other arts "speak only of the shadow, but music of the essence." If one could ever give a complete explanation of music, Schopenhauer concludes, one would have at the same time a complete explanation of the world—"the true philosophy."

The composer Richard Wagner had already completed the majority of his works when he first encountered *The World as Will and Representation*. In certain ways, its theories didn't fit his practice. Wagner wrote his own librettos, and he aimed to create a "total work of art" that combined music with poetry, painting, costume design, and even architecture. To that end, he took an obsessive interest in the nonmusical elements of his "musical dramas," and he wrote long, polemical essays defending his approach. But a composer with Wagner's ego couldn't help being seduced by the suggestion that music lay at the center of existence itself. He became a committed Schopenhauerian.

Wagner spent much of his life moving around Europe to outrun debts and escape the inevitable trouble with local authorities that his radical politics caused. After participating in the failed liberal revolutions of 1848, he fled Germany, eventually settling in Switzerland. There he befriended Friedrich Nietzsche, thirty years his junior, who was at that time a promising young philologist, a music lover, and a fellow Schopenhauer devotee. Wagner saw the younger man as a kind of apostle.

Nietzsche was born into a devout Prussian family in 1844. His father—a minister in the establishment Lutheran Church—died when he was just four years old, and he was raised by his mother to follow into the ministry. As a young man Nietzsche abruptly gave up both his theological studies and his religious beliefs. Though it shocked his surviving family, the decision doesn't seem to have entailed a great emotional struggle. Nietzsche continued to idolize his father, and he expressed no personal resentment toward establishment Christianity or individual Christians. (In Nietzsche's view, resentment was one of the worst sins imaginable.) It was just that Christian belief seemed to him impossible for an intellectually honest nineteenth-century European.

The discipline he chose in place of theology had played a central role in creating this condition. Philology is the historical study of languages through close textual analysis. In practice, this often involves demythologizing ancient texts. Throughout the eighteenth and nineteenth centuries, Germany was the great center of philological analysis, much of it dedicated to the Hebrew Bible. This naturally entailed viewing the book as a collection of historically contingent texts that had evolved over centuries of Jewish practice, rather than the word of God handed down to Moses and the other prophets. Philologists also set to work on the New Testament, attempting to separate the historical Jesus from the Christ of the Gospels.

Nietzsche focused on Greek and Latin, and he excelled in this study, so much so that he was awarded a chair at the University of Basel when he was just twenty-four, making him the youngest ever to receive the honor. After taking up his position in Switzerland, he visited Wagner frequently. The two men bonded over their appreciation of Schopenhauer, whom Nietzsche had begun reading after giving up his theological studies. (It was not Schopenhauer who brought him to atheism, he would later insist, but atheism that brought him to Schopenhauer.) They also shared the view that Wagner himself represented the culmination of Schopenhauer's ideal.

IN 1874, Nietzsche published his first book, *The Birth of Tragedy Out of the Spirit of Music.* In it, he argued that the early Greeks had two opposing artistic tendencies, which tragedy had ultimately united. The first was exemplified by the Greek god Apollo and expressed in sculpture, an art marked by "beauty and moderation." Greek statues are notable for their "measured restraint" and "freedom from wilder emotion." They are also highly representational, mostly depicting the gods. But unlike so many gods from the ancient world, these deities are not fearsome monsters; they are simply images of human beings at their most powerful.

Apollo was the god of prophecy or soothsaying, and Nietzsche associates him with dreams—not in the sense of the nightmarish or irrational but in the sense of life as illusion and play. In dreams we are all sculptors of a sort, fashioning representations and giving ourselves over to them even as some part of us knows we are dreaming: "Even when this dream reality is most intense, we still have, glimmering through it, the sensation that it is *mere appearance.*" Thus it is that in dreams "the deepest pathos can be merely aesthetic play."

Not just Apollo but the entire Olympian pantheon treats life with this spirit. Above all, the gods *enjoy* being gods; they take pleasure in their powers: "There is nothing here that suggests asceticism, spirituality, or duty. We hear nothing but the accents of an exuberant, triumphant life in which all things, whether good or evil, are deified." Because the life of these gods is so much like our life, the affirmation of their life is an affirmation of humanity: "Thus do the gods justify the life of man: they themselves live it—the only satisfactory theodicy!"

The Apollonian side of Greek life was matched by another, represented by Dionysus, the god of wine and festival. The quintessential Dionysian art form was music, used at Dionysian festivals to drive participants into religious ecstasy. Where Apollo is associated with dreams, Dionysus is associated with intoxication. Under his sway, the musical artist has none of the sculptor's dispassionate control. He cannot step back from his creation; he is wholly absorbed by it: "He is no longer an artist, he has become a work of art." The Dionysian spirit is volatile, and the Greeks felt it particularly strongly. They put such emphasis on formal restraint, Nietzsche insists, precisely because they were in such close contact with a power in need of restraining.

The division between the Dionysian and the Apollonian parallels Schopenhauer's distinction between will and representation, and Nietzsche follows Schopenhauer in judging artworks according to their relationships to these two aspects of the world: Schopenhauer had said not just that music was pure will but that sculpture was pure representation. Yet Nietzsche breaks with Schopenhauer by utterly rejecting the goal of negating will, and he rejects the idea that tragedy turns us away from life and all its suffering.

The great tragedies are a celebration of life, Nietzsche tells us. They show us the worst that life can give a person while also showing us that life is nonetheless something to be affirmed. All of life, in Nietzsche's view, has its Apollonian and Dionysian sides. Every artist is "either an Apollonian artist in dreams, or a Dionysian artist in ecstasies." The genius of the

Greeks was that they put the two into proper balance. The Greek tragedian was "at once artist in both dreams and ecstasies."

THE GREAT AGE of Greek tragedy was short-lived, lasting roughly the span of a single human life. If it had achieved such balance, why did it not endure? The spirit of tragedy was killed, Nietzsche argues. And the culprit was Socrates.

A nice bit of circumstantial historical evidence supports this claim: Socrates was born around 470 BCE, when the plays of Aeschylus, generally considered the form's apex, were appearing regularly on the Athenian stage. By the time he drank his hemlock seventy years later, the last of the great tragedians, Euripides, was dead, and the genre was essentially exhausted. But what about Socrates might have made him responsible for this fact?

Nietzsche believes that the spirit Socrates brought into the world—the spirit of science,* "the faith in the explicability of nature and in knowledge as a panacea"—was inimical to the tragic view of life. Socrates teaches us that the world is rationally ordered, that the good and the true are intimately connected, that the highest form of human life is dedication to the pursuit of knowledge. Such a life produces lasting happiness, and since happiness is our natural goal, the failure to pursue the good life is a simple misjudgment. All evil stems from intellectual error.

These beliefs leave no place for the Dionysian spirit, which tells us that there are wild and dangerous forces at work in the world, ones that can be tapped into only through irrational means. But it isn't Apollonian either,

---

* The German word for science—*Wissenschaft*—is very important to Nietzsche's work. It suggests the systematic pursuit of knowledge, but without the heavy emphasis on the study of the natural world that *science* has in English. The relevant contrast is not between the sciences and the humanities but between science and "art," in the sense of practice or application. Science is disinterested, theoretical study. Philology viewed itself as the most scientific of the humanities.

for it refuses to affirm worldly pleasure. Socrates (by way of Plato) expresses disgust at the hedonistic behavior of the Olympian gods and at the treatment of such behavior as an image of divinity. In their place, he gives us an abstract, unified god—the good, the beautiful, the true.

Unfortunately, the Platonic-Socratic spirit proved far more enduring than the tragic one, for it bequeathed us Christianity—"Platonism for the masses," as Nietzsche would call it—which in Nietzsche's account swallowed up Europe for nearly two millennia. Modern readers will hardly think of Christianity as the historical guardian of the scientific spirit, but it derives from Plato its view of the universe as ordered and comprehensible through reason, as well as its faith in the connection between the good and the true. As Nietzsche sees it, the Socratic and Christian metaphysical belief in an enduring reality with which we will ultimately be joined for eternity renders the truly tragic view of life—one that recognizes the unavoidable reality of suffering and loss yet affirms life in the face of that reality—impossible.

SHORTLY AFTER NIETZSCHE completed a first draft of *The Birth of Tragedy*, Prussia led the German states into war with France. Nietzsche served briefly as a medic on the front lines, which contributed significantly to his already declining health. Following a quick and decisive victory, Germany was unified in 1871 under Prussian king Wilhelm I, crowned kaiser of the German Reich, and his chancellor, Otto von Bismarck, who became the new nation's de facto political leader. Sixty years after Napoleon's near conquest of Europe, Germany had dealt France a humiliating loss and become the Continent's great power.

Many Germans saw this result as cultural more than military, a victory for German Romanticism over French Enlightenment rationality. For all his celebration of the "German spirit," Nietzsche was disgusted by this jingoistic response. He began a series of essays he called *Untimely Meditations*—"untimely" because he was so out of step with the climate of the new German Reich.

He intended to write a long series of these meditations, but he completed only four. The third, "Schopenhauer as Educator," expressed his great admiration for the thinker who had influenced him so much while also making clear that he had moved beyond him. "No one can construct for you the bridge upon which precisely you must cross the stream of life," he wrote. "No one but you yourself alone." It was a kind of declaration of intellectual independence, and anyone who was following the matter closely could see where this declaration was really aimed.

By the time of German unification, Wagner had returned from exile under the protection of the Bavarian king Ludwig II. He now established residency in the Bavarian town of Bayreuth, where with Ludwig's financial and political support he built a theater to be devoted exclusively to the performance of his works. A man who had spent his entire life out of favor with political authorities was now an official court artist. His performances at Bayreuth would become something like religious festivals, ritualistic expressions of the German spirit.

Nietzsche initially threw himself into the developing plans for Bayreuth, but he quickly became disillusioned by Wagner's nationalism. This break proved to be the defining experience of his life. Having fallen under the sway of such a powerful influence—and having successfully resisted it—would become the model for all his future thought. Whenever he seemed to have settled somewhere, he asked himself, Can this, too, be overcome?

His rejection of Schopenhauer and Wagner also taught him to be suspicious of profundity. "A profound thought can nonetheless be very distant from the truth," he writes in *Human, All Too Human*, "as, for example, every metaphysical thought is." Here and in the works that immediately follow—generally grouped as the "Free Spirit" trilogy—Nietzsche embraces the positivistic worldview of modern science, but he seeks to do so *as* a free spirit, as the "musical Socrates" he'd earlier prophesized.

Nietzsche doesn't make any sustained case against metaphysical truth. That would involve precisely the kind of Germanic heavy-handedness he wants to avoid. Anyway, that work is already done. Even after breaking with Schopenhauer, he held on to the essentials of Schopenhauer's vision of existence: We are trapped in a world of appearances; all life is the blind and irrational struggle of will to assert itself; the world is utterly without purpose or meaning. We need now to comprehend the full implications of the antimetaphysical view and to figure out how to live with the results.

The Gay Science—the last of the three Free Spirit books—contains Nietzsche's classic parable of this condition:

> Have you not heard of that madman who lit a lantern in the bright morning hours, ran to the market place, and cried incessantly: "I seek God! I seek God!" —As many of those who did not believe in God were standing around just then, he provoked much laughter. . . . The madman jumped into their midst and pierced them with his eyes. "Whither is God?" he cried; "I will tell you. *We have killed him*—you and I. All of us are his murderers. But how did we do this? How could we drink up the sea? Who gave us the sponge to wipe away the entire horizon? What were we doing when we unchained this earth from its sun? . . . Do we hear nothing as yet of the noise of the gravediggers who are burying God? Do we smell nothing as yet of the divine decomposition? Gods, too, decompose. God is dead. God remains dead. And we have killed him.

God is dead: perhaps the most famous declaration of atheism ever made. But it is a strange one, addressed not to believers but to those who already do not believe. Such people don't need to be convinced that there is no God; they need to be made to feel this fact as a grave *loss*. They need to understand that God did once exist, that the believers of an earlier age were not wrong, and they need to be made to understand their own responsibility for this change. *We have killed him*: We scientists, we seekers after knowledge, have made belief impossible—not just belief in God but belief in all higher or elevated human goods. And even we scientists ourselves have refused to acknowledge the significance of this fact.

So, for example, Kant demolished the Scholastic proofs for God's existence and demonstrated the total impossibility of metaphysical knowledge, but he insisted that a binding morality and even a kind of religion could be had "within the bounds of bare reason." Schopenhauer went even further than Kant in rejecting Christian dogma, yet he couldn't help resurrecting "the whole of medieval Christian conception of the world and of the nature of man."

Philosophy is the greatest of the sciences because it has the power to put all the others on properly scientific footing; modern philosophy has instead given itself the thoroughly unscientific task of replacing religion, meeting the "metaphysical need" by other means. The idea that philosophy, art, politics, or science might give foundational meaning to a godless world, that through them we can have morality and even religion without God: This is the final illusion that science has yet to pierce. Taking science to its limit means finally treating all these still-sanctified features of human existence to proper scrutiny, undertaking "a chemistry of the moral, religious and aesthetic conceptions and sensations."

BEFORE NIETZSCHE, the effort to place human goods on a "scientific" footing meant trying to gain for moral or aesthetic or political judgments the certainty of objective fact—that is, using science to justify one worldview or another. That's a very different project from subjecting human goods *as such* to scientific scrutiny. The ruthless picking apart of morality that will become the signature undertaking of Nietzsche's later work begins in the Free Spirit trilogy: "Mankind can no longer be spared the cruel sight of the moral dissecting table and its knives and forceps."

Nietzsche's modern predecessors insisted that the great religions and the wild diversity of their myths all expressed the same core moral truth—roughly, that we should concern ourselves with the collective good, rather than our own narrow interests. Given the universality of this core, they argued, we ought to be able to preserve it in the absence of those myths. As a historical matter, Nietzsche responds, it's simply not true that all cultures have admired those who sacrifice for the greater good.

The ancients generally associated goodness instead with *power*. The good man "has the power to requite, good with good, evil with evil, and also actually practices requital—is, that is to say, grateful and revengeful." The bad man "is powerless and cannot requite." Together, the "good" form "a community which has a sense of belonging together because all the individuals in it are combined with one another through the capacity for requital," while the bad make up "a swarm of subject, powerless people who have no sense of belonging together." In this age, Nietzsche concludes, "good" and "bad" are respective synonyms for "noble and base, master and slave."

The master morality of good and bad was eventually replaced by a slave morality of good and evil, one that valorized meekness over strength, forgiveness over revenge. How this came about is treated at great length in Nietzsche's later work, but the broad outlines are already present here. Suffice to say that the change itself was not motivated by generosity and selflessness; it was an entirely understandable assertion by the many—those counted as "bad" under the old dispensation—of their power over the few.

Like everything else that we take as elevated or sanctified, this morality is "human, all too human." It arose to meet the basest human needs. (This is not an argument against it; the moral scientist is not concerned with "for" and "against.") An entire system of religious myth supports this change, even up to the point of imagining an all-powerful God allowing himself to be humiliated and put to death. When we moderns strip this myth away, we don't find a core truth; we find a naked expression of power. The rise of selflessness as a moral good may for all that still seem like an obvious improvement to us, but that is only because we have internalized the new values. We are judging competing ethical systems from within one of them. Once we try to find some ground for the system *outside* the system itself, we are left at a loss.

This is a problem not just with the morality of selflessness but with any morality at all that seeks a "scientific" footing. Utilitarianism grounds morality in maximizing pleasure and minimizing pain, but why do we take pain to be inherently bad? As the tragedians knew, pain is as much a part of life as pleasure, and to deny suffering is finally to deny life. ("Man does *not* strive after happiness," Nietzsche later wrote. "Only the Englishman does that.") The greatest human achievements were bought at the cost of great suffering. To eliminate suffering would mean eliminating greatness. One might find this trade-off worth it, but one would first need some evaluative basis for making that judgment. A truly "objective" morality—one that does not proceed by embracing some insufficiently justified foundational value—is simply impossible.

ONE REASON THAT philosophers have been so insistent that some basis could be found for reconciling reason with such human goods as morality and art is that they have assumed that the truth must be ultimately good for humanity. This belief dates back to the origins of the scientific spirit in Socrates. But if we apply the scientific spirit to itself and ask whether the truth is always beneficial in the here and now—whether it is conducive to human happiness—the evidence is mixed. We have no scientific cause to think that losing our religious and metaphysical illusions will be to the good: "Man may bleed to death from knowledge of truth."

Aristotle suggested that humans naturally strive for the truth, that we are the animals that *want to know*. But the history of humanity is a history of falsehood, suggesting that we not only want but even need untruth. The clearest defense of truth in this world is Baconian: Knowledge is power. But this is not a defense of a will to truth; it is a defense of a will to power that might put truth to work as means to its end. And we know from experience that a good lie can be at least as powerful as any truth.

Just as a deeper selfishness lies at the root of morality, perhaps error and untruth can even be found at the root of knowledge itself. "Over immense periods of time," Nietzsche speculates in *The Gay Science*, "the intellect produced nothing but errors." Inevitably some of these errors proved advantageous for survival: "Those who hit upon or inherited these had better luck in their struggle for themselves and their progeny." These falsehoods became incorporated by humanity "as a condition of life."

We have now come to the real limits of science, the point at which the scientific spirit dissolves even itself. Science, too, proves to have an unexamined value behind it—the value of objective truth—and a brave scientist must scrutinize even this value: "Knowledge can allow as motives only pleasure and pain, utility and injury; but how will these motives come to terms with the sense for truth?" Having shown itself to be just as much without foundation as every other human good, the scientific spirit—the will to truth—becomes one more thing to overcome.

WHAT NEXT, after one has seen through every illusion—including the illusion that it is possible to live without illusions? How *does* one live?

Nietzsche was perhaps the first philosopher to engage explicitly in the project I found myself undertaking—trying on different worldviews to see which one *fit*. He correctly identified the impossibility of judging the various options from some neutral position. The question of how to live, he said, can't be answered theoretically—that is, scientifically—because "life is no argument." But what is the alternative?

One human activity has long shown us how to live with untruth *as* untruth. The arts are a "kind of cult of the untrue," where appearance revels in itself as appearance, and they can render bearable "the realization that delusion and error are conditions of human knowledge and sensation." Without them, "honesty would lead to nausea and suicide."

In *The Birth of Tragedy*, Nietzsche made his famous observation that "it is only as an aesthetic phenomenon that life can be justified." Of course, to speak of life's being "justified" is still to presume some solid position from which different forms of life might be judged. Nietzsche has by now given up any such position. In *The Gay Science* he puts things in slightly starker terms: "As an aesthetic phenomenon existence is still bearable for us."

Speaking not of what is justified but what is *bearable* makes the answer to the question of how to live entirely subjective. The way to appreciate any set of values is to try them on and see how they feel. Because we are all different, the answer will be different from person to person, and indeed different for any given person at different points in life. But while you're testing a worldview, you must in a sense mean it. You can't wear it as a costume, something foreign to you, for you will never experience it fully without experiencing what it's like to believe in it. This is a different kind of experiment in living than the one Mill proposes.

The Nietzschean ideal is a mix of the Apollonian—recognizing life as an illusion, never taking it too seriously, treating yourself as an artist of life—and the Dionysian—nonetheless throwing yourself into that illusion, living inside of it with your whole being, becoming not just an artist but a *work of art*. Just as certain people have a genius for making art, certain people have a genius for life. They know how to take it seriously without taking it solemnly—they treat it ultimately as a form of play. They choose their myths *as* myths—that is, they worry not about their supposed historical or metaphysical truth but about whether they are conducive to greatness.

Why aspire to greatness? Why affirm life, rather than negating it? Nietzsche can't answer such foundational questions. He can only say that he has tried on the life-negating philosophies—he has been both a Christian and a Romantic pessimist—and so he is in a position to compare them to the alternative. (Here he does sound a bit more like Mill.) If someone else insists on life negation, Nietzsche will leave them to it, with one caveat: "Your evidence will be of no weight until you have lived for years on end without Christianity, with an honest, fervent zeal to endure life in the antithesis of Christianity: until you have wandered far, far away from it."

THE GOAL OF making life bearable, finding some reason to affirm the world as it is in the face of suffering, was not academic for Nietzsche. Around the time of *Human, All Too Human*'s publication, his chronic illness (almost certainly syphilis, along with a host of other ailments) forced him to leave his academic post for good. For the rest of his life, he was in near-constant physical pain, which made even the act of sitting and writing almost unbearable. He lived for the next decade on a small pension, publishing about a book every year—an astonishingly productive rate, especially given his condition. These books sold poorly (sometimes in the double digits) and further alienated him from the Wagner circle that included his few close friends. He made a virtue of his isolation, but it clearly pained him. He prized intellectual independence while feeling an obvious compulsion to make his ideas understood.

During this time, he spent his summers in the Swiss mountains at Sils Maria and his winters in the cities of southern Europe, and he developed a new metaphor for his dual drive to be independent and to bring his work to others, to stand outside of life seeing clearly through its illusions and also immerse himself in life, illusions and all: A strong soul will have the health to live at high altitudes, in solitude, well above general human company, but he will also have the strength to go down from the mountain, to breathe the pollutants of society. Nietzsche considered the decade he spent writing the Free Spirit trilogy to be a mountaintop time, calling for clean air, clear prose, purity of vision, a spirit resistant to illusions of every kind. He followed this with a book that both describes and enacts a going down from the mountain.

Thus Spoke Zarathustra is Nietzsche's attempt at precisely the thing he'd said philosophy ought not attempt: creating a substitute for religion. The historical Zarathustra (or Zoroaster) was an ancient Persian prophet, the founder of Zoroastrianism, a monotheistic faith that views the world as a battleground for the struggle between good and evil. For Nietzsche, this Zarathustra represents the original theist and moralist, and *his* Zarathustra will be the first figure to see beyond theism and morality.*

As the book begins, Zarathustra has spent a decade in solitary contemplation on the mountaintop. The fruits of this contemplation have become overabundant and overripe and made him weary of wisdom, "like a bee that gathered too much honey," so he comes down from the mountain, into the villages, to distribute these fruits. Like the madman of *The Gay Science*, he brings news of the death of God, but he is also a prophet of what comes next. In the first village in which Zarathustra arrives, he finds

* Zoroastrianism is perhaps the oldest world religion still in active practice; its main challenger for this title is Judaism. Placing humanity's two great mistakes—theism and morality—at Zarathustra's feet is among other things Nietzsche's way of rejecting Schopenhauer's view that the Eastern philosophies dealt in the perennial truths because they were uncorrupted by Judaism.

a crowd gathered in the marketplace to watch a tightrope walker, and he announces to them the heart of his philosophy: "*I teach you the Superman.* Man is something that should be overcome."

Zarathustra's Superman stands in relation to humanity as humanity does to our evolutionary ancestors. We have made our way from worm to ape to humankind, but this process is not meant to end there. The true meaning of the species rests in being a "bridge" rather than a "goal." We are called to continue evolving into the next thing: "Man stands at the middle of his course between animal and Superman."

It's difficult to say exactly how we are meant to take this idea, especially since it's being declared by a fictional character with a hint of madness to him. Nietzsche clearly did believe in a form of Lamarckian evolution that proceeded not by random variation but by adaptation and the inheritance of acquired traits. He also believed—like Rousseau—that the very attributes that separated us from our animal ancestors had denatured us, turned us into something decadent and weak. Because error has been bred into our very being, it's not sufficient simply to recognize it as error in order to overcome it, but we also don't have to treat it as a permanent feature of our nature. A generation of humans prepared to do the difficult work of living by the truth, forgoing all life-supporting falsehood, might give rise to a new kind of creature, one who does not need these falsehoods, one who will not just survive but thrive on the truth.

What kind of man heralds the appearance of the Superman? He's utterly lacking in pity or compassion or any sense of duty to the mass of humanity, and he asks no such things from humanity in return. Because he never allows another person to fall into his debt, because he takes what he wants wherever he is strong enough to take it, he feels no resentment or injustice. He lives with a good conscience. He never judges the actions of others, for he knows that there is no free will and thus no basis for moral responsibility. At the same time, he experiences himself as enjoying total freedom. How is this so? Because he affirms everything that life brings his way. Of every fact, every experience, he says: Thus I have willed it.

What Zarathustran man does more or less consciously, with the active intention of bringing the Superman into being, the Superman himself will do naturally, without reflection, with no thought to any life above or beyond this one. Will this Superman really be a new *species*, as different from *Homo sapiens* as we are from, say, *Australopithecus*? Or will it just be a form of humanity that is capable of living robustly without our noble lies? Will it be a stronger, healthier version of us or have entirely different physical attributes? To ask such questions may be taking the idea too literally. As much as it is grounded in a version of evolutionary science, the Superman is also clearly a kind of fiction whose primary significance is *as* a goal, an aspiration toward which our overcoming might be directed. Zarathustra's real concern—the real subject of his preaching—is not the Superman but the kind of human life that could serve as a bridge to it.

The very desire to set oneself a goal clearly conflicts with the free spirit's ideal of wandering without ever traveling *to* a fixed destination. Nietzsche would not deny this fact—as we know, he did not prize consistency. He might reply that keeping in constant motion without a destination is best of all, indeed precisely what a Superman would do. Any human already capable of this should go forth. For the rest of us, the Superman is a fiction that can teach us to one day live without fictions. It gives life a meaning, and this meaning is: Strive to be one of those who can do without meaning. The alternative to assigning oneself this illusory goal is taking man as he now appears as an end point, which is the worst of all options.

A POPULAR NINETEENTH-CENTURY belief—one that returned to popularity at the end of the twentieth—held that the rise of modern, liberal democracies was not just the latest stage of history but the end of history as such. The combination of liberalism and democracy would defuse the social and political struggles that had dominated humanity from time immemorial. Technological and economic advances would allow the increase in resources to exceed the increase in population, eliminating the Malthusian scarcity and competition that had been history's prime engine.

In a liberal democracy, this view holds, the conflicts that once gave rise to violence are resolved through reasoned discourse and impersonal expertise. Even such enduring human foibles as jealousy, drunkenness, and petty crime can be rationally managed. Instead of dominating and exploiting each other, citizens engage in mutually beneficial exchanges of goods and services. A similar dynamic would pertain internationally. National differences of culture and religion would persist as a kind of agreeable variety, sources of entertainment and tourist interest rather than fundamental disagreements worth killing or dying over. The values that truly matter are marketplace values, which can always be peacefully negotiated. The citizens of an ideal liberal democracy are maximally free, but they practice their freedom in a way that's entirely consistent with the freedom of others.

The possibility of this reconciliation of freedoms was held across the modern philosophical spectrum. Locke and Spinoza, Hume and Rousseau, Mill and Kant—all agreed that real human interests were (or could be) aligned in such a way as to allow universal freedom to coincide with universal peace. Some people might need to be "taught" to be free—freed from their own passions, freed to act rationally, freed to be citizens rather than bourgeois—but this educational project was simply another technical problem to be solved.

From Nietzsche's standpoint, this vision isn't wrong because it is false. Of course, it *is* false: Real freedom does not consist in willing the general will or making a maxim of the universal law; it consists in making one law for yourself and yourself alone, willing what you will. Struggle is not a problem to be rationally managed; it is life itself. But none of that means that the vision of perpetual peace can't be brought about in practice. Humans could very well have their passions—their very *life*—bred out of them. They could be made to believe that reconciling themselves to others was the true definition of freedom. They could be forced to internalize the latest life-negating illusion.

The real problem with this vision is that these rational citizens—Zarathustra calls them the Last Men or Ultimate Men—are "contemptible":

> The earth has become small, and upon it hops the Ultimate Man, who makes everything small. . . . They still work, for work is entertainment. But they take care the entertainment does not exhaust them. Nobody grows rich or poor any more: both are too much of a burden. Who still wants to rule? Who obey? Both are too much of a burden. No herdsman and one herd. Everyone wants the same thing, everyone is the same: whoever thinks otherwise goes voluntarily into the madhouse. . . . They still quarrel, but they soon make up—otherwise indigestion would result. . . . "We have discovered happiness," say the Ultimate Men and blink.

This is precisely the outcome that the ideal of the Superman is meant to avoid.

One might expect the Nietzschean view that there are no ultimate truths, that we all have our owns truths, would go well with the liberal vision. The beauty of liberalism lies in the fact that you can be a Nietzschean and I can be Catholic and our neighbor can be a scientific materialist and we can all get along. You can hold whatever view you want, so long as you don't want to impose it on others.

But what of the worldviews that can't be held in any meaningful way without becoming impositions on others? Standing above the fray, calmly saying, "To each his own," is the act of a Last Man, not a Superman. The will to power includes the will that your own view be victorious over its competition, even if your view is precisely that no single view is definitive. Because there's no rational basis for achieving this victory, these questions *must* be fought out: "And do you tell me, friends, that there is no dispute over taste and tasting? But all life is dispute over taste and tasting!"

Settling this dispute in the liberal's marketplace of ideas means granting victory to the marketplace ideology before the dispute has even started. So Nietzsche takes the dispute to the place where disputes were always settled before the rise of the Last Man—the battlefield: "You say it is the good cause that hallows even war? I tell you: it is the good war that hallows every cause." Doesn't settling disputes on the battleground still allow one side—in this case the side that says "might makes right"—dictate the terms of engagement? The beauty (if one could call it that) of Nietzsche's approach is that it doesn't have to bother with such questions: It takes two parties to enter into a contract, but only one to start a war.

To lots of people the prospect of being an Ultimate Man sounds more appealing than the prospect of being a pitiless Superman. When Zarathustra finishes telling his audience about these figures, they respond: "Make us into this Ultimate Man! You can have the Superman!" Then a strange thing happens: The tightrope walker they have gathered to see is disturbed by a buffoon who jumps on his rope. The performer falls to his death. We suddenly understand this performance—a typical bit of marketplace entertainment—as having been all along fraught with real danger. We understand that even the Last Man's life needs the spectacle of such danger in order to be bearable. We also understand that life is a fragile thing that can be ended at any time by some malicious clown, and that such figures will always exist.

Zarathustra does not *explain* any of this to the crowd; that would be beneath him. He simply puts the dead tightrope walker on his back and heads off in search of another audience. Rather than making any logical or (God forbid) moral case for the Superman, Nietzsche seeks to make his project feel dangerous and exciting and attractive: "Man is a rope stretched between the animal and the Superman—a rope over an abyss." One of the most appealing things about Zarathustra's vision is the sense that he doesn't really care whether people listen to him, agree with him, follow him. He speaks his truth not so that you will agree with it but so that you will be inspired to live your own truth in your own way. He wants to find people "who follow me because they want to follow themselves—and who want to go where I want to go."

ZARATHUSTRA'S OVERHEATED rhetorical pitch would prove another thing for Nietzsche to overcome, and his next several books would again be written with the purity of mountain air. Yet he would continue to play out the war of "Dionysus versus the Crucified," as he would later put it in *Ecce Homo* (at a time when he had returned to overheated rhetoric).

"Christianity arose to lighten the heart, but now it must first make the heart heavy in order to be able to lighten it afterwards." So Nietzsche claims in one of his earliest aphorisms. The same could be said about Nietzsche himself. He needed to convince materialists that their godless lives were empty and meaningless in order to show them a way to lead full and meaningful lives without God. To those who do not see the problem in the first place—who do not feel the absence of God as a kind of death—his work has little to say. To the rest of us, it can be remarkably powerful.

Like me, Nietzsche suffered from ill health and wanted to be one of the fit and strong. He championed "living dangerously," and he made the life of a literary invalid somehow seem a risky adventure. Like Schopenhauer, he went completely ignored throughout most of his life, but he handled this fact rather differently from his first intellectual hero. He refused to give in to resentment. His song could not possibly be heard by those without ears for it, but he had complete faith that his terrible news would have its world-historical impact.

And so it has. He started to get his due in his own lifetime—again like Schopenhauer—though he was not able to enjoy this change in fortune. In 1889, he suffered a complete mental collapse. A series of strokes left him mostly paralyzed. He survived in this state for more than a decade—living until 1900. By the time of his death, he was world-famous.

"Die at the right time," Zarathustra advises his followers. Nietzsche failed on this front. He and his work fell into the care of his sister, a nationalistic and anti-Semitic philistine of precisely the kind Nietzsche hated so much. Elisabeth Förster-Nietzsche eventually became a close confidante to Hitler, and she brought about Nietzsche's close association with the Nazis, which long shaped the reception of his work.

Nietzsche was perhaps even less of a proto-Nazi than Schopenhauer. He detested German nationalism and he was never an anti-Semite, even when still under the sway of the arch-anti-Semite Wagner. (The Jews are in fact a model culture for Nietzsche: They don't seek converts, and they make no moral claims on those outside their clan. They have no wish to universalize their way of life, and they suffer without giving in to ressentiment.) Nietzsche did not want disciples, and he didn't aim to be the house philosopher of any movement. Millions of people conforming to the orders of a single man or a small clique was the opposite of his vision for the future.

The image of Nietzsche as a mentally enfeebled ward, become world-famous by way of being gravely misunderstood, evokes more than anything a sense of pity, but pity is exactly what Nietzsche didn't want. And it may let him off the hook too easily to see him simply as a victim of his ill-intentioned sister and various bad followers. For starters, Nietzsche did not believe in victimhood. And while he was still sane, he knew very well that he was trying to bring something unstable and dangerous into the world. He also knew that he was apt to be misunderstood, and he wrote in a style that even invited misunderstanding.

The things that the Nazis took from Nietzsche—the celebration of war and domination, the vision of a higher type of man driving the weak and the sick into extinction, the disgust with democracy—are all right there in his writing, even if he meant by them something different. If the Nazis used his ideas as stepping stones, a bridge rather than a goal, isn't that just what he called on good followers to do? What's more, he explicitly rejected any basis—beyond the aesthetic basis of its sheer ugliness—by which one might condemn Nazism. Even granting that the Nazis represented a betrayal of so many things he cherished and an embodiment of so many things he hated, a Nietzsche who lived to see their rise and their embrace of his work would perhaps have had no choice but to say: *Thus I willed it.*

Eighteen

IN THE FACE OF NOTHING

One of Nietzsche's greatest insights is that the scientific picture of the world does not oblige us to embrace any particular values—even the value of truth itself. He tells us that the disinterested pursuit of objective knowledge that Enlightenment thinkers take as reason's great project is not really possible, since everything human is ultimately dictated by our interests, not our reason. This is an ethical view but also an epistemological one, insofar as it concerns what kind of knowledge is possible for us.

But Nietzsche leaves the scientific materialist metaphysic largely untouched. In this sense, he is perhaps not as revolutionary as he initially appears. His view is not so far from Hume's empiricist contention that reason is ultimately passion's slave, even if Nietzsche follows this contention to a very different conclusion. As far as Nietzsche is concerned, the world described by materialism—in which God is dead and the horizon has been wiped away—is the ultimate reality. It's just that this world by its nature can make no claims on us, not even the claim that we accept its reality. Yet one still imagines that Nietzsche's Superman would be a thoroughgoing materialist, strong enough to embrace a world with no horizon.

For the Nietzschean ethic of self-creation to become the centerpiece of a radically new worldview, it needed to be combined with a different metaphysical and epistemological approach, developed around the same time that Nietzsche was doing his work. This combination was enacted by another German thinker, one ranked by many as the greatest philosopher of the twentieth century, just as Nietzsche is ranked by many the greatest of the nineteenth.

MARTIN HEIDEGGER WAS born in 1889, the year of Nietzsche's mental collapse, into a devoutly Catholic, working-class family. While still a teenager, he began training for the priesthood, but his career path was altered when the rector at his seminary gave him a copy of a work by the philosopher and former Catholic priest Franz Brentano.

Equally steeped in medieval Scholasticism and the most up-to-date thought of Mill and Comte, Brentano had been responsible for introducing to modern psychology the Scholastic notion of "intentionality" that we've already discussed at length. But he did not treat intentionality as a challenge to scientific studies of consciousness, as I have. He shared the positivists' goal of making psychology properly scientific, and he believed that the concept of intentionality could help achieve this goal.

If every thought has an "intentional" object other than itself, Brentano argued, it follows that it also includes some additional something other than the object. (Otherwise the thought would simply *be* the object.) If I call the image of a chair to mind, I am conscious of the chair but also conscious of the thought—a physical phenomenon and a mental phenomenon are at once present in my mind. Brentano sought to isolate the latter and make it the subject of a properly scientific psychology.

In his view that mental phenomena have real existence and thus can be studied empirically, Brentano was strongly influenced by Aristotle's metaphysics. He'd written an early work on the "senses of being" in Aristotle, and this is the one that first made its way to Heidegger. Reading Brentano on the subject sparked Heidegger's passion for philosophy, along with an abiding belief that what he would come to call "the question of Being" was *the* great philosophical problem.

Like Brentano, Heidegger hoped to combine the practice of academic philosophy with his priestly vocation. He eventually moved to a seminary at Freiburg while continuing his studies at the university there. Poor health forced him to leave the seminary, but he continued to consider himself an explicitly Catholic philosopher—a distinction that mattered because the church was paying for his education and because the University of Freiburg had a special chair in philosophy reserved for a Catholic thinker. Heidegger was ultimately passed over for that job, but he was still teaching there in 1916, when Brentano's greatest student, Edmund Husserl, arrived in Freiburg near the tail end of an illustrious career.

While Brentano simply hoped to practice an empirical psychology that stood comfortably beside the natural sciences, Husserl believed that Brentano's isolation of mental phenomena was the first step toward something far more ambitious, a science that could transcend the empirical entirely—a "science of the essential being of things."

The first step in this science is setting aside every possible object of thought. This means all the physical objects we come to know through "outer perception" but also all the generalized essences and concepts we use to organize this object. Kant treated categories like quantity and unity as a kind of built-in mental architecture that conditions the raw material of sensory intuition, but we clearly have thoughts *about* these essences, and in this sense they are themselves objects of intuition. These too should be set aside.

Husserl doesn't propose denying the reality of any of these things. He asks instead that we place them "in brackets." When something has been placed in brackets, he explains, it has not been negated but simply put "out of action." We are treating it *as though* it were not there. The result is what

Husserl calls an "epoché," after the Ancient Greek word for the suspension of judgment. Husserl proposes that we adopt a "phenomenological epoché" in which we "put out of action" every possible object of consciousness. Having done so, he argued, we are still left with a remaining "phenomenological residuum." This is what Husserl means to study by way of his new science—the science of phenomenology.

To show phenomenology in practice, Husserl offers the example of walking around the table in his office. The table's color and shape appear different from moment to moment, but we are conscious of the fact that these are just "appearances," that the "actual" color and shape remain unchanged. We are conscious of this fact even as we take one of these attributes (color) as secondary and the other (shape) as somehow inherent in the table. We take our divergent perceptual data as different perspectives on a single object, though "an experience has no perspectives."

Experience gives us a constant flux that passes through the ever-present *now* of consciousness. The man of science, Husserl tells us, treats reality as a kind of mathematical abstraction in which "the whole essential content of the perceived thing, all that is present in the body, with all its qualities and all that can ever be perceived, is 'mere appearance,' and the 'true thing' is that of physical science." This particular table—just as much as the broad concept "Table"—is a transcendent essence we have derived from experience without ever fully experiencing it.

As Husserl sees it, the opposite is the case with immanent perceptions. When we reflect upon our own conscious experience, our reflection takes its object whole. It does not have this problem of perspective: "The experience of a feeling has no perspectives. If I look upon it, I have before me an absolute; it has no aspects which might present themselves now in this way, and now in that." What's more, we do not have to concern ourselves over the "real" existence of the object in question: "Every immanent perception necessarily guarantees the existence of its object."

When we experience the table as an intentional object, it is given to us "essentially." That is, various data points lead us to infer the table as an essence, and we then posit the existence of this table in its essence. Our own conscious self, on the other hand, is "given in a primordial and absolute sense, not only essentially but also existentially." All transcendent objects—everything I experience from the "world of things"—have "only a presumptive reality," while "I myself . . . am *absolute* Reality."

UNDER HUSSERL'S DIRECTION, Heidegger soon became a committed phenomenologist, and he decided to make his first mature work a phenomenology of religious life. He'd begun reading Protestant theology, particularly Luther, and in 1917 he married a Protestant woman, Elfride Petri. They had a Catholic wedding but decided against baptizing their first child, born two years later. Heidegger wrote to the priest who had married the couple (and would have been expected to perform the baptism) that "epistemological insights extending to a theory of historical knowledge have made the *system* of Catholicism problematic and unacceptable to me."

His growing commitment to phenomenology clearly played a large part in his rejection of the church. (Husserl—who was Jewish—joked of being brought up on the Socratic charge of corrupting the youth of "arch-Catholic" Freiburg.) He had also begun reading Nietzsche, and he shared the Nietzschean view of philosophy as not just a career but a way of life that might supplant his earlier religious calling. He could not submit himself to an institution that placed limits on his thought. At the same time, the letter noted his continuing belief in "Christianity and metaphysics—these, though, in a new sense."

After serving briefly as a meteorologist in World War I, Heidegger returned to Freiburg, and his study of the phenomenology of religious life at some point became instead a work on Aristotle. He wrote a short summary of this project, one of the few pieces of writing he published in these years, in order to secure a teaching position at the University of Marburg. There, he took up his first serious consideration of the meaning of time, which again changed the trajectory of his ongoing work. He also initiated a lengthy affair with his own most illustrious student, Hannah Arendt. (She was a nineteen-year-old undergraduate when the affair began; he was thirty-five.)

When Husserl decided to retire from his professorship at Freiburg, Heidegger was the leading candidate to replace him. He'd already developed a near-legendary reputation as a teacher, but he had published little of significance. Husserl urged him to get a presentable manuscript into the world so that he could be considered for the appointment. In 1927, Heidegger published *Being and Time*, which weighed in at nearly six hundred pages, though he considered it only a small fragment of his ongoing investigation of the nature of being.

AS HEIDEGGER EXPLAINS in the book's opening pages, philosophers have argued for millennia over what sorts of things—material objects, universal concepts, moral values, mathematical truths, transcendent gods—can be said to exist. Every discipline, every worldview, has an ontology—that is, its own enumeration of the kinds of entities that it treats as real. But philosophy has largely given up on a *fundamental* ontology, a consideration of what it means for something really to exist in the first place.

The meaning of Being is understood to be at once obvious and indescribable—we all know what it is, though none of us can put it in words—which makes inquiring into it seem like a singular waste of time. For Heidegger, however, "the very fact that we already live in an understanding of Being and that the meaning of Being is still veiled in darkness proves that it is necessary in principle to raise this question again."

Being is obviously not an entity that exists alongside other things; it is a thing that entities must possess in order to *be* entities. But nor is it simply an attribute of some (or even all) entities. Both Hume and Kant made this point in their rejection of the ontological proof: We cannot imagine a mythological creature that has the head of a human, the body of a horse, and the being of a dog. We can posit or deny the actual existence of a thing we have imagined, but this affirmation or negation does not change any of the thing's attributes.

So: What is Being? Heidegger notes that the very question already contains an *is*; we can't formulate it without a "vague average understanding of Being" in place. Furthermore, in order to ask the question, one must already *be*, and so a natural first step in our inquiry is for "we, the inquirers" to consider our particular kind of Being. Indeed, the ability to ask the question of Being is constitutive for that particular kind of Being that we are. Heidegger's name for this kind of Being—"this entity which each of us is himself and which includes inquiring as one of the possibilities of its Being"—is *Dasein.**

When we undertake a preliminary phenomenological analysis of Dasein, a few things jump out. The first is that the Dasein I'm considering is inevitably *my own*: Dasein is always personal to the entity doing the asking. Second, Heidegger tells us, "the essence of Dasein lies in its existence." What does this mean? Husserl suggested that the conscious ego is the one entity whose essence entails existence. (Not coincidentally, this is precisely the claim the ontological proof makes about God.) The essence of a chair—the thing that makes it what it is—consists in its form or in the way it serves its purpose. It is because of this essence that a nonexistent chair can be an intentional object. We can represent to ourselves a seat

* *Dasein* is one of two common German words that are generally translated as "existence." Heidegger contrasts it sharply with its synonym, *Existenz*, which makes it impossible to render both the same way, and pretty much everyone just leaves *Dasein* untranslated.

with a back and four legs without positing the real existence of this particular chair. But whenever we have a thought as an intentional object, that thought *must exist.* Heidegger's claim goes even further than this. For Heidegger, the potential for working through the possibility of existence is precisely the thing that makes Dasein what it is, the essence of its particular way of Being.

These two facts—Dasein's personal nature and its existential nature—lead to a third fact: "Because Dasein is in each case essentially its own possibility, it *can*, in its very Being, 'choose' itself and win itself; it can also lose itself and never win itself; or only 'seem' to do so. But only in so far as it is essentially something which can be *authentic*—that is, something of its own—can it have lost itself and not yet won itself." Dasein has authenticity and inauthenticity as possible modes of Being.

When we live in a way that keeps the working out of our own Being at the forefront of our existence, we live authentically as Dasein. When this question slips into the background, we are living inauthentically. Most of us pass most of our lives at a distance from the question of Being, in a state that Heidegger calls "average everydayness." But the question can never be entirely effaced; we are always living in relation to it—"even if this is only the mode of *fleeing in the face of it* and *forgetfulness thereof.*"

To understand what this authenticity or inauthenticity looks like in practice, we must recognize another key feature of Dasein: The Being of Dasein is always Being-in-the-world. Heidegger does not mean that we are each situated in the world as one entity among other entities. We have no Being apart from the world that we are Being in. Furthermore, the term *the world* "is not a way of characterizing those entities which Dasein essentially is *not*; it is rather a characteristic of Dasein itself."

Heidegger is trying here to overthrow the stark Cartesian dualism that divides the spatial world of objects from the conscious self. A core implication of the Cartesian view that there is a world "out there," wholly separate from our subjective experiences of it, is that science can transcend the limits of our subjectivity to study that world in its objective fullness. While it is certainly possible and sometimes even fruitful to take such a stance, Heidegger tells us, this is not at all the way we generally relate to things.

One of the major features of the framework Heidegger opposes—the one in which Being and World are separated as subject and object—is a particular view of the meaning of truth. In this view, an idea is true when it corresponds to some state of affairs in the world. Heidegger wants to restore what he takes as the ancient view of truth as an "unveiling." We experience truth when something shows itself to us in its Being. For a Cartesian, we get at the "truth" of this object in front of us when we get beyond our subjective use for it. For Heidegger the exact opposite is the case: It is when we are putting it to use, when we are lost in our familiarity with something, that it properly shows itself to us.

The best way to "know" a hammer is not to examine it objectively in the scientific manner but to grab ahold of it and start hammering. When the hammering is going well, we hardly notice the hammer—or the nail. We don't experience ourselves as subjects putting a number of different objects to different uses. Everything is one. If the hammer breaks or if we simply find it too heavy to do the job, however, it suddenly becomes conspicuous. We become aware of ourselves as subjects dealing with objects. But when we are engaged in an authentic relationship, this distinction tends to fall away. For the Cartesian, it is precisely when the hammer is conspicuous—when we can properly identify it as an object apart from ourselves and our needs—that we can be said to "know." For Heidegger, the opposite is the case.

ANOTHER NOTABLE PROBLEM with the Cartesian scheme is the way it handles other people. I may presume that other people are subjective thinking things like me, but I can access them only as objects in the extended world, much like any other objects. In such a scheme it becomes possible to theorize about "philosophical zombies" and ask ourselves whether other people actually have subjective experiences like my own or simply display the objective signs of doing so.

For Heidegger, we are not genuinely faced with that problem, because our relationship with the entities he calls "the Others" is fundamentally distinct from our relationship with objects. Like "Being-in-the-world," the expression "Being-with-Others" describes something essential about us. We are not first of all atomized beings that can choose to relate to others. At the same time, the Others are not radically separate, waiting out there for us to stumble upon them.

Heidegger's point about truth as "unveiling" becomes clearer when we apply it here. It's possible to possess every imaginable objective fact about a person without really knowing that person. There are people we see and even interact with on a daily basis—the man who sells our morning coffee, the woman two desks over at work—whom we wouldn't really claim to know. Most of us even have friends or family members who we suspect have never shown us their "true self."

Most of the time, we encounter the Others in this inauthentic way, as an undifferentiated mass. Because our Being *is* Being-with-Others, this distancing actually distances us from ourselves. We stop being authentic and fall prey to the "dictatorship of the 'they'": "We take pleasure and enjoy ourselves as *they* take pleasure; we read, see, and judge about literature and art as *they* see and judge; likewise we shrink back from the 'great mass' as *they* shrink back; we find 'shocking' what *they* find shocking."

The truth of a person is discovered for us when we are engaged in an authentic relationship of care. This isn't simply a matter of finally seeing an object clearly. Something about *us* "brings out" this truth. The only way to have an authentic encounter is to unveil our own selves, and so it is in Being-with-Others that we come to an authentic Being-one's-Self.

BEING-IN-THE-WORLD, BEING-WITH-OTHERS, AND Being-one's-Self are the three "equi-primordial" modes that together comprise Dasein's way of Being. But a final element must be introduced to complete Heidegger's initial existential analysis. That is our state of mind, our mood.

For the Cartesian, subjective attitudes are something wholly other than the objective reality with which we are faced. We must transcend these attitudes in order to arrive at true judgments about reality. Conversely, both Brentano and Husserl argued that our emotions can't really be separated from perception and understanding. They are all components of every cognitive act.

Predictably, Heidegger goes even further in this direction. He considers mood a "primordial kind of Being . . . *prior* to all cognition and volition." We don't have certain thoughts and experiences to which we respond by falling into a corresponding mood. Our mood is always already there, and it determines in important ways the form our thoughts and experiences take. Nor can we stand outside our mood and control it. We are never not in some mood or another.

Our mood is closely related to something Heidegger calls "throwness." (The vocabulary is starting to pile up, I know.) We don't choose to Be in the first place, and we can't ever take a break from existing. At times, Dasein is a great burden to itself; at other times that burden lightens. Not only can you not stop Being, but you can't stop Being-in-the-world, Being-with-Others, or Being-one's-Self. You are constantly faced with the particular situation you are in. Nor can you simply shrug this situation off, because the world, others, and yourself are all things that *matter* for you. Your mood is an expression of that mattering.

In the empirical view, we take in perceptions through sensory intuition, and our understanding works on this raw material to make coherent experience. Heidegger's treatment of state of mind makes intuition instead derivative of understanding. How things appear to us in sensory intuition is decisively determined by their significance for us. We are constantly engaged in acts of interpretation, and these acts do not simply modify the raw material of intuition: "When something within-the-world is encountered as such, the thing in question already has an involvement which is disclosed in our understanding of the world, and this involvement is one that gets laid out by interpretation." To return to a common refrain, even when we adopt the disinterested scientific stance, we are choosing to interpret the world in a particular way.

Here Heidegger follows closely on Nietzsche's famous insistence that "there are no facts, only interpretations." Heidegger's own term for his philosophical approach is *hermeneutic*—i.e., interpretive—*phenomenology*, and this is the point at which it joins Nietzsche's ethic of value creation with Husserl's epistemological and metaphysical understanding of the conscious ego as ultimate reality, pointing the way toward an entirely new worldview.

A FUNDAMENTAL COMPONENT of our interpretative work is language, a subject that obsessed Heidegger as much as it did his analytic contemporaries. For Heidegger, the significance of the world is disclosed through discourse or talk. Needless to say, he utterly rejects the linguistic view that we generate language in order to make a picture of the world as we find it, and that we must constantly examine whether our language is transparently rendering this world. In Heidegger's view, language is world making.

Like so many existential elements, discourse has its authentic and inauthentic manifestations. Inauthentic discourse takes a form that Heidegger calls "idle talk." This is the talk of everydayness, gossip and chitchat. Idle talk gives us the impression that something has been unveiled, but in fact it is only talk talking itself. It is through idle talk that the dictatorship of the They establishes itself. In such moments, we see the basic character of everyday Dasein, which Heidegger calls "falling."

Falling is a constant temptation for Dasein. As we've already seen, following the lead of the They is a way of giving up the heavy burden of responsibility for our own significance. It promises us ease and tranquility. But falling is also alienating. We feel the loss of this separation from ourselves. We are fleeing from something we can never really escape. The result is a state of *anxiety*, which Heidegger takes as Dasein's paradigmatic mood.

The defining feature of anxiety as a mood is that it doesn't have any obvious intentional object. We feel fear "in the face of" something threatening. We can relieve our fear by distancing ourselves from this threat. In anxiety, we feel threatened "in the face of" *nothing*, and for this very reason we cannot relieve the feeling. What threatens "is so close that it is oppressive and stifles one's breathing, and yet it is nowhere." Because it is nowhere, we can never distance ourselves from it.

Heidegger argues that the *world as such* is that in the face of which we feel anxiety. This threat seems to be "nowhere" because the world as such *is* nowhere: There is no spatial "out there" where the world occurs. And it is "nothing" because in the absence of our own Being-in and Being-with, the world *is* nothing, utterly insignificant. Anxiety is a recognition that we are responsible for the meaning of our world. In the face of this burden, we flee into inauthenticity, into the They-self. We dull our anxiety with the tranquilizing effects of idle talk.

But the thing we are trying to escape is ourselves, and so it remains always right there behind us. In the moments we feel most comfortably enmeshed in average everydayness, anxiety creeps up to suggest the inauthenticity of this experience. But anxiety can't simply show us the authentic world in which we might instead live, because that world does not exist until we engage in the authentic living that might unveil it for us.

We are thrown into a definite situation that is not of our choosing, called to enter into an authentic relationship in which the truth of existence might be unveiled, but that truth can't simply be possessed and filed away. It will fall back into obscurity unless we continuously make something of it. And so we are anxious of our own Being as potentiality, the fact that existence can be won or lost at any moment. We are never done becoming ourselves.

WITH THE INTRODUCTION of potentiality, our consideration of Being finally arrives at Heidegger's other great theme: time. Our Being as potentiality is thoroughly temporal in nature; it is a Being in which we are constantly projected into the future.

We have been trying to comprehend Dasein in its totality, but with this realization we see that total comprehension won't be possible. Generally, we believe we have taken in the totality of something when we have captured its essence. But Dasein's essence *is* existence, and we can never capture the totality of our own existence. We always have more existing to do—that is, of course, until we don't, but at that point we aren't around to capture anything: "In Dasein there is undeniably a constant 'lack of totality' which finds an end with death."

A proper working out of the question of Being will have to include a working out of death, but death is not something we can ever possibly grasp. We think we know about death because we have witnessed the death of others and we live with the certainty that it will come eventually for us.

But we don't ever experience the death of another. Like Dasein itself, death is always *mine*.

If we are to live authentically in the truth of existence, we must live authentically with death, which means "holding death for true"—that is, facing up to its certainty. We must grasp the possibility of nothingness, nowhereness. This possibility is precisely what anxiety shows to us. When we stand with courage before our own death with all the anxiety this entails, we are finally able to grasp the full truth of our existence. And this is, of course, what we've been after all along. So we arrive at the conclusion that authentic Being-toward-death *is* the answer to the question of existence that we have been trying to work out.

In our average everydayness, the "certainty" of death is really just the certainty that "They" die. Death becomes an event within life rather than an existential condition. They die, but because They are everyone and no one, They are still there. So death becomes something almost trivial. "The 'they' provides a constant tranquillization about death." When we are settled in the tranquilizing comfort of average everydayness, we are not just surrounded by the They, we *are* the They-self.

How are we ever brought out of this state? We can't stand outside ourselves—outside our own mood or state of mind—and point the way toward some other manner of Being. In any case, there is no other Being to which we can point until we have become that Being ourselves. As with depression, we can only begin to talk ourselves out of it once we are already on our way: "Because Dasein is *lost* in the 'they,' it must first *find* itself. In order to find *itself* at all, it must be shown to itself in its possible authenticity." This possibility is shown to us by a phenomenon that Heidegger names "the call."

Like so many phenomena that Heidegger examines, the call is something about which we already have a vague everyday understanding. It is the "voice of conscience" that tells us we have done wrong, that there is some other way we ought to be. But what is the voice actually *saying*? It can't tell us what it is calling us to be, because it is only in our authentic Being-one's-Self that this "to be" is unveiled. So the call doesn't really say anything: "The call discourses in the uncanny mode of keeping silent."

The appeal of the call is always made from the authentic self to the They-self, which means that we hear the call always in our fallenness. The thing the call says to us is *that* we are fallen—that we are guilty. We are always projected toward some potentiality, but we are always falling short, never getting there. Being there is an impossibility, because the only way to get there is to stop Being. Like anxiety, guilt must be faced rather than escaped.

The call is more than just a voice in our heads, our constant internal monologue. Because the call is a call toward a potentiality that hasn't yet been achieved, the call comes "from beyond me." This sense makes it tempting to understand the call as coming from God, but that temptation arises from the mistaken view that anything that *is* must be an entity present at hand. If the call comes from beyond me, the thinking goes, there must be a thing in that beyond doing the calling, and we can name this thing God. To understand the call this way, Heidegger insists, not only fails to clarify the call's uncanniness but actually "annihilates" it. The fact that it comes at once from me and from beyond me is the call's very meaning: The thing that the call is calling me toward is myself. To understand the call instead as coming from God is an inauthentic response.

This is not the only reason that living authentically means living as an atheist. A world created by God does not depend on me for its meaning or its existence. In such a world, we don't need to work out the answer to the question of our own Being, because God *is* the answer. The hope of eternal life allows us to deny finitude rather than facing the possible impossibility of our own existence. Belief in God means belief in an entity that might forgive us of our guilt, relieve us from the burden of it.

But the truly inauthentic response to the call is to deny its very existence. To acknowledge the call—to stand before death in anxiety and guilt, to choose to be our authentic selves—this is the manner of Being that Heidegger calls "resoluteness," and it finally represents the answer to the question we've been asking all along: "The phenomenon of resoluteness has brought us before the primordial truth of existence."

HEIDEGGER CONCEIVED *Being and Time* as a massive two-part work, with each part containing three divisions. The book he rushed into publication included only the first two divisions of part one, stopping before he even moved from the particular sort of Being that is Dasein to a consideration of Being in general. Still, it was enough to get him hired—and to make him one of the world's most famous philosophers.

From the very beginning, a vocal minority of serious readers found Heidegger to be a total charlatan. His use of obscure jargon to gesture wildly at vague, all-encompassing concepts is precisely the kind of thing the analytic tradition lives to combat. For an analytic philosopher, the problem of Being is a pseudo-problem, and Heidegger's endless verbiage quite literally signifies nothing.

For others, Heidegger's work contains a genuine profundity, despite (or perhaps even because of) all its convolutions. If you have had the experiences Heidegger describes—the feeling of spiritual homelessness, the call to resist the allure of the They and take responsibility for the meaning of your own existence—then his descriptions simply resonate. There is perhaps no better preparation for reading Heidegger than being forced at a young age to face your own mortality and finding yourself unable to flee from this encounter. After my own illness, death was not for me something that happened to the They. Heidegger suggested that my anxiety over this fact was not a failing but a sign that I was living authentically, listening to my own call.

Nineteen

A TOTAL ABSENCE OF HOPE

There are some obvious problems with Heidegger's view, beginning with the question of *why* we ought to live authentically, why we ought to listen for that call that calls out in silence, rather than letting ourselves be tranquilized and absorbed into the They. Why not silence our anxiety, with drugs and drink perhaps, or with idle talk, or for that matter even with a theistic belief that death is not the end of Being? Heidegger can't answer this question, because there is no basis for normative claims within his approach.

Heidegger says repeatedly that he is not making such claims. He does not mean to suggest that authentic Being is a "higher" state than inauthentic Being. Yet he consistently describes these divergent ways of Being in morally charged ways. You can't honestly speak of authenticity versus inauthenticity, resoluteness versus fallenness, truth versus untruth, while insisting that you don't mean to suggest that one is superior to the other. For all his careful caveats, it is simply not possible to read *Being and Time* without a profound sense that values are being expressed.

This fact seems to have been part of why Heidegger never completed the book's remaining divisions. At some point in the 1930s, he underwent what he called "the Turn." He remained committed to inquiring after Being, but he gave up on the approach he'd been taking. For all its rejection of Cartesian thinking, Heidegger concluded, his focus on Dasein could not help confirming the subject-object separation. What's more, the declaration of resoluteness toward death as the ultimate meaning of authentic existence inevitably leaves the reader with a secondhand disclosure. The book seems to convey an ultimate truth that can be paraphrased and delivered to one who has not first wrestled it from existence. (My own summaries of his arguments betray them in just this way.)

For the rest of Heidegger's life, his work took the form of classroom lectures on the one hand and poetic essays on the other. He became even more gnomic, more and more interested in embodying thinking as such, rather than producing work that expressed conclusions arrived at through thought. Needless to say, this didn't alleviate the sense from some quarters that he was basically full of shit.

In April 1933, a few months after Hitler came to power, Heidegger was elected rector at the University of Freiburg, and he officially joined the Nazi Party. He greeted the end of Weimar democracy with great excitement as a defeat of the dictatorship of the They and a call for German authenticity. He cut off communication with Husserl, removed his mentor's name from *Being and Time*'s dedication page, and participated in the purging of other Jewish faculty members. He would give up the rectorship after a year, but his disillusionment with Nazism seems to have stemmed more from his failure to establish his own brand of hermeneutic phenomenology as Nazism's house philosophy than from any moral outrage.

Heidegger was still a Nazi in good standing when Jean-Paul Sartre was introduced to *Being and Time* by a Catholic priest with whom he shared a cell in a German POW camp. While the postwar denazification was removing Heidegger from his teaching position, Sartre, Simone de Beauvoir, and Albert Camus were turning the charged language of his early philosophy—authenticity and inauthenticity, anxiety and alienation, finitude and Being-toward-death—into atheist existentialism. "Existence precedes essence" became a rather unlikely bohemian rallying cry.

Ironically, Heidegger's early philosophy seemed to offer a proper atheist response to the war's horrors. What had happened in Germany exemplified the dictatorship of the They, in which no one was responsible because everyone was simply doing what They did. In a famous 1946 essay, "Existentialism Is a Humanism," Sartre even suggested that existentialism could be the source of a kind of categorical imperative: "Everything happens to every man as though the whole human race had its eyes fixed upon what he is doing and regulated its conduct accordingly."

Heidegger might easily have embraced this legacy as a means of rehabilitating his reputation. Instead, he responded to Sartre with his own "Letter on Humanism," in which he warned against "the seductions of the public realm as well as the impotence of the private" and insisted that any form of humanism—Christian, Marxist, or Sartrean—was ultimately a misbegotten retreat into metaphysics.

To the great frustration of his followers (including Arendt, who became totalitarianism's most acute diagnostician), Heidegger never publicly reckoned with his actions during the war. A man who made facing up to guilt the meaning of existence never expressed true remorse over his participation in Nazism. He admitted the evil of Hitler, but he placed fascism alongside American-style consumer capitalism and the cult of technology in a ranking of modern ills. He refused to classify the death camps as a unique moral catastrophe. Perhaps his sense that we are *all* guilty—that Dasein is guilty—made acknowledging his particular guilt impossible.

AFTER THE WAR, the Allied Denazification Committee held a hearing to determine whether Heidegger should be rehabilitated and allowed to teach again. Arendt testified on his behalf. Among those making the case against him was Arendt's former dissertation adviser, Karl Jaspers.

Born in 1883, Jaspers began his career as a man of science, a medical doctor specializing in psychology. Though the positivistic age in which he trained tended (like our own post-Freudian era) to treat mental illness as fundamentally physiological, properly understood through the study of the human body, Jaspers felt that medical science could not wholly capture the work of the mind, a view encouraged by his reading of Spinoza's *Ethics* and Kant's *Critique of Pure Reason*. He shifted his focus to philosophy in the years after the publication of *Being and Time*, and Heidegger's work had a profound influence on the formation of his own *Existenzphilosophie*. The two men became correspondents and, briefly, friends, though this friendship ended with Heidegger's embrace of Nazism.

In 1937, Jaspers—whose wife was Jewish—was removed from his university position and placed under a publication ban for being politically suspect. Before the removal, the German Academy of Frankfurt had invited him to give a series of lectures on the philosophy of existence, the fashionable new movement with which he and Heidegger had become associated. The academy honored the invitation despite the ban, so Jaspers prepared and delivered these talks with the knowledge that they would be his last public statements so long as the Nazis remained in power.

He begins the first lecture by clarifying that the philosophy of existence is not something fundamentally new but "really only a form of the one, primordial philosophy." Jaspers understood philosophy as standing between the two other primary modes of thought, science and religion. He believed science to be an essential conduit for knowledge about the world, but he opposed the prevailing view that science could "give what had been sought to no avail in philosophy," particularly by telling us "what goals to pursue in life." People asked too much of science, and science inevitably failed to make good on these unreasonable claims, resulting in a constant wavering "between a superstitious faith in science . . . and an antagonism to science that rejects it as meaningless and attacks it as destructive."

In contrast to these extremes, the Kantian critical tradition achieves two things. First of all, it shows science's limits: Science can tell us only about determinate objects, not being itself; it can "provide no goals whatever for life"; and it can "give no answer to the question of its own meaning." Yet this same critical tradition also demonstrates "the indispensability of science for philosophy." Science gives us real knowledge about the world of objects, something philosophizing simply can't do. In the process, science shows us all the more clearly what work is left for philosophy—that is, the consideration of being as such.

The task of philosophy has always been "to catch sight of reality at its origins," and "*Existenz* is one of the words for reality."* The philosophy of existence looks new only because the modern scientific era requires an emphasis on one particular view of this reality. Like Heidegger, Jaspers argued that being can't be fully comprehended through the study of existent objects. It is always there in front of us yet somehow recedes every time we attempt to grasp it and put it under examination. It is not an object in the world, but nor is it simply the sum total of such objects, capable of being approached through aggregation. Instead it is the ground of all objects. Jaspers called this ultimate ground of being "the encompassing."

"Never appearing to us itself," the encompassing "is that wherein everything else appears." Following Spinoza and Schopenhauer, Jaspers sees the encompassing as having two modes—the world and consciousness. But he diverges from both his predecessors in his belief that it is possible

* Just to keep things simple, Jaspers reverses Heidegger's approach, using *Dasein* to refer to existence as commonly understood and *Existenz* in the more specialized sense of a form of being that is concerned with its own being.

to transcend these immanent modes. It is possible to "leap out of immanence, in two ways at once: from the world to deity, and from the existence of the conscious spirit to *Existenz*."

Transcending our own existence as consciousness, we become *Existenz*. In this leap, ultimate freedom is found, for "freedom exists only with and by transcendence." The immanent world offers an apparent freedom, but this is ultimately illusory: "I cannot disregard myself as possible *Existenz*—and therefore also disregard transcendence—without betraying myself and sinking into a void."

The possibility of transcendence brings us to that other mode of thought that competes with philosophy, namely religion. Jaspers respects religion as an essential path to wisdom, just as he respects science as an essential path to knowledge. Religions are symbolic systems for working through the possibility of transcendence. But we err whenever we take them as giving us determinate truth about the transcendent, as though it were itself an object within the encompassing. As Kant showed, we can't ever meaningfully reason about the transcendent.

The job of philosophy, then, is to allow us to make the leap into transcendence, but to do so without attempting to cognize the transcendent. Philosophy is an *activity*, not a body of knowledge. It begins with taking the leap, facing up to the possible nothingness into which we may be leaping but willing with love the truth that we will find awaiting us. This project is fraught with danger: "In *Existenz* there is faith and despair," but we naturally desire "the peace of eternity, where despair is impossible and faith becomes the vision." And so we are constantly being called away from the path to truth toward various more comfortable untruths.

Nowhere in these lectures does Jaspers mention the political climate in which they are taking place. (To do so likely would have condemned him and his wife to death.) But listeners would have very well understood the implications of his talk about freedom, authority, and exception. They also would have understood the contrast Jaspers drew with Heidegger when he insisted that existential philosophy was fundamentally rational, a continuation of a long-standing tradition, rather than a radical break with Enlightenment thought. Granting that Jaspers's personal situation would not have allowed him to embrace Nazism in any case and that he responded to the Nazi threat mostly by way of silence, one can't help concluding that his more rationally grounded version of existentialism could not be reconciled with Nazism in the way that Heidegger's antirational version could.

Why, then, did Heidegger's version prove so much more influential?

In *The Myth of Sisyphus*, written during the German occupation of Paris, Albert Camus classed Jaspers alongside Søren Kierkegaard and other religious existentialists. All of these thinkers recognized what Camus considered the fundamental absurdity of the human condition: Humans long for meaning in an utterly meaningless world. The world itself is not absurd in its meaninglessness, nor is humanity absurd in its rationality. Absurdity arises from the fundamental disjunction of the two. Seemingly alone among all creatures, humans are capable of choosing whether or not to go on living, and the world around us gives us no cause to choose life. Yet if we choose the alternative, we have given up the possibility of any future choice. For this reason, Camus called suicide the "one truly serious philosophical problem."

On one hand, to give in to suicide is obviously a form of defeat. But to accept the palliative fictions that make life seem worth living is another defeat. For Camus, truly facing up to the problem requires "a total absence of hope (which has nothing to do with despair), a continual rejection (which must not be confused with renunciation), and a conscious dissatisfaction (which must not be compared to immature unrest)." Anything that "destroys, conjures away, or exorcises these requirements"—especially anything that tells us that the absurd logic might somehow be resolved—"ruins the absurd."

The religious existentialist recognizes the absurdity of our condition but believes that it can be escaped by way of the religious leap. Jaspers represents a particularly notable case of this belief, precisely because he does not share the orthodox believer's faith in God. Without God, Jaspers is "powerless to realize the transcendent, incapable of plumbing the depth of experience, and conscious of that universe upset by failure." Still he asserts the transcendent without any justification: "Thus the absurd becomes god (in the broadest meaning of this word) and that inability to understand becomes the experience that illuminates everything."

For Camus, the leap is not an answer to the problem of suicide; it is itself a *form* of suicide. What else would we call leaping without any reason to believe there is something there to catch our fall? The existentialist is right to say that empirical study of the world of objects can't ever provide meaning or value, but he is wrong to think these things can be found in some other source. This mistake is made by existentialism in general, going back to its sources in Husserl. Phenomenology "confirms absurd thought in its initial assertion that there is no truth, but merely truths," but it goes wrong in its quasi-Platonic embrace of eidetic essences. For Husserl, "all things are not explained by one thing but by all things." This still amounts to a belief that explanation is possible, that sense can be made of the world. To the existentialist, "reason is useless but there is something beyond reason." To the absurdist, "reason is useless and there is nothing beyond reason."

It's not enough to come to grips with the reality of our situation, Camus notes—"the point is to live." How do we do this if all our resources are useless? The absurdist still has some fundamental truth on which he can rely. He cannot know whether the world has some transcendent meaning. But like Socrates—the wisest of all men because he knew that he knew nothing—the absurd man *knows* that he cannot answer the question of meaning. He has two certainties: his own hunger for the absolute and the utter impossibility of satisfying that hunger in the world. Because he knows that he is free to stop living—suicide is always an option—he also knows that continuing to live is his own choice. That is his "absurd freedom." In practicing this freedom, he makes "the heart-rending and marvelous wager of the absurd." It is not a wager on meaning like the one Pascal advocates but a wager on life in the face of meaninglessness. The absurd man "wants to find out if it is possible to live *without appeal*."

WHAT DOES THIS MEAN in practice? Camus's answer to this question was profoundly influenced by the facts of his own life.

He was born into a working-class family of French descent in Algeria. Less than a year later, his father was killed in World War I, and he was raised in poverty by a deaf, illiterate, and extremely loving mother. By his own accounts, Camus's childhood under these conditions was largely happy. He had a great love of soccer, girls, and the Mediterranean sea and sun that surrounded him. He studied philosophy on a scholarship at the University of Algiers, after which he ran a theater troupe and worked in journalism. When a story he wrote on the treatment of the minority Kabyle tribe put him under suspicion with the Algerian authorities, he moved to Paris.

Even if they were quite poor and socially disadvantaged, as Camus was, the so-called *pieds noirs* were generally treated by Indigenous Algerians as colonialist outsiders. Most of them (Camus included) never learned the Arabic or Berber languages predominantly spoken in their native land. Arriving in the metropole, however, Camus found that he was considered not quite French. The sense of foreignness was further compounded by the fact of German occupation. Camus was actively involved in the Resistance, editing and writing for an underground newspaper, *Combat*, that also served as an information network.

All of this contributed to Camus's acute sense of the outsider as an exemplary figure. (The title of his reputation-making first novel, *L'etranger*, is probably best translated as "The Foreigner.") In *The Myth of Sisyphus*, Camus offers some examples of the form that an absurd life might take, and each borrows from an aspect of his own personality. There is the seducer (also a favorite of Kierkegaard), who lives to gratify every wish as it occurs to him. There is the actor (by which Camus means particularly the stage actor, whose work is not memorialized on film), who makes an art out of the ephemeral gestures of existence. There is the traveler, constantly on the move in search of new experiences. There is the conqueror, the man of action who makes himself equal to the gods but can never be satisfied by his conquests and must go always in search of another.

What seems to unite all these figures is that at the end of their lives they have nothing to show for themselves—and that they have known all along that this would be the case. They have not set out to have something to show for themselves, only to fill their lives with activity. Camus is quick to note that he means these figures as illustrations rather than models. An absurd life can be lived equally by "a sub-clerk in the post office" as it can by any of these more dramatic figures. Besides, the kind of life that might provide an example to follow, engendering new ways of being, is a life lived with an eye on the future, and thus lived with hope. "In the absurd world," on the other hand, "the value of a notion or of a life is measured by its sterility."

In contrast to this sterility, Camus considers the possibility of "absurd creation," specifically through a consideration of novelists who have taken the absurdity of the human condition as their starting point. There are two exemplary figures in this tradition—Dostoyevsky and Kafka—but both end by making their own version of the religious leap. Indeed, Camus suggests that the very act of writing a novel, dedicating yourself to the creation of a work that might outlast you and have some meaning for others, is a wager on significance, a leap in the direction of the transcendent. The lesson of these writers is that hope "can beset even those who wanted to be free of it."

In Camus's view, Nietzsche alone maintained in his work a "sterile and conquering lucidity and an obstinate negation of any supernatural consolation." But this "sterility" means that he cannot have any real followers, as Nietzsche himself noted so often in his work. Anyone who attempts to follow Nietzsche's example has simply proved that he has not really understood it, for to have properly understood his message would demand living without any examples at all. And so "the only artist to have derived the extreme consequences of an aesthetic of the Absurd" could not be called upon as a model.

THROUGHOUT THE OCCUPATION, Camus published a series of "Letters to a German friend," in which he made a philosophical case for resistance to Nazism. Many of the Resistance forces were Marxists who opposed National Socialism on ideological grounds. Some others were conservative Catholics. Camus attempted to make a case for resistance in the absence of belief in any totalizing system.

The last of these letters was written in July 1944, after the D-Day invasion had made the end of war in Europe seem inevitable, and in it Camus explains to his hypothetical German "how it is possible that, though so similar, we should be enemies today":

> For a long time we both thought that this world had no ultimate meaning and that consequently we were cheated. I still think so in a way. But I came to different conclusions from the ones you used to talk about, which, for so many years now you have been trying to introduce into history. I tell myself

> now that if I had really followed your reasoning, I ought to approve what you are doing. And this is so serious that I must stop and consider it, during this summer night so full of promises for us and threats for you.

Camus concludes that the difference between the two men is simple: "You readily accepted despair, and I never yielded to it." One of them, in recognizing "the injustice of our condition," took it as a license to add more injustice to the world. The other felt compelled to "fight against eternal injustice." But he did this without ever giving in to the metaphysical belief that justice could be found in the world. "I continue to believe that this world has no ultimate meaning," he tells his friend. "But I know that something in it has a meaning, and that is man, because he is the only creature to insist on having one."

In Camus's account, the war had forced the French to follow the Germans into despair, and for a time this had forced the French down to the Germans' level. But the French had survived by refusing to forget happiness: "We tried to preserve in our hearts the memory of a happy sea, of a remembered hill, the smile of a beloved face." Camus had become one of those beset by the hope from which he had tried to free himself.

In the years after the war, he became even more committed to a vision of clear-eyed resistance that never gave in to the belief that some meaning might exist out in the world. His rejection of Marxism and his pointed disgust with Stalin put him out of favor with Sartre and other more fashionable existentialists. Throughout the fifties, Algerians fought a bloody war for their independence, which de Gaulle granted in 1958. The rebel fighters in this asymmetrical contest often resorted to guerrilla tactics, including acts of terror against the *pieds noirs*. Camus's criticism of this approach led him to be branded a colonialist reactionary by the French Left. He argued that proper rebellion—the act of saying no to the conditions under which one has suffered—is an assertion of value, a rejection of both despair and the absurd, and to live up to this assertion meant respecting certain moral limits.

In his 1957 Nobel Prize acceptance speech, Camus claimed that he had envisioned from the beginning of his writing career a series of "cycles" on a progression of themes. *The Myth of Sisyphus* and *The Stranger* were part of a cycle on "negation," which he followed with a cycle on "rebellion" that included *The Plague* and another book-length essay, *The Rebel.* In the speech, he indicated that he would be writing a third cycle, on love. He spent his last years working on another novel, *The First Man*, which included a surprisingly sentimental portrait of his childhood in Algeria. Here he gave full voice to the memories of a happy sea and the smile of a beloved face. The manuscript was found in the wreckage of the car crash that killed him—absurdly—at the age of forty-six.

Twenty

AMONG THE IRONISTS

As I again near the end of my historical account and attempt a complete description of this second atheist worldview, I have to acknowledge something that is probably obvious: I found—and continue to find—romantic idealism far more compelling than I ever did scientific materialism.

Though it took me time to articulate precisely what I found so inhospitable about scientific materialism, it didn't take long to realize that I couldn't live that worldview out. But I *did* live out the romantic idealist version of atheism. When I describe what it's like inside it, I am not engaging in a theoretical exercise. I am describing what it was like *for me.* Elements of that experience continue to influence me. In fact, this book's very framework owes something to it. The assumptions that none of us have unmediated access to "the world," that we are instead fated to occupy different possible worldviews, and that a given worldview can't be judged from the vantage of another are all drawn directly from this tradition.

In 1962, the historian of science (and former physicist) Thomas Kuhn published a classic study, *The Structure of Scientific Revolutions*, in which he questioned the common history of scientific progress as a steady accumulation of knowledge that gradually fills out our picture of the natural world. Kuhn argued instead that certain scientific achievements create disciplinary "paradigms" in which science is normally practiced. These paradigms determine not just a given discipline's methods for answering questions but what kinds of questions the discipline deems relevant and even what objects the discipline studies. The practice of "normal science," Kuhn argues, involves working within the prevailing paradigm to solve "puzzles"—that is, cases where observed facts fit imperfectly within prevailing theories and the two must somehow be brought into line.

At rare times, however, anomalies arise that can't be assimilated within an existing paradigm. Most practitioners (particularly older ones who have more invested in the status quo) will either treat these anomalies as yet-unsolved puzzles or simply shunt them aside. But as it becomes gradually clearer that these problems can't be solved within the paradigm and are too important to ignore, a crisis occurs. Then some within the field begin to practice "revolutionary" or "abnormal" science, in which new methods are tried, new questions asked, accepted answers to old questions reconsidered. Eventually, a new paradigm emerges that can solve the new problem without unsettling too many old ones.

It's not simply that old data is interpreted in new ways or that new data is added to the picture. "When paradigms change," Kuhn suggests, "the world itself changes with them." Here Kuhn uses precisely the vocabulary I've been using: A revolution, he says, is "a change in world view." You can't arrive by "normal science" at a new paradigm. It is only when the old paradigm falls into crisis and "revolutionary science" becomes possible that the change can occur. (Kuhn explicitly refers to "the transfer of allegiance from paradigm to paradigm" as a "conversion experience.") Furthermore, different paradigms are incommensurable. You can't judge one from the standpoint of another, and there is no neutral ground from which competing paradigms can be compared.

Kuhn recognized that he had not somehow solved that problem and found a neutral point from which to judge the progression of scientific paradigms. Like science, history is often treated as "a purely descriptive discipline," but Kuhn admits that his own historical account is "often interpretive and sometimes normative." He also understood his own discipline to be suffering one of those crises that lead to revolution. What had fallen into question was "the epistemological viewpoint that [had] most often guided Western philosophy for three centuries," namely the view that "sensory experience" is "fixed and neutral," and that "theories [are] simply man-made interpretations of given data." Kuhn couldn't help still feeling some allegiance to this view, but he was becoming increasingly convinced that it didn't fit well with the data under study.

This point is already found in Nietzsche, but it really comes into its own after Heidegger, and Kuhn was one of several thinkers grappling with it in the postwar era. Michel Foucault had just published *The History of Madness*, the first in a series of books that applied a similar attention to the history of the human sciences. Foucault argued throughout his work that various seemingly objective categories—insanity, sexuality, even humanity itself—were creations of the disciplinary discourses that emerged from the Enlightenment dream of a universal science. In order to make the study of humanity properly "scientific," the complexities of human behavior needed to be made legible, and this meant the creation of normative categories that could be treated as objective facts. Influenced by Nietzsche, Foucault saw these interpretive acts as fundamentally driven by the power dynamics of social control. (A generation later, Judith Butler and other feminist theorists would argue that gender was another such constructed category, and that it could be liberated from this control by being treated as a matter of individual "performance.")

Among philosophers and intellectual historians, the "paradigm shift" (to use the Kuhnian term, which has since become a business cliché) in which Kuhn and Foucault participated is called the "hermeneutic turn." After Heidegger, Continental philosophy became increasingly doubtful that it was possible to acquire through sense perception and reason anything like objective knowledge about an external world of fact. As phenomenology taught, an interpretive act was "always already" built into even the most seemingly neutral observation.

The American philosopher Richard Rorty, whose work engaged both the analytic and the Continental traditions, puts this in terms of the longstanding search for a "first philosophy" to serve as the foundation for all of knowledge. Medieval Scholastics gave the job to metaphysics. Locke and Kant initiated the turn to epistemology, in which a proper theory of knowledge became the new foundation. When positivism made core epistemological concepts seem too subjective, dualist, even metaphysical, Russell and others turned instead to linguistic analysis as "first philosophy." But Wittgenstein and Heidegger demonstrated various problems with treating language as foundational. There was no objective method for establishing linguistic significance in even the most seemingly straightforward cases. One could not avoid interpretation.

For Rorty, it's essential to understand that the "hermeneutic turn" does not seek to make interpretation the new foundation. It seeks instead to give up on foundations entirely. Kuhn believed that scientific crises ultimately had to be resolved by the emergence of a new paradigm. It is only in rare historical moments that "abnormal" science gets practiced, and the goal is always to get back to some sense of normalcy. (A "science" that remains in crisis eventually stops being a science.) Borrowing Kuhn's terms, Rorty speaks of "normal" and "abnormal" discourse, citing Heidegger and Wittgenstein as exemplars of the latter, but he doesn't think that "abnormal" discourse can lead us to a new theory that better fits the facts out there in the world and allows us to return to normalcy. No theory is better than any other at fitting the facts in this way, because there are no theory-neutral facts "out there." Truth does not consist in a correspondence between theory and fact. It is created, not discovered.

At the same time, Rorty recognizes that most if not all of us require a worldview. Our challenge is to adopt a worldview while acknowledging it as such. We must act *as though* certain values are foundational while always recognizing that we might just as easily have taken up some other set of values. We must also understand that we have no rational basis for convincing others to adopt our values. This puts us in the position that Rorty calls "irony." The ironist, Rorty says, will "remind herself of her rootlessness by constantly using terms like 'Weltanschauung.'"

In other words, what I'm going to call the romantic idealist worldview is one of those rare worldviews that conceives of itself *as* a worldview, rather than a privileged vantage point from which the world as it actually is can be properly addressed. It might be better to call it a metaworldview, insofar as it ultimately concludes that every one of us is responsible for the creation of our own *Weltanschauung*.

Here we get into a classic case of circularity, for this metaworldview cannot claim to be some foundational position from within which the work of creating our worldviews can be undertaken. "The truth is made, not discovered" has no more claim to truth than any other statement, including the statements "the truth consists in a correspondence between our ideas and objective reality" and "the truth is the eternal infinite absolute Good." A good ironist, says Rorty, won't be troubled by that fact. For the ironist, "foundational" values are just those values that can't be defended without falling into this kind of circularity.

HAVING SAID ALL THAT, I'm now going to attempt just the kind of discursive quasi-neutral account of romantic idealism that an ironist would say is not really possible.

As the name I've given it suggests, romantic idealism is metaphysically idealist. Having its origins in Cartesian and Spinozistic rationalism, it takes subjective experience rather than objective matter as its fundamental starting point. It does not (necessarily) embrace what Kant calls "empirical idealism"—that is, the belief that reality is a purely mental phenomenon and that no world exists outside our own heads. But it believes that reality as we experience it is conditioned by the mind to such a degree that we could never possibly separate a material reality from our conscious experience and use the second to gain access to the first.

This has obvious epistemological (or hermeneutic) implications. Truth is not a correspondence between an idea or proposition and an objective world against which it can be compared and verified. After all, we can only ever experience the idea and not the world. How, then, is a proposition verified? What could we possibly "check" it against? The answer is that truth is not primarily propositional or discursive; it can't simply be stated and thus itself turned into an object to be passed from hand to hand. We must participate in making truth.

Furthermore, this truth making is not done dispassionately. It is emotionally charged. We can't possibly separate emotion from reason, and even if we could, we would only be doing damage to ourselves. Whatever "truth" resulted from this separation would necessarily be incomplete. This is the "romantic" part of romantic idealism: Not only must the truth be lived out, but it must be lived out as a question only we can answer, a question whose answer *matters* for us.

This demand gives rise in turn to the romantic idealist ethic, which is grounded in authenticity. We are called to take up the project of making truth, living in a way that honors our own reality. For the romantic idealist, the greatest ethical good is personal freedom, and this freedom is absolute: It is not just a freedom of action within certain limited boundaries but an interpretive freedom to make our own meaning out of the world.

How is this freedom to be squared with the freedom of others? In the Spinozistic view, we are all parts of a rationally ordered whole, and so our free actions can be naturally reconciled. True freedom entails transcending our narrow perspective and viewing the world under the aspect of eternity. From this viewpoint, there is no conflict between our desires and those of others. Rousseau gives up the idea that the world is rationally ordered but still holds to the idea that proper freedom entails willing the general will. There is a tension here that demands a paradoxical coercion in freedom's name: Some people will have to be taught to be free. Finally, Kant turns Rousseau's general will into the categorical imperative to universalize your maxim.

Beginning with Schopenhauer, the tradition rejects the idea that differing wills can be reconciled through reason and adopts instead the idea that will itself is an irrational, antagonistic force. It is not possible to placate the will; the fact of its being violent is what *makes* it will. We have to choose between freedom and peace.

Schopenhauer chooses peace. Romantic pessimism does not argue that there is an ethical imperative to avoid action, because its view of the world as will does not allow a rational basis for ethical imperatives of any kind. But it treats suffering as the fundamental condition of existence, and it assumes that recognizing this condition will naturally bring about compassion for fellow sufferers. It also suggests that negation of the will might allow us to escape our own suffering. The romantic pessimist has an abiding attraction to self-annihilation but ultimately rejects it on the basis that suicide, too, is an act of will.

The other romantic idealist option is the Nietzschean affirmation of the will, which acknowledges the practice of freedom as a form of violence against others and chooses freedom nonetheless. Like romantic pessimism, this view utterly rejects both the rationalist idea that our wills are reconciled by the order of the world and the utilitarian idea that our wills can be reconciled through technical management. It sees the contest of wills as the inevitable feature of life. Unlike romantic pessimism, it celebrates this fact.

This version of the romantic idealist ethic gets read back into the romantic idealist epistemology. If truth is something we are responsible for making, then it is another product of the will, and subject to the contest of wills. The fact that we have no objective reality against which truth can be verified means that truth must be "proved" through action. Rather than attempting to transcend the narrow limits of our own perspective and arrive at some hypothetical shared reality, we must fight to ensure the victory of our viewpoint against its competitors. In some cases, the opponents whose truth we are confronting do not even know there is a war going on. So much the better. Since the war of truths is fought without ground rules, many romantic idealists are not above appealing to the standards of objective truth when it serves their interest. This seems to be an obvious hypocrisy, but hypocrisy is a problem only if one accepts consistency and honesty as virtues.

In other cases, this war is fought in more or less explicit terms. For we can't even be reconciled with our fellow romantic idealists. We cannot rely on a common understanding that we are all "entitled" to our views. What if my view does not grant you this entitlement? Peace can't be negotiated; it can come only through unconditional surrender.

TO DECLARE FREEDOM and authenticity as supreme goods is to imply the preexistence of some scale into which goods could be placed. It suggests a standard outside the self against which a life might be judged. But this is just what the ethic of authenticity seeks to deny. Here we have the problem of the transvaluation of all values, which Nietzsche identified. It is not enough to reshuffle the list of human goods, to find some new standard. We must do away with norms entirely. But that is itself an imperative; it seeks to serve as a norm.

There is a kind of double vision common to many prominent romantic idealists. On the one hand, they hold the belief that no worldview is inherently better than any other, that the only way to justify a view is to live it out in contest with other views. On the other hand, they believe in their own worldview with all of the commitment this entails. They must do so, for that is what it means to live it out. Part of the reason that Nietzsche and other avatars of this tradition write in literary forms and adopt various authorial personae is that romantic idealism demands that we truly believe something while also acknowledging that it is "only" a belief. There is an inherent tension—perhaps even an incoherence—at play here, but exemplary romantic idealists know this fact; they are ironists in Rorty's sense, and living with this tension is part of their achievement.

Some romantic idealists aim to overcome this tension, to arrive at the point where they can simply live out their viewpoint without combining it with the implicit recognition that it is just one viewpoint among many. This is the dream of Nietzsche's Superman. Romantic idealists sometimes express nostalgia for a time when such uncomplicated expressions of meaning making were possible. Like Rousseau, they may blame reason itself for sending us down the path of self-consciousness. Or they blame the Enlightenment for undermining religious certainties without thought for what might be put in their place. They might become religious nostalgists, but they don't think the problem can be solved through returning to religion, since we can't unlearn what we know. For other romantic idealists, getting past our knowledge that all values are inventions is not even a goal. The point is to engage in the meaning-making act in full knowledge that your meanings are "mere" creations.

This is a difficult balancing act, and most romantic idealists are not up to the task. Most of us, it seems, don't just want values; we want our values to be "real." We want to have some justification for universalizing them. (That is to say, imposing them on others.) Faced with an obvious moral outrage—say, the torture of a child—most of us will insist that there simply *must* be some objective standpoint from which all rational people could agree to call this wrong.

From this same standpoint, we might criticize romantic idealism for its complicity in some of history's greatest horrors. You can't simply wave away the extent to which Rousseau inspired the French Terror or Schopenhauer and Nietzsche inspired the Nazis. Well, a romantic idealist might tell a scientific materialist, we are responsible for the death camps, and you are responsible for the bomb, and we'll see which one winds up causing more suffering in the long run.

More pointedly, he would say: What does suffering have to do with it? Who says there's anything wrong with suffering? You can't judge me according to the standards of your worldview. Or rather, you can—and must—judge me according to the standards of your worldview, but I need not submit to the judgment. Meanwhile I judge *your* worldview, with its obsession with shallow human comforts and its childlike fear of the slightest physical harm, to be empty and insipid, and I would rather live my life with a passion that occasionally risks overspilling into violence. Nietzsche would go further with his response and say: I have tried your way. Your faith in the Golden Rule, your faith in science, your faith in reason. I have tried them all, and I have overcome them all. Do you have the courage to try things my way?

HAVING TRIED AS much myself, I can say a few things about the experience. The first is that constructing your own worldview is incredibly isolating. Shared worldviews are one of the things that bring people together. When we each construct our own world, we each live alone. Other people exist as paper cutouts, characters in our world-making drama rather than fellow inhabitants of a shared world, and we exist for them in just the same way. An unbridgeable gap separates us, and real community across the gap is impossible. Yet most of us feel very strongly the need for community, even if it only takes the form of sitting beside another person in the dark cave, watching the same shadow show on the wall.

This raises the second point, which is that living out romantic idealism is incredibly *difficult*. Unlike scientific materialism, romantic idealism can be done badly or well. It is possible to hold to the truth of scientific materialism and still maintain the occasional superstitious practice—knocking on wood or throwing salt over your shoulder—that you can't rationally justify. A scientific materialist who finds himself praying in a moment of crisis has not failed to live his worldview authentically, because his worldview does not demand authenticity.

In this sense, romantic idealism is much closer to the typical religious worldview. Indeed, scientific materialism may be the real outlier here in its refusal to make such demands. But most worldviews tend to be rather explicit about what they demand. Romantic idealism is a way without a way. It asks each of us not just to live up to a standard but to create that standard ourselves. For many people, this is precisely its attraction. Yet there is no mistaking how hard this work really is. To this end, the worldview's exemplars are not average people but heroes, geniuses, saints—even Supermen. (Rorty admits that the ironic pose is really only appropriate for "we intellectuals," not for the common run of people.)

Romantic idealists talk often about the anxiety of living without external certainties, and they understand this anxiety not as something to be transcended but as something to be embraced. A striking number of romantic idealists admit to being profoundly unhappy. Here the romantic idealist obsession with suicide is notable. It is all well and good to recognize that you are free at any time to end your own life. But if you continue finding yourself truly faced with this choice—if suicide seems on a day-to-day basis not like an abstract possibility but like a live option—something seems to have gone wrong.

Even those romantic idealists who claim to affirm life show something of the strain. It is a well-known fact that obsession with healthy vitality is itself a kind of morbidity. To put things in Wittgenstein's terms, true health shows itself rather than stating itself. Actually healthy people don't spend a lot of time talking about their health. Exercise and eating well might be signs of good health, but continually telling people how much you exercise and how well you eat is a sign of sickness.

It's tempting to say that romantic idealism is so difficult—even impossible—because it is simply false. There is, in fact, a shared world of objects beyond our individual control, and the belief that the world is totally malleable to our own wills is a recipe for endless frustration. Even if this is the case, the romantic idealist would reply, the failure of my worldview to correspond to this reality does not falsify my worldview, for this correspondence theory of truth is precisely what romantic idealism rejects.

Instead of judging its truth in this sense, we might ask whether romantic idealism is conducive to human flourishing. In making this judgment, we need not accept the utilitarian standard of flourishing. Let us take an appropriately romantic approach. Does romantic idealism foster sublime human achievement? Does it make the world beautiful, exciting, interesting? Does it transform our lives into something as compelling as the finest works of art? Is a world in which romantic idealism is the prevailing view even an attractive one?

I DON'T THINK we need to speculate about the answers to these questions. We have them right in front of us.

When I began my journey through the atheist responses to the riddle of life, scientific materialism was far and away the dominant form of disbelief in mainstream Western culture, but it wasn't entirely unchallenged. Throughout the nineties, scientific materialists working within universities had sounded the alarm about a distinctly secular threat to reason on the rise among their colleagues. Daniel Dennett decried the "postmodernist science critics and other multiculturalists" who argued "that Western science was just one among many equally valid narratives." Steven Pinker complained of graduate students in the humanities being shut out of the job market "unless they write in gibberish while randomly dropping the names of authorities like Foucault and Butler." E. O. Wilson mordantly remarked that "scientists, being held responsible for what they say, have not found postmodernism useful."

At the time, scientific materialists mostly treated postmodern antirationalism as a curiosity, unlikely to survive outside the hothouse environment of the academy. This changed after 9/11. As I've already suggested, the New Atheist movement was in large part a scientific materialist response to the rise of Islamic terrorism. Many New Atheists—most notably Hitchens and Harris—vocally supported the war on terror. In the light of this support, they came to view the postmodernists within their own atheist camp as a kind of fifth column, undermining reason in its fight against religious extremism. From their perspective, the postmodernists were the people who excused the treatment of women in the Muslim world on grounds of cultural relativism. They were the ones who insisted that Western-style liberal democracy and its bundle of human rights were not universal goods we could simply impose on the rest of the world. They were quislings and collaborators. Still, they remained an afterthought compared with the primary threat.

Twenty-five years on, this has largely changed. One simple way to track the rise of the competing secular worldview is to examine the fortunes of the political approach that goes hand in hand with scientific materialism. I came of age between the collapse of the Berlin Wall and the collapse of the Twin Towers, during the high-water mark of liberal triumphalism. This was the age of the "end of history," when Francis Fukuyama predicted the "universalization of Western liberal democracy as the final form of human government." It was a fairly widespread belief at this time that secularism, economic liberalism, and political liberalism would together conquer the globe. Because it was accepted as fact that secular democracies did not make war against one another, this global marketplace was expected to be a world of perpetual peace.

Some theorists of liberalism allowed that it could not meet every human need. The full title of Fukuyama's famous book was *The End of History and the Last Man*, and he was very much alive to the Nietzschean idea that some people would find the triumph of peace and prosperity to be unlivable. The liberal order of the future would no longer be faced with the challenge of feeding and clothing its people or protecting them from hostile neighbors, but it would need to find some way to keep its people entertained. Fukuyama himself professed ambivalence about life in a perfectly managed liberal state, and he wondered whether the "very prospect of centuries of boredom at the end of history will serve to get history started once again."

As it happens, of course, history never ended at all. Today, large portions of both the Left and the Right are—by their own description—anti- or postliberal. Illiberalism is more prevalent on the political right, and right-wing illiberals have acquired considerable electoral power, making them a far greater threat to the liberal project. But there is no question that a strain of unapologetic illiberalism exists on the left. Young people who identify as left-wing are far less likely than they once were to describe themselves as liberal or to champion liberal values. They are far more likely to embrace the Rousseauian-Nietzschean idea that so-called universal rights are a front by which the elite oppress the marginalized.

The dramatic internal conflicts on the left in response to Hamas's October 7, 2023, attack on Israeli civilians strongly echoes the disagreement between Camus and the French existentialists over the tactics of Algerian resistance. As I was finishing a draft of this book, a young man named Luigi Mangione shot and killed health care executive Brian Thompson outside a Midtown Manhattan hotel. During the police manhunt that followed, Mangione became a kind of romantic-existentialist folk hero. Half of American college students viewed the murder as justified, with nearly the same portion of people under age thirty calling the action "acceptable." Both age cohorts are far more likely than the general population to occupy the political left.

The moderate secular liberals who have observed the recent retreat of liberalism with (quite justified) horror have generally seen the forces of illiberalism as closely related to a familiar enemy: religion. Because scientific materialism views itself as the default secular worldview, it naturally treats any rival as fundamentally a form of religious belief. In this view, Christian nationalism is the primary motivating ideology behind right-wing illiberalism. Meanwhile, many liberals of a strongly atheist bent insist that left-wing antiliberals are equally under the sway of a kind of religion—the "cult" or "church" of identity politics. Richard Dawkins speaks for many of them when he declares "woke" to be a "latter-day Torquemadism . . . with its own religiously enforced dogma . . . which makes no sense to anyone outside but which resonates perfectly with cult insiders—the evangelical leaders and their sheeplike followers."

"Religion" is a famously malleable sociological category, but if we stick to the criterion of theistic belief, the argument that modern-day illiberalism is primarily a religious movement does not hold up to much scrutiny. Perhaps the crudest way to make the point would be simply to note that the rise of illiberalism has gone hand in hand with a decline of theistic belief and religious practice—both in America and around the world. In the year before the 9/11 attacks, about 70 percent of Americans went regularly to church. Fewer than half do today. In most of the European countries that have faced a rise in neofascist, xenophobic, and other illiberal movements, the vast majority of citizens don't identify as adherents of any faith.

The avatar of right-wing illiberalism is the least religious U.S. president of my lifetime, the first in several generations who does not even pretend to be influenced or motivated by Christian faith. While he relies on the support of conservative Christians, he is better understood as our first Nietzschean president, a man who explicitly embraces the will to power as the ultimate value, a force to which even the truth itself must give way. On the left, meanwhile, illiberalism is far and away most prevalent among the young and highly educated cohorts that are also the least likely to identify themselves as religious believers.

For all their differences, I think that both right-wing and left-wing illiberalism are species of romantic idealism. Both camps champion the importance of authenticity and identity. Both tend to treat the gap between themselves and those who disagree with them as fundamentally unbridgeable. Both are doubtful of the existence of objective truths that can be arrived at through free inquiry. Both believe instead that "truths" are expressions of power dynamics. Since I have already said that romantic idealism has many similarities to religion, perhaps I might even concede to liberal atheists their contention that the great threats to liberalism are religious in nature. But these religious threats are predominantly atheist ones.*

Scientific materialism remains the default secular worldview. Atheists and believers alike are expected to show allegiance to it, at least so long as they are in the public square, debating matters of general concern. Simi-

* Even those within these camps who claim to be Christian tend to do so as an expression of particularist identity rather than metaphysical belief. Speaking to Tucker Carlson, Elon Musk declared himself a "cultural Christian," while quickly adding, "I have trouble believing all these religious stories."

larly, most people living in most Western democracies remain liberal in the broadest sense, even if they are liberal ironists who don't claim to be able to justify their liberalism. But both of these facts seem to be changing, and the changes appear to be obviously related. It hardly seems a coincidence that the threats posed to liberalism today are the same threats that romantic idealism has always posed to liberalism.

Richard Rorty was a dyed-in-the-wool liberal, despite his belief that his own philosophy could not justify liberalism. He thought seriously about the possibility that functioning liberal societies needed the kind of glue that shared metaphysical values provide, and he considered what might result if "ironism replaced metaphysics in our public rhetoric." It was possible, he allowed, that "the prevalence of ironist notions among the public at large, the general adoption of antimetaphysical, antiessentialist views about the nature of morality and rationality and human beings, would weaken and dissolve liberal societies." He posed this question in 1989, when liberalism did not seem to face any serious challenges on the world stage, and he concluded that liberalism would survive this change. I wonder what he would say now.

IF I'M RIGHT about all of this, we might look around ourselves for answers to the questions I've already posed: Is a world dominated by romantic idealism one in which we want to live? Is it liberating? Is it interesting? Is it beautiful? Or is it repressive, tedious, and ugly? Granted, these are matters of taste, but let us accept the Nietzschean dictate that we can—and must—argue about matters of taste.

One of the most widely remarked-upon features of contemporary culture is the rise of anxiety—that emotion that romantic idealists so closely associate with authentic existence. Many commentators have attributed this rise to technological changes, particularly the prevalence of the smartphone and social media. I am sympathetic to this explanation. But what, after all, is the world of social media if it is not the purest imaginable expression of romantic idealist ideology?

Here is a place where you can make yourself from scratch, where you can do so again and again, where you can have as many different personalities, identities, realities, as you want. But it is also a place where you *must* make yourself from scratch. You can't rely on other people to trust your good faith, to know where you're coming from, because every day you must start over. It is a place where you are constantly being judged, and these judgments are always ultimately aesthetic even when they pretend to be ethical. It is a place where people are bullied into silence rather than reasoned with, a place where the loudest voice gets to be right, a place where whoever can mobilize the largest army gets to determine the terms of the debate.

Above all, it is a place of constant dispute. It is a place where even the most well-meaning conversation can be hijacked at any moment by nihilistic trolls who want to amuse themselves by making real communication impossible. Everything is up for debate, including the very terms by which any debate might possibly be settled. (In Rorty's view, this is a key characteristic of "abnormal" discourse.) Truth is not a function of correspondence to the real world, because there is no real world. It doesn't matter how you treat other people because they aren't real either. It is a place that brings out the worst in almost all of us, and it is making us miserable. It is making us miserable in part by encouraging us to deny the reality of other people. It is making us miserable by making us feel alone.

Is it possible to live without appeal? Camus asks. For most of us, the answer is no. We can say this with some confidence because we are attempting to do just that, and it doesn't seem to work. Because he did not believe that his own approach could be defended rationally, Rorty suggested that we ought to give it a try and "see how we get on." So far, we don't seem to be getting on very well.

Twenty-One

THE WAY OUT OF THE BOTTLE

Ludwig Wittgenstein didn't stay long at the monastery. In 1929, he returned to Cambridge to take up teaching again. When asked by administrators what title they should give his course, he answered that his subject was "Philosophy." He lectured on this topic for the next two decades, until just before his early death from cancer in 1951.

His work in the thirties and forties would end up being even more influential than his work before the First World War, but he was once again reluctant to put his ideas into print, and he didn't publish another book in his lifetime. When his *Philosophical Investigations* finally appeared two years after his death, it was greeted as perhaps the greatest work of twentieth-century philosophy.

What brought him back? As the fame of the *Tractatus* grew, Wittgenstein had come to think that the logical positivists and his other champions had not really understood what he'd been trying to say. With more philosophical history in hand, we can see how Wittgenstein was dealing in ideas handed down by Spinoza, Schopenhauer, and other thinkers well outside the tradition in which he was being situated. (A close friend from these years spoke later of "well-meaning commentators" who made

Wittgenstein's ideas seem "easily assimilable into the very intellectual milieu they were largely a warning against.")

As he attempted to resolve this misunderstanding, however, he found his earlier ideas themselves to be mistaken in important ways. In his own fashion, Wittgenstein had come around to the central insight of romantic idealism—that there is no neutral position from which questions of ultimate meaning can be settled. Indeed, there is no such thing as ultimate meaning.

The later Wittgenstein did not entirely reject his earlier views. He believed that the picture theory of language was incomplete rather than false. Picturing states of affairs is certainly one way that language signifies, but it is not the only way. Thus the *Tractatus* can be taken as correct if we stipulate that it describes a particular class of what Wittgenstein came to call "language-games," but it is mistaken to claim that it described all meaningful language-games, that any language not fitting its description is really a species of nonsense: "It is as if someone were to say, 'Playing a game consists in moving objects about on a surface according to certain rules . . . '—and we replied: You seem to be thinking of board-games, but they are not all the games there are."

Could we find a more comprehensive description than the picture theory, one that properly captures all forms of meaningful signification? What form could such a description take? Well, what is the definition of a "game"? That is, what distinguishes game playing from other forms of human behavior? This turns out to be a surprisingly difficult question to answer. We might say that a game is a pastime played by children for enjoyment, until we call to mind the professional athlete who plays for money and approaches this job with great seriousness. We might say that a game pits individuals or teams against each other, until we remember solitaire. But even in solitaire there is an objective and a clear way to win or lose, so perhaps this is the essential feature? Then what about a child's game of "house"? There doesn't seem to be any obvious definition that includes everything we mean by the word and excludes everything that we don't.

For Russell or the early Wittgenstein, this presents a problem in need of clarification. How can we say we know the definition of the class if we can't state the rule for membership in it? Yet our use of the word *game* is neither arbitrary nor incoherent. All of the things that we call games share a "family resemblance," as Wittgenstein puts it. They appear to be related, even if we can't in every case say they share the same features. Do I really know what a game is, if I can't give a better definition than this? Well, I use the word all the time without confusion. Other people seem to understand what I'm trying to say. What makes me think that they understand? Because they respond in a way that is consistent with my own sense of the term.

Still, is this enough? Without an explicit definition, how can I teach the word to a person who isn't familiar with it? By giving some examples of the way I use it. I will name or point out some games and say (or imply), "These are the kinds of things I call games." If it's important to me that the person have a sense of the full range of the term, I will be sure to include ball games and card games and board games among my examples. But if the question has come up in a particular context, this will alter my response. For example, if it's a rainy day, and I've asked my friend if he wants to play a game, and he asks what I mean, I will mention some of the games that we might play under the circumstances. It will be left to some future occasion for him to learn that outdoor sports can also be called "games."

Wittgenstein's example does double duty here. In trying to define the term *game*, we have noticed something important about the way language works, but we have also come to understand what he's getting at when he says that language itself might be understood as an assortment of language-games. He offers a brief list of different ways we can use language to signify, including "giving orders, and acting on them," "describing an object by its appearance, or by its measurements," "reporting an event," "cracking a joke," "solving a problem in applied arithmetic," "requesting, thanking, cursing, greeting, praying." Again, we see an obvious "family resemblance" here, but it's difficult to pull out a single feature common to all of these behaviors, such that we could say: *This* is what it is for something to signify; *this* is what makes certain vocalized sounds or marks on a page into language.

The way we learn how to play these language-games is much like the way we learn other games. Some games do have explicit and detailed rules, but reading the rule book is rarely the best way to learn the game. Instead someone who already knows it shows you how to play. This might involve explaining the game's purpose and letting you pick up the rest as you go. At what point in this picking-up process can you be said to know how to play? It isn't uncommon for a professional athlete to make a mistake that reveals he didn't understand some rather technical rule, but we would certainly not say in that case that he didn't "really" know how to play.

In the case of professional sports there are official arbiters plus high stakes that make properly following the rules feel important. And so it is for certain language-games—say, writing a term paper or a legal brief. But in most cases the rules are just worked out between the players. If a disagreement comes up, we settle it between ourselves. We may have recourse to a formal rule book if one exists and it is close to hand, but we might alternatively just rely on what we did the last time a similar case came up, or else just agree on the most sensible solution to keep the game moving. We might get halfway through a game before discovering that we've been taught to play it in slightly different ways, and we will have to arrive at some compromise. Of course, there are also times when we can't compromise, and the game breaks down.

There are rule books meant to cover the ground of all possible language-games within a particular language—i.e., dictionaries and usage guides. But they are inevitably incomplete, and we generally don't feel bound by their rules. If I say that I'm nauseous and someone notes that I've just said that I *cause* nausea rather than that I am experiencing it, I will tell that person he's wrong. It doesn't matter that he can produce a dictionary that insists I am really *nauseated.* I have always used the word *nauseous* this way, and so has everyone else I know. In my world, this just *is* what it means. If this use becomes sufficiently widespread, the dictionary will be updated to reflect this fact (as most actually have been in this particular case). But if the dictionary is simply a descriptive record of evolving usage, it has no final authority as a prescriptive rule book. Defining words is itself a language-game, rather than a necessary precursor to playing other language-games.

Without explicit definitions of things, isn't there always the possibility that people aren't really understanding each other? This was precisely the problem that concerned the early Wittgenstein. As he showed then, an explicit definition won't actually solve this problem, because it will have to be made out of words, and there will be the problem of defining all of them. Meaning can't be explained; it can only be shown.

If I point to a piece of paper and utter a sound, do I mean that sound to signify the material paper or the shape of the sheet? Or am I perhaps making a command: *Draw something* or *Bring that to me.* If I point to the paper, then point to the wall, then point to a cloud in the sky, repeating the sound each time, you will come to understand that I'm indicating the color white. But this is just showing you through use, in the same way I taught you the meaning of *game* by giving you examples of things I call games.

All of this might seem of only abstract interest, but it has profound implications. It is not just that the same word can mean different things in different contexts but that there is no such thing as what the word means outside of any context, because there is no such thing as meaning outside of contexts.

Taking words out of their context to establish some absolute atomic meaning is precisely what analytic philosophy was trying to do, and it did seem to be part of the early Wittgenstein's project, but the later Wittgenstein comes to sound at times like the most thoroughgoing postmodern relativist. "What a Copernicus or a Darwin really achieved," he wrote in a notebook from the time, "was not the discovery of a true theory but of a fertile new point of view."

One might object that the fact that meaning is relative does not mean that truth itself is relative. But how can there be truth without meaning? "What is true or false is what human beings *say*; and it is in their *language* that human beings agree," Wittgenstein tells us. "This is agreement not in opinions, but rather in form of life."

When we are ensconced in a particular form of life, we generally don't ask ourselves the kind of questions philosophers like to ask. "Philosophical problems arise when language *goes on holiday*," Wittgenstein writes. In other words, when we take language out of its context, when it stops doing its usual work, it becomes strange and perplexing. The rest of the time it simply gets the job done. We do have occasional confusions about game play, but these can usually be settled on a local level. This is familiar analytic-philosophical cleanup work, and that work is never done, because new problems always arise.

Not only can such problems generally be resolved, but we may actually be helped in resolving them by the implicit understanding that, after all, it's "just" a game—not in the sense that it's a trivial undertaking but in the sense that there is no absolute right answer to be discovered, that we are free to modify the rules in whatever way keeps things going smoothly. What won't help—what will likely only lead to more confusion—is seeking out the definitive answer to our question in some standard that transcends our particular game and gets to the essence of things. For there is no essence of things.

SOON AFTER RETURNING to Cambridge, Wittgenstein became obsessed by the need to offer confessions to various people in his life. He understood confession to be a particular kind of language-game: When we make a confession to another person, we don't simply want to convey some bare information about our prior actions; we want to get ourselves into a certain relationship with that person. We want to restore a lost sense of wholeness. "A confession," he noted to himself, "has to be a part of your new life."

The most significant of these efforts entailed returning to Otterhal, the Austrian town where he'd worked as a schoolteacher, to apologize to the boys he'd harmed. But other confessions involved relatively trivial matters. After the Nazis came to power, Wittgenstein grew deeply bothered by the fact that he had obscured his Jewish heritage, telling people that he had just one Jewish grandparent instead of three. He also confessed to one friend that he'd allowed him to believe that he'd never slept with a woman, though this was not the case.*

It's strange to see someone with such a seemingly relativistic view of the truth worrying so much over dishonest statements, but nothing was more important to Wittgenstein than integrity. He maintained throughout his early and late phases the sense that the great problem of life was ethical—the question was how to live. At the same time, he maintained that the generation of ethical rules was not philosophy's job. Indeed, ethical rules could never be stated outright.

Here the analogy of the game might help us one more time. It's obviously possible to play a game well or badly. To play a game well is, in a

---

* Most of Wittgenstein's romantic and sexual relationships were with men.

sense, the point of playing a game. But doing so is not simply a function of knowing and following the rules. The rules tell you how to play, but not how to excel.

This is further complicated by the fact that the best players are often unable to articulate how they do what they do. Either they are simply naturals or lengthy hours of practice have turned them into naturals. There is no truth to be conveyed here apart from these natural predilections and these practice hours. In fact, our self-consciousness, our need to keep asking unanswerable questions about flourishing, is part of what keeps us from flourishing. What we need are not explanations but examples. And we aren't meant to interpret these examples, to turn them into explanations. We are just meant to follow them.

Apart from helping to resolve the everyday disputes that come up in game play, philosophy can help us to live precisely by showing us again and again that there is no answer to the questions we've been asking: "Philosophy is a struggle against the bewitchment of our understanding by the resources of language." Here we find more of the common romantic idealist sense of life—that language and reason might be best understood as a kind of curse that alienates us from living instinctually. "The task of philosophy is to soothe the mind about meaningless questions," Wittgenstein wrote in one of his notebooks. "Whoever doesn't tend to such questions doesn't need philosophy."

Apart from soothing our mind, philosophy might actually liberate us, not by giving us the rule for life but by showing us that life can't be lived by a single rule. We are being held captive, Wittgenstein writes, by a *picture*. The reference to his own earlier work is explicit here. The desire to answer philosophy's questions is part of our problem. The goal of his later philosophy, Wittgenstein wrote, is to "show the fly the way out of the fly-bottle."

One of the implications of this approach is that an idea or an example might mean nothing to you at one point in your life, because it does not serve any purpose in the game you happen to be playing, but can feel decisive at some other point, when you have a use for it. This was the case for me with Wittgenstein's work. In the earlier parts of the story I've been telling, the early Wittgenstein exercised a major influence on me. It showed through the sublimity of logic the limitations of a particular form of atheism that I'd been trying to practice. I loved the austere, impersonal rigor of it, the fact that I was not meant to be communing with another mind but climbing up a ladder to self-evident truth. The more conversational later Wittgenstein didn't interest me. But when I returned to the later work in my early thirties, I responded much more powerfully, perhaps because I wanted to talk to somebody.

In one of the *Philosophical Investigation*'s most famous and influential passages, Wittgenstein considers the possibility of a "private language." The question is not whether you can play a language-game by yourself, which is clearly possible, or even whether you can play a made-up game that no one else knows. The question is whether there could be a language that one person knows that could not in principle be taught to another person. In other words, could a word be said to have a meaning if that meaning could never be shown or told to someone else?

Wittgenstein gives as a possible example a person who marks a calendar with the letter *S* every time he experiences a particular sensation. Let's say this sensation is one for which there is no word in common language: It is not exactly a pain or a pleasure, a tingle or an itch, and it does not occur in a particular place in the body to which you can point. There is no way to describe the sensation to someone else except as the sensation that causes you to write *S*, and no way to define *S* except as the thing you write to mark having experienced the sensation. Does this *S* have a meaning? Is it a sign of something?

How can you be entirely sure from day to day that you are using the *S* to describe the same sensation? What does it even mean for two sensations experienced on different days to be the "same" sensation? How close in kind do the qualitative experiences have to be? How could you distinguish a proper use of the sign from an improper one?

Wittgenstein concludes that private languages are not, after all, possible. Some commentators have taken him to be saying that there is no such thing as private *experience*, as though he shared Daniel Dennett's view that qualia are a philosophical invention, a bewitchment of language. But he makes quite clear that he doesn't mean this. His point is not that a private experience without a public expression is "a Nothing," but that "a Nothing would render the same service as a Something about which nothing could be said." In rejecting private language, he has "only rejected the grammar which tends to force itself upon us here."

Wittgenstein clearly believes in the existence of ineffable subjective experiences. But such experiences just *are*. Taken alone, they do not have any significance. It is by way of language (understood in the broadest sense) that experience is given significance, and unlike experience itself, language cannot be private. Here we find one way out of the nihilism of extreme relativism. We can't just make up the rules as we go along, because if we do, no one can play along with us. Experience, thought, being—these may be things we can have entirely to ourselves. But for meaning we need someone else.

POSTLUDE

The Man Who Needs Infinite Help

Tempted to Exist

The someone else that I needed arrived the same week my first novel came out.

This was not the novel with the Nabokovian title that I'd labored over throughout my twenties, though I had managed to complete that one. By the time it was done, it had turned into the story of an orphaned young artist living in the ruins of the old capital soon after the fall of a great imperial civilization. He wanders the city, trying through his art to recover what has been destroyed. In retrospect it seems an almost comically obvious metaphor for the situation I'd placed myself in, but I'd had no interest in using the boy's situation to work through my own. I meant for the story to feel completely unconnected to life, a great monument to my own imagination, sealed off hermetically from the reality around it. The result was mannered, overwritten, cold to the touch. The agents and editors who read it professed admiration for my ambition and a willingness to read whatever I wrote next, but they wanted no part of this effort. My would-be masterpiece would never see the light of day.

Plenty of writers spend years on apprentice work that winds up consigned to a desk drawer, but I didn't think I had much time left, and giving up on the novel devastated me. To distract myself, I started a less ambitious project, inspired by some other books on my grandmother's Long Island shelves, a fifty-one-volume set called the Harvard Classics. I suggested to one of the more enthusiastic agents that I might write a memoir about reading the entire set in a year. She assured me that she could sell the proposal. After seven years of painstaking effort had amounted to nothing, seven weeks of relatively straightforward work earned me my first book contract.

The advance was modest, but it allowed me to spend a year reading and writing, which was all I wanted to do. Though the whole undertaking felt slightly frivolous—I was riding a boom in "annualist" stunt books, the opposite of my idea of artistic seriousness—I was nearing thirty with nothing to show for myself, and I liked the idea of having a book under my belt. My postmodern doorstop could wait for another day; in the meantime I'd be published.

The memoir recounted in somewhat different terms many of the life experiences I've described above. (I left out the angels.) It also memorialized the last days of my mother's sister, Mimi, who was my godmother and one of the most devout people I knew. She was diagnosed with melanoma near the beginning of that year, and she was gone before the year was through. I spent many days in between sitting beside her while she suffered. She had lived a hard life, widowed while pregnant with her second child, always scrambling to get by as a single mother, and just as both her sons had been launched into the world, she died a painful death. I marveled at this cosmic injustice, and I attempted to use the classics of Western civilization to make some sense of it. I came to understand the project I'd backed into as part of my larger effort to displace my family's religious tradition with a secular literary one.

The result was not a major work of art, but it was a breakthrough for me, because it taught me that the struggle I was going through might be my real subject. I realized something that every worthwhile artist must realize eventually—that art must be made *out* of something, something other than just the desire to make art. Even Flaubert had not in the end written a great book about nothing. He needed the commonplace predicament of Emma Bovary to create something worthy of his talents. If he could not make meaning out of pure style, I certainly could not. What happened on the page had to be an expression of what I already found meaningful.

As soon as I sent the finished manuscript off to my editor, I began work on a new novel, set unmistakably in the world I actually occupied, about a young, lapsed Catholic writer and his fascination with an old girlfriend who has converted to Catholicism. I put into it all my quarrels with God, but I also tried to address the fact that I couldn't quite get over him. The book took four years to write, and it was the first thing I'd done of which I felt really proud. After many revisions, I sold it to a well-respected literary publisher.

Given all that I wanted (or thought I wanted), this should have been the highlight of my life to that point. Instead it coincided with the most severe bout of depression I had ever faced. For several months, I was almost completely paralyzed with dread. I thought seriously about killing myself. What kept me from it was not any sense that I wanted to go on living but the thought of the pain my death would cause my family, who had supported me through all my misbegotten days. With their help, I pulled myself out of the worst of it, made the necessary journey described by Freud, from neurotic misery to ordinary unhappiness. That's where I imagined I would stay for the rest of my life.

It's not that I was never happy. I was still capable of moments of profound joy, moments when I felt lifted out of my troubles, up to a higher plane. Usually these moments were prompted by an encounter with art or a stretch when my own writing was going especially well. Time would quicken, and I would find on the page words that were smarter, funnier, more interesting than I was, words that seemed to come from something greater than me. I would feel again that I had been given access to some larger truth about the world. But when the moment passed, I was quick to shut that feeling out. For there was no greater truth. And I would remind myself of those angelic visitations from my childhood and their perfectly mundane explanation.

While still at the lowest point of my depression, I ended a relationship I'd been in for several years. I'd been dissatisfied in it almost from the beginning. I'd been dissatisfied in all of my relationships. As the common element between them, I could only assume that I was the problem. I was a frustratingly ambivalent partner. I drank too much and fell into dark moods in which I cut myself off from the people around me. I could never really commit myself to anyone, although not for what I take to be the usual reasons that men in their late twenties and early thirties can't commit. I was secretly sure that I wouldn't live long, and leaving behind some significant work seemed a far more urgent task than having a happy, functional life in the meantime. I wanted companionship, but I also wanted to dedicate myself entirely to the creation of my own meaning. That a life shared with others might play some part in that creation hardly occurred to me.

I told myself that the relationship I was ending would be my last. I wanted to live in a cell, read and write, and shut out the world. If there were such a thing as atheist monasteries, I would have joined one. Instead I answered an email about a room for rent in Fort Greene. My roommates were two men who'd become friends as undergraduates at NYU. They were both a decade younger than I was, fun-loving, and gay. They liked to host all-night parties catered by shirtless bartenders. I liked to drink alone and read works of Romanian existentialism with titles like *The Temptation to Exist*. We got along wonderfully.

After finishing the memoir, I had taken an editorial job at a magazine. The pay was bad but sufficient to live on when combined with my writing income. The first novel had not yet been published, but I was hard at work on the next, an angry drama about the superficiality of contemporary culture in which a failed actor sells a sex tape and becomes a reality show star.

(I'd settled on the subject because the woman I'd just broken up with had hated the idea.) The room was a sublet, and I figured I'd be there for a few months while I pulled myself together. After a year, I re-upped the lease. I was in one of those transitional phases that don't transition into anything, eventually just becoming your life. Some mornings I would wake up especially hungover and think, *You can't go on like this.* Then I would give up drinking for a while. After several unhappy weeks or months, I would remember drinking as one of my few sources of relief from misery, and I would start again.

I might have made other efforts at change, but I wasn't at all sure I *wanted* to be happy. Happiness seemed like a rather shallow response to the realities of the human condition. Life was suffering. Everything that I believed told me that. We were all living in a dark cave, and none of the things we took for meaningful were even real. I had freed myself from the chains, and I had come to recognize the shadows on the wall for what they were—insubstantial appearances. But I had also come to understand that there was no way out, apart from death. The idea that one could somehow escape to some higher reality was just another shadow dream. I vacillated between a romantic pessimism that wallowed in these facts and a romantic affirmation that attempted to will meaning in the face of them. This proved easier said than done. After all, didn't it take a Superman to do that?

In the midst of such edifying thoughts, I ran into an old friend at a party, and she offered to introduce me to a woman she thought I'd like. I politely agreed but never followed up, which was my general approach in such situations. It was simpler than admitting you'd decided to become an atheist monk. My friend prodded me, so I finally emailed to make a date.

Everything changed that night. Almost immediately I felt something coming back to life in me that I'd thought was gone forever. I could tell you that A—— was beautiful, smart, and funny, all of which is true but seems almost trivial beside the deeper truth. She was, in a way I could not articulate, *right* for me. I realized very quickly that I wanted to spend as much time with her as I possibly could. I also realized that I was making a terrible impression. It had been a long time since I'd enjoyed myself around another person, and I was out of practice. Usually under such circumstances I would drink to calm my nerves, but I knew that getting drunk would not make me look good, and I suddenly cared very much about looking good. At the same time, I suspected that abstaining from drinking entirely would suggest I had a problem (which I did, but that didn't mean I wanted to suggest it). So I closely monitored both my intake and my behavior, acting wooden and self-conscious.

In an effort to impress, I talked at length about my writing and my editorial job. A—— loved books as much as I did, and she had worked briefly for a literary magazine herself, but she had no interest in that world and she was not the kind of person who judged other people on what they did for a living. When I told her about my sex tape book, she responded to the idea immediately, and I finally felt I'd found a toehold.

"I love comic novels," she said.

"It's not a comedy," I explained with patience. "It's a drama of moral choice, an indictment of the superficiality of contemporary culture."

She nodded diplomatically.

"It sounds like a comedy."

She agreed to a second date, which didn't go much better than the first, though it confirmed my feelings for her. I later learned that she was ready to give up on me at this point, but she talked it over with another mutual friend, and she decided to give me one more chance. I knew none of that at the time, but I sensed that the situation called for a different approach. Instead of trying to impress her, I tried to make her laugh. This turned out to be exactly what she wanted. We discovered that we had the same sense of humor. I realized that I was still capable of being happy, that I was capable of making someone else happy. And making A—— happy seemed the best possible way I could be spending my time.

Within six months I'd moved out of the room in Fort Greene. Within another six, we were engaged. Somehow I was giving in to the temptation to exist. On the day I proposed, a publisher made an offer on the sex tape book. (It was now a comic novel.) A week before we got married, I quit drinking. Though my struggles with alcohol had been a dominant feature of my entire adult life, the end of these struggles did not come with any great drama attached. I wasn't quitting in an effort to find happiness; I was quitting *because* I was happy. After fifteen years, I had wandered quite by accident out of the cave. I was standing in the sunlight.

This change created a strange new problem. For I had already committed myself to unhappiness. It was more than a disposition: It was a worldview. *Get out as early as you can, and don't have any kids yourself.* What if I didn't want out anymore—and even wanted kids? It was not just that I was happy but that this happiness was not of my own making. It had not come about by a heroic act of Nietzschean will. It had come from outside my own head. My overwhelming feeling in those days was not despair but gratitude, not just toward A—— but toward the world that had brought us together. I had no framework for this gratitude, nowhere to put it that might make sense of it. Pessimism had finally provided a plausible answer to questions I'd been working over for so long. What would it mean to give it up?

The best thing that had ever happened to me had undone fifteen years of work. Perhaps you'd think that it had made such work unnecessary, that the quest for meaning would no longer be relevant. The opposite was true. My life was filled with love, but there was something in this love that demanded I make sense of it. The light and the warmth of this sun were baffling. Where were they coming from? What did they mean?

I don't want to suggest that everything was suddenly perfect, and that this perfection struck me as a problem. Of course I was still subject to all the usual ups and downs of life. I still worried a great deal about mortality. One of the reasons that pessimistic philosophies encourage detachment is that attachment can be a source of suffering. I understood that I might lose A—— at any time. For that matter, I might lose my own life just as I'd come to want to live it. If reality were all joy or all suffering, I thought, the matter would be simple. Instead it was both, and this was the perplexing thing.

Piercing the Cloud

One way to understand the historical story I've told in this book is as an ongoing battle against skepticism. To modern ears, that word has a largely positive connotation. Skepticism should not be battled but encouraged. A skeptic is someone who refuses to get taken in.

If you are an atheist who doesn't want to be identified as an atheist—perhaps because you don't want to be defined by your rejection of one particular nonexistent entity among all the entities that don't exist—you might call yourself a skeptic, and this suggests that you don't believe anything without sufficient cause. You might take pleasure in debunking superstitions and conspiracy theories and all manner of unwarranted beliefs beyond the strictly religious. The point is simply that you don't take things on faith.

But in the early modern era, skepticism was a problem for precisely those people who wanted to move beyond the old religious ways. While Montaigne believed that skepticism could temper religious passions, he also believed that it left us little choice but to take certain points on faith. Nearly everyone who followed after him took Montaigne's Pyrrhonian skepticism as the danger they were trying to avoid. We need beliefs in order to put one foot in front of the other, and if we want the world to be a livable place, we need at least some of these beliefs to be *shared* beliefs. The skeptic does not believe without sufficient cause, but what amount of cause is sufficient? What standard could be established that is not itself subject to skepticism?

Here a better contemporary analogy than religious skeptics might be climate skeptics or vaccine skeptics, the people on social media who insist that they're "just asking questions" about some settled empirical matter, the ones who post a link to a long piece of pseudoscience with the comment "Something to think about . . ." This kind of skeptic is the spreader of conspiracy theories rather than the debunker of them. (The opposite of believing something, C. S. Lewis once wrote, is not believing nothing but believing everything.) There's a healthy dose of romantic idealism to this contemporary skepticism; it presumes that expert consensus is largely driven by power structures rather than disinterested study, and it views the questioning of settled facts as the expression of one's own reality.

The epistemic chaos this view has brought to our culture is just the thing that the early modern thinkers feared most. At the time, religious figures insisted that such chaos was the unavoidable alternative to a reliance on tradition, revelation, and ecclesiastic fiat, so skepticism became a problem to solve for those who wanted to move beyond these forms of authority. They needed some firm foundation on which to build real knowledge of the world. For Bacon, that foundation was practical efficacy, i.e., the ability to achieve material ends. For Descartes it was the indubitable existence of the thinking thing. For Locke it was sense perception. Hume mitigated skepticism with custom. Kant tried to contain it to the noumenal world. For Schopenhauer the one certain thing was the will. For Camus it was the absurd.

All of these appeals had proved insufficient to me, leaving only the romantic idealist option: There is no foundation; we are standing over an abyss. But this had proved unlivable—and now it was proving untrue. For

I could tell that my foundation was sound. I just wanted to know what was underfoot. So I told myself, *Suppose you start with love.* That was the one clear and certain thing in my life. What would it mean to start there? To begin with the certain reality of that love and build whatever could be built on top of it? If I took this for true, what else would have to be true with it?

To believe in love—not as a physical sensation, a neurochemical process in the brain, an adaptive strategy blindly hit upon by the genes in control of us survival machines, but as a foundational reality—means abandoning strict materialism, for the kind of love I'm talking about simply can't be reduced to physical processes. It also means abandoning the idealism that says that the world we experience is entirely or even largely our own creation, that we project upon the raw facts whatever meaning and value and order we find there. From this perspective, love is a "mood," part of the subjective apparatus with which we take in the objects of experience. But to really feel love is to be certain that it is not simply a projection, just as to stand in the warmth and the light of the sun is to be certain that the sun exists outside ourselves.

Starting with love means acknowledging the reality of other people—the people we love, the people who love us, but also the people we fail to love, those whose love we lack but might one day earn. The cardboard cutouts of the romantic idealist world are not fit objects of love. Truly loving someone requires taking their joys and sufferings seriously on their own terms, recognizing their subjective world as every bit as rich and full and important as yours. Accepting the possibility of love from someone requires the same.

It also means acknowledging the reality of the physical world. Love makes us aware of the boundaries of time and space; it makes us feel the pain of separation as well as the pleasure of proximity, the frustration of waiting and the joy of fulfillment. Love is an intimation of the infinite that brings an acute sense of finitude. The people we love will turn to dust. We ourselves will die without ever having enough of what we love. In many ways, these were the very realizations that had set me on this journey, and I didn't have any better response to them now.

Real love requires freedom, for it cannot be coerced. This freedom includes the freedom to reject love, to turn away from the good of the world. At the same time, to love another person is to recognize them *as* a person—that is, as something with an essential self, not just a collection of free choices. It requires that certain things endure even as most things pass away.

Everything I'd learned in my years of study told me that this could not all be true. No one yet had explained how subjective mental selves could operate within an objective physical space. No one yet had reconciled individual freedom with a law-governed world. One way or another, you had to choose. All I could say in response was that my starting point, my foundational principle, told me otherwise.

AROUND THE TIME of our engagement, I suggested to A—— that we go to church one Sunday. I didn't imagine making a regular habit of it, but I wanted to give it a try. You might object that I must have skipped a step somewhere. How do I get from "starting with love" to going to church? But I didn't make the suggestion out of any metaphysical commitment. It was just a thing to do. We both agreed that it would be nice to have a sense of community, time for reflection, the experience of ritual. These happened to be among the things my own religious upbringing had offered me, and now that I was opening myself up to the world, I found myself missing them. I'd been given a great gift, and everyday life didn't provide many ways to express gratitude for such gifts.

Like me, A—— was an atheist, but she had been raised Episcopalian, and there was a popular Episcopal parish right up the block. The church had a large organ and a full choir. The liturgy was beautiful, the priest kind and welcoming. The Episcopal Mass is nearly identical to the Catholic one, but they welcome any baptized Christian to join in Communion. On our second Sunday there, I did so for the first time in a decade. Of course, it was not precisely the same thing as the Catholic sacrament. I was not really being asked to commit to anything when I walked up to the altar that day. If I had been, I wouldn't have done it.

We returned a few more times in the months that followed. This practice should have been perfect for me. It provided the things I thought I was after—community, reflection, ritual. We could go when we wanted, stay home when we didn't, and we didn't have to question too deeply whether or how we believed what was being said there. The progressive parish we were attending seemed particularly careful not to make doctrinal demands. I had nothing but respect for the regular parishioners for whom this church was an important part of a life of service to others. But its very nearness to Catholicism made me feel I was missing something. This was an entirely personal response; it would obviously not have occurred had I not been raised in the Catholic faith. But I couldn't help it. I felt like a lifelong smoker sucking on a vape pen that delivered all the necessary chemicals without the hit to the lungs. The very thing that had allowed me to participate—the fact that participation didn't require belief—began to feel like a problem. Something in me wanted to be asked to believe. I wanted to find out whether or not I could do it.

This desire had arrived one Sunday morning while I listened to a reading I knew well, from John's First Epistle:

> Beloved, let us love one another, for love is from God, and whoever loves has been born of God and knows God. Any-

> one who does not love does not know God, because God is love. In this the love of God was made manifest among us, that God sent his only Son into the world, so that we might live through him. In this is love, not that we have loved God but that he loved us and sent his Son to be the propitiation for our sins. Beloved, if God so loved us, we also ought to love one another. No one has ever seen God; if we love one another, God abides in us and his love is perfected in us.

The claim that "God is love" has become a spiritual cliché, and it can be hard to recapture its full force. Analytic philosophers talk often about the confusion that arises from the deceptively simple verb *to be.* To say "James is tall" is to attach an attribute to James. It does not follow from this statement that "tall is James." To say instead "James is the third one on the right" or "James is my dad" is to identify James, and here the transitive statement holds up. When listening to that familiar reading in that moment, I understood that the statement "God is love" identifies rather than describes. God is love, it says, and love is God.

It is stated repeatedly and explicitly throughout the Bible that love is the meaning of the world, the sum total of God's teaching and his great demand of us. "Faith, hope, and love abide," Saint Paul writes in a passage read so often at weddings that even most atheists could probably quote it by heart. "But the greatest of these is love." He goes on to say that even a "faith that moves mountains" is worth nothing if not accompanied by love.

This passage from John says something more than all that. It does not just say that God is loving, not even infinitely loving. It does not just say that love is God's great desire for all of us. It says that God *is* love. It says that when we love, God becomes a part of us. In other words, it says that the thing I had come to understand as my foundation, the thing that had united me with A——, the thing that had brought order to my shambolic life, was the same thing I had been running away from all this time. The warmth and the light in which I was standing were God.

Wittgenstein remarked that all statements of identity, if they are true, must be tautologies. But if they are tautologies, they don't need to be stated at all. If *God* and *love* are simply two words for the same thing, why not stick to one? As I considered this biblical passage anew, I could already hear the New Atheist objection in my head: "If you want to use *God* as a synonym for *love*, that's your business, but you and I both know what people actually mean by the word *God* and what they actually mean by the word *love*, and they're not the same thing."

But what *do* people actually mean by the word *God*? I have intentionally avoided that question throughout this book, but now it must be faced.

THE IDEA THAT we might know God directly—that God might "abide in us," as John puts it—through love is the core of the Christian mystical tradition, whose works I began reading around this time. It's significant for this tradition that love is God's identity rather than an attribute, because Christian mystics generally advocate the *via negativa*—that is, the negative path toward an understanding of God, which strips away attributes rather than applying them.

Like the Kantian thing in itself, God exists outside of time and space, beyond the range of human understanding through reason. The *via negativa* tells us that any attempt to describe God through conceptual terms—even terms like *goodness* or *perfection*—is bound to get things wrong. All of the language we attach to God risks taking us further from him. (For example, I have just used a masculine pronoun, though God certainly has no gender.) But this does not mean that God must remain, like the thing in itself, forever unknown to us. Because we are creatures made in God's image, we do have a capacity for a kind of knowledge of God.

The fourteenth-century English treatise *The Cloud of Unknowing*—one of the great guides to the Christian contemplative life—claims that all rational beings have both a "faculty of knowledge" and a "faculty of love." "God can well be loved, but he cannot be thought," the *Cloud*'s author tells us. "By love he can be grasped and held, but by thought, neither grasped nor held." There stands between us and God a great cloud of unknowing. The goal of the contemplative life on earth is not so much to reach God but to reach that cloud, which can be "pierced" through "thrusts of love." We are called away from conceptual thought, away from acts of the intellect, toward acts of the heart. It is only when we arrive at the unknowing place that some glimpse of God becomes possible.

"There are three things which prevent us from hearing the eternal Word," writes the thirteenth-century theologian Meister Eckhart. "The first is corporality, the second is multiplicity and the third is temporality." When we detach from our own bodily and temporal self through love, when we transcend multiplicity for the union of love, we become "God's only begotten son," and

> then God presses so urgently upon us and acts as if his divine being were about to collapse and become nothing in itself so that he can reveal to us the whole abyss of his Godhead, the abundance of his being and his nature. God urgently desires that this should become ours just as it is his. Such a person is established in God's knowledge and in God's love and is nothing other than what God is.

Around the same time and place as the composition of *The Cloud of Unknowing*, an anchoress named Julian, who lived in seclusion at a church in Norwich, had a series of visions while suffering from a near-fatal illness. Among them was this:

> And in this vision he also showed me a little thing, the size of a hazelnut, lying in the palm of my hand, and it was as round as a ball, as it seemed to me. I looked at it and thought, "What can this be?" And the answer came to me in a general way, like this, "It is all that is made." I wondered how it could last, for it seemed to me so small that it might have disintegrated suddenly into nothingness. And I was answered in my understanding, "It lasts, and always will, because God loves it; and in the same way everything has its being through the love of God."

This is a common refrain throughout the mystical tradition—that the objects of time and space that are within the realm of human comprehension are vanishingly small beside the love of God, which makes them possible. Yet God spends his love on this creation. This is the only reason it exists at all. Julian of Norwich was filled with the sense that all of God's work had been done for her alone, and she encouraged others embarking on the way of contemplation to see things in this way.

A hundred years later, the Carmelite nun Teresa of Ávila, who also suffered from severe bouts of painful illness, became famous for the states of rapturous ecstasy she entered through the practice of contemplative prayer, which she described in erotically charged language. "It doesn't seem He is satisfied in truly bringing the soul to himself," she wrote of these experiences, "but it seems he desires the body even though it is mortal and, on account of the many offenses it has committed, made of such foul clay."

A striking number of the most significant Christian mystics were women. This is certainly in part because such direct experience of the divine could be had outside the institutional mechanisms that have always favored men. Both Julian and Teresa were treated with suspicion by many church authorities, who were threatened by their direct access to religious experience. But both were eventually recognized as saints of the church, and Teresa (who had been brought before the Inquisition in her lifetime) became the first woman named a church "Doctor"—one of the most significant theological thinkers in the church's history.

There have been very few women's voices heard in this book, and I'd like to blame this fact entirely on historical prejudices—women's voices were generally not heard during the historical periods I've been considering. But there may also be some prejudice of my own. After all, this is not simply an intellectual history but a record of the books I chose to read during these years. I don't want to compound the problem with speculation about gender differences, but I have often noted how many of the great spiritual examples I've had in my life have been women, including members of my immediate family.

While my intellectual upbringing owes a great deal to the Jesuit priests who ran my high school, the school's student life was largely managed by a nun named Nora Cronin, a member of the Sisters of the Presentation of the Blessed Virgin Mary. Sister Nora died more than twenty years ago, but to this day when I want to call to mind the virtues of a Christian life toward which I aspire, I picture her.

It has been widely noted that the New Atheist movement was largely populated by men, and particularly by men of an intellectually aggressive sort. I'm not suggesting for a moment that women are on the whole less suited to intellectual approaches to spiritual questions. Perhaps Wittgenstein's greatest student was the Catholic philosopher G. E. M. "Elizabeth" Anscombe, whose reading of her mentor has influenced my own religiously tinged sense of his work. It may, however, be that the drive that dominated my life throughout these years—the tendency to treat life as a problem to be solved by the intellect, a thing that must be mastered by being understood—is more common among men, while the humility and the willingness to live with perplexity that mysticism requires is more common among women.

Teresa insisted that she was forced into the contemplative path toward God because of her "inability to work discursively with the intellect." In a slightly comic moment in her autobiography, she speaks of the many learned men who "wanted to explain what the Lord was giving me so that I would be able to speak about it," and she admits that her "dullness was truly so great that their explanations benefited me neither little nor much." But while she struggles for the words to explain her experiences, "His Majesty when He desires, teaches me everything in a moment."

Contemporary atheists often treat mysticism as a kind of intellectual cheat. Now that science has rendered absurd the actual claims of actual theists—claims about a magic bearded man in the sky who built the world in six days six thousand years ago—those who want the comforts of belief without embarrassment have retreated to this philosophical mumbo jumbo. They want to place their belief safely outside the reach of empirical science, because they know it can't be defended there.

In reality, the mystical conception of the divine is not a modern response to scientific threats. It is as old as humanity's effort to understand our place in the universe. It played a prominent part in ancient Greek philosophy from the pre-Socratics to the second-century Neoplatonists who influenced early Christianity. *The Cloud of Unknowing* is a gloss on an earlier Christian mystical text that likely dates to the fifth century. Mysticism is present throughout various non-Western traditions that are generally treated as pantheistic or animistic or even athcistic. It is so widespread that Schopenhauer, among others, thought it was the default position for anyone who had not been ruined by the materialist and rule-bound tradition of Jewish monotheism.

Ironically, the Jewish mystical tradition is actually among the most robust and complex. It was formalized into the Kabbalah in the early medieval era, around the same time that Julian and the *Cloud* author were writing, but it dates to biblical times. Several works in the Hebrew Scripture (along with the Book of Revelation in the New Testament) are best understood as accounts of mystical experience. The term *mystical* comes from the Greek for "hidden," and early mysticism was grounded in reading scripture for secret meanings. One of the chief texts taken up by mystical readers was the Song of Songs, the Hebrew Scripture's collection of surprisingly erotic love poems, which mystics took as expressions of God's love.

The great twentieth-century rabbi and philosopher of religion Abraham Joshua Heschel was a scholar of Jewish mysticism. He spoke of religion emerging from our "sense of the ineffable," and he sought a way for philosophy to recapture the "treasures of higher incomprehension" that it had surrendered to poets and mystics. Philosophers had been "enticed by the promise of the known," but "without the sense of the ineffable there are no metaphysical problems, no awareness of being as being, of value as value."

In my experience, such talk tends to exasperate scientific materialists. How can you claim to believe in something if you can't say anything *about* the thing in which you claim to believe? What does that belief even entail? The answer is that the belief entails a form of life. (The author of the *Cloud* frequently uses this expression, so beloved by Wittgenstein.) If you accept the empiricist belief that truth is a matter of a correspondence between a mental picture and the physical world, this mystical view will not make any sense. But what if the correspondence view itself does not make sense?

Well, the scientific materialist says, if you can't describe what it is you believe, you can hardly expect to convince me of it. But mystics by and large are not trying to convince anyone of anything. The *Cloud* and most similar guidebooks are addressed to novices who have explicitly sought out their teaching. Such books often spend a great deal of time warning away those who don't have the capacity for the contemplative life. This exasperates scientific materialists all the more. If you won't even *try* to change my mind, what are we supposed to argue about?

But mystics—like Rorty's ironists—are not concerned with argument. They are engaged with what Rorty would call "redescription." They are simply saying how it is for them. Many mystics—including Julian and Teresa—wrote down their experiences only after their superiors compelled them to do so for the sake of other believers. In the process, they were constantly aware of the ways that language fell short of capturing their experience.

Mysticism is so widespread that it becomes tempting to detach these thinkers from their particular traditions and see them as together comprising a single tradition. The mystics of all traditions appeal to spiritual seekers who don't want to be bound to explicit expressions of faith. Such seekers might fruitfully read the Zohar on one day and the Sufi poet Rumi on the next. But most mystics do understand themselves as practicing within particular traditions. Another twentieth-century scholar of Jewish mysticism, Gershom Scholem, has written powerfully about the complex interplay between mysticism and tradition. Many mystics have the same fraught relationship to authority experienced by Julian and Teresa. Formal religious institutions have a fairly shameful history of treating mystics as a threat to their teaching authority, but they also recognize profound religious experience as the ultimate lifeblood of all they teach. Meanwhile, the mystics themselves generally understand that their experiences have their full meaning only within their traditions.

For Heschel and Scholem, the Jewish self-conception of their status as chosen people was central to an understanding of God's need for mankind. Julian and Teresa both went to great lengths to insist that everything they described was consistent with the teaching of "Holy Church." Nearly every faith attempts to strike some balance between creedal doctrines that can be conveyed explicitly and practices that are meant to provide direct contact with the ineffable truth of the divine. Toward the end of his life, Saint Thomas Aquinas—the greatest of all Catholic philosophers and the one most committed to putting church teaching into rationally comprehensible terms—had a mystical experience after which he said that everything he'd written "seemed as straw" to him.

A Superabundant Light

One weekend when A—— did not feel like joining me on our new Sunday-morning routine, I left our apartment and headed instinctively in the opposite direction, toward the local Catholic parish. Over the next month or two, I went there whenever A—— stayed home. I knew that she had serious reservations about the Catholic Church—about the status of women within it, about its official teachings on various social questions, about the manifest institutional corruption that showed itself in things like the horrifying clerical abuse scandals. While she was happy enough to come along to Episcopal services, she would not have wanted to go to Catholic Mass, and I had not asked her to.

I shared many of her reservations, but when I found myself free to go where I wished, the Catholic church was where I wished to go. I could not explain this impulse even to myself. I was simply answering a call in my heart. This went on for several more weeks, until A—— explained kindly that we were making a compromise that pleased neither of us. I did not really want to go to the Episcopal church, but she did not really want to go to church at all. She proposed that we take our Sunday mornings for ourselves: If I wanted to go to the Catholic church, I should just go, and she would spend the time as she wanted.

For several months, I told no one but A——that I was going to Mass every Sunday. It would have pleased my parents to hear it, but I still wasn't sure from week to week whether I would keep it up. If anyone had asked, I would not have said that I'd returned to the fold. In fact, I still considered myself an atheist. I didn't take Communion, and I didn't say the creed when the time came to declare our faith. Mostly I just listened—listened in a way I might never have done without having taken all those years away.

What I heard surprised me. It wasn't that the teachings had changed over the previous decade, or that I had not really understood them when I rejected them. Granted, I understood them differently after years of wandering, but what surprised me was the extent to which what I heard spoke to my deepest needs.

I heard the expression of a worldview that recognized both our human freedom and our human limitations, one that had room in its picture of reality for great suffering and great joy, one that acknowledged that our lives on this earth were short and bound to come to dust but gave us cause to do something with them in the meantime. I found a balance between the material reality of the physical world and the spiritual reality of the individual person. I found beauty and humanity's capacity both to create and enjoy it treated as essential features of reality rather than evolutionary accidents. I was told that I wasn't going to figure everything out, that certain things would remain always mysterious, that my greatest problems could be solved only through love. Perhaps most important, I was told to stop worrying so much over the riddle of my own existence and to try to serve others.

This all sounds rather vague, so I will do my best to describe this worldview in the terms that I've been using throughout this book. Simply put, the purpose of our existence is to know and love the created order and through doing so to know and love God. Love is the cause of the world, in the full Aristotelian sense of that word: It is the efficient cause, the thing that brought the world about, and it is the final cause, the end or purpose for which the world exists. We are physical matter animated by spirit, that is what makes us whole persons, and any picture that leaves out one or the other is incomplete.

Because we are both matter and spirit, we have the capacity to know both the natural and the supernatural order, to know the physical world, to know other people and ourselves, and even to know God. Human reason is one of God's greatest gifts to us, and science of all kinds—that is, the application of human reason to sense perception—is a powerful tool for understanding God's creation. But there is a limit to what can be known through reason, and we also have a capacity for knowledge that does not come by way of sense experience. This knowledge comes through the grace of God, and it is knowledge we gain through love. The Scriptures and the historical church are a great repository of this knowledge, but they both attempt to put a truth beyond human understanding into human terms, and so they must always be understood as provisional, incomplete, imperfect.

What these provisional, incomplete, and imperfect messengers are telling us is simple: We are here to love. We are pilgrims on this earth, it is not our final resting place, and the goods of this world are not what ultimately matters, but there is goodness here. Because the material world is God's loving creation, we cannot understand it as fundamentally debased. We are not simply meant to endure our time on earth, and we are not meant to escape our physical bodies. We are meant to enjoy the fruits of God's creation. We are also meant to be stewards of this creation, to care for it and for each other.

Taking all this together, I found a metaphysics, an epistemology, and an ethics that all converged on the thing I had already accepted as my foundational starting point. This may sound like an eccentric rendering of Catholic thought, but it is actually more or less the official one. "If man exists," the very first chapter of the Catholic catechism tells us, "it is because God has created him through love, and through love continues to hold him in existence." The catechism speaks of a universal religious impulse—the heart's desire for God—that has been expressed in various forms throughout human history. It says that we can know God through study of the world and examination of our own selves, but that we also have the revelation found in Scripture and church teaching.

Because God is "the inexpressible, the incomprehensible, the invisible, the ungraspable," the truth of biblical and ecclesiastical teaching is limited. "Our human words always fall short of the mystery of God," and that includes the words of the church itself. We are constantly at risk of mistaking God for our human representations of God. The catechism's first chapter ends with a quote from Aquinas's expression of the *via negativa*: "Concerning God, we cannot grasp what he is, but only what he is not, and how other beings stand in relation to him."

I can already hear the objections: That catechism goes on for another eight hundred pages! All this business about love could describe nearly any faith, but Catholics believe quite a bit more than that. Catholics believe in the virgin birth, and the Resurrection of the body, and the transubstantiation of the Eucharist, and the existence of hell. They believe in clerical celibacy and papal infallibility and abstaining from meat on Fridays during Lent.

And so they do. I'm not attempting to deny these beliefs, or even to downplay them. But there is a difference between a worldview and the beliefs that worldview sustains. Scientific materialists believe that light is both a wave and a particle, but knowing this tells us very little about scientific materialism. To understand the worldview, you need to know *why* they hold this belief, and what they think it means to believe it. What I've been trying to convey for the past few hundred pages is that your worldview determines not just what but how you believe. For two people ensconced in two different worldviews to examine each other's individual beliefs out of context and attempt to determine their plausibility without first settling that question can only lead to confusion and misunderstanding. That is why I've spent so much time in this book trying to consider different worldviews from within.

That is also, incidentally, precisely why the catechism begins where it does:

> Before expounding the church's faith, as confessed in the creed, celebrated in the liturgy, and lived in observance of God's commandments and in prayer, we must first ask what "to believe" means. Faith is man's response to God, who reveals himself and gives himself to man, at the same time giving man a superabundant light as he searches for the ultimate meaning of life.

I would not read those lines for several more years, but a superabundant light to guide my continued search for the ultimate meaning of life is a pretty good way to describe what I found when I started going to Mass again.

WHILE TELLING THE STORY of romantic idealism, I largely left out a key figure who contributed to the tradition but falls uneasily within it. Søren Kierkegaard was born in Copenhagen in 1813, halfway between the birth of Schopenhauer and the birth of Nietzsche. Like the first, he rejected the

Hegelian idealism that was dominant in his day. Like the second, he rejected the various nineteenth-century efforts to put morality on rational footing. He was trained in theology at the University of Copenhagen, but he rejected the official Danish church's respectable version of Christianity.

Kierkegaard wrote in penetrating fashion about anxiety and absurdity, those two central existentialist concepts, but he gave them a very different meaning than atheist existentialists do. His sense of anxiety comes from the combination of our intuitive knowledge of God's love and the impossibility of rationally comprehending what this love requires from us. We cannot meet love with reason; we can meet it only with love. Meanwhile, the real source of absurdity for Kierkegaard was not the disjunction between man's capacity for meaning and the senselessness of reality but that between the magnitude of God's love and our insignificance as objects of that love. We are nothing, but he treats us as everything.

The Christian existentialist is called to embrace the absurdity of belief. Part of this means recognizing that the worldview of belief, like any other worldview, can't be justified for us in advance, from the outside. We must leap into it. Only then can we possibly know what it means to believe. Furthermore, we must accept the irony of our condition. For Kierkegaard this doesn't mean—as it does for Rorty—accepting that our values are entirely contingent and that we might just as easily hold other ones. But it does mean accepting that we could well be wrong. It means recognizing that we can never justify our faith. We can never *know*. If we had knowledge, we would not have need of faith. Belief is something that we must live out. We must keep choosing it, and we won't know until we are done whether we have chosen correctly.

I eventually met with a priest at the church I'd been attending. I explained to him a bit about my situation, and he mostly listened without remark. He made no attempt to clear up my uncertainty, but when I'd finished talking, he offered to take my confession. I hadn't prepared myself for it, and I did not know what I meant to say until I said it, but I found myself telling him mostly about the people I'd mistreated over the years. I told him about all the ways I had used my quest for understanding as an excuse for selfishness. I told him how long I had resisted allowing real love into my life. By the time he offered me absolution, I was in tears. That day I took Catholic Communion for the first time since bringing *Why I Am Not a Christian* down from the shelf.

I had thought that once I'd faced down death without God, I could never possibly have need of him again. It turned out that the thing I couldn't face without God was love.

Now Believe!

One evening in the late 1940s, Robert Lowell and Elizabeth Hardwick brought their young friend Flannery O'Connor to dinner at the house of Mary McCarthy. O'Connor was in her early twenties, with a recently minted MFA from the University of Iowa. She had published a handful of short stories, but she was known to most of the company there primarily for being a devout Catholic country girl from rural Georgia. McCarthy too had been raised Catholic, but she'd left the church at fifteen, an experience she had described in the autobiographical novel that made her famous. She was a decade older than O'Connor. Like Lowell and Hardwick, she was among the most prominent of the era's New York intellectuals.

O'Connor would later remember sitting for hours without opening her mouth. "Having me there," she wrote to a friend, "was like having a dog present who had been trained to say a few words but overcome with inadequacy had forgotten them." Long after midnight, the topic turned to the Catholic Eucharist, which O'Connor was encouraged to defend. Perhaps in an effort at magnanimity, McCarthy allowed that it was a beautiful symbol. "If it's a symbol," O'Connor replied in a shaky voice, "to hell with it." Recounting the exchange years later, she went on: "That was all the defense I was capable of but I realize now that this is all I will ever be able to say about it, outside of a story, except that it is the center of existence for me; all the rest of life is expendable."

O'Connor did not believe that if some debunking skeptic waited in the front pew until the moment of the consecration, then tore the host from the priest's hands and placed it under a microscope, he would find human cells with DNA that matched that of the historical Jesus. The church holds that the "accidental" features of the bread and wine remain unchanged while their "inner reality" is transformed. Of course, this is just the kind of talk that infuriates materialists—and, indeed, Christians of many other denominations. What does it mean to claim something has been transformed, if it gives no visible signs of this transformation? What does it mean to insist that this change is not merely symbolic? What difference could whatever change you're talking about even make?

For O'Connor it made the greatest difference in the world. While still at Iowa, as she moved from a journalism program into the fiction workshop and began to understand the nature of her vocation, she'd started a journal that she considered a form of prayer. She had come to find that when praying in the traditional way, her "attention [was] always very fugitive." Writing made such distraction impossible: "I can feel a warmth of love heating me when I think & write this to You." She prayed for the strength to dedicate her life to God. "Help me to feel that I will give up every earthly thing for this," she wrote, while clarifying, "I do not mean becoming a nun."

She meant instead becoming an artist, which she understood to require not just effort and sacrifice but grace: "If I ever do get to be a fine writer, it will not be because I am a fine writer but because God has given me credit for a few of the things He kindly wrote for me." Like any student at a place like Iowa, she was dedicated to mastering her craft, but she also knew that this craft could come to something significant only if it was directed at a larger truth: "All our lives are consumed in possessing struggle but only when the struggle is cherished & directed to a final consummation outside of this life is it of any value."

What happened to O'Connor next was this: A few years after finishing her journal and her Iowa degree, probably not long after that dinner party with McCarthy, when O'Connor was still just twenty-five years old and before she had published any of her significant work, she was diagnosed with lupus. She returned to her family farm in Milledgeville, Georgia, where she spent the remaining fifteen years of her life in overwhelming physical pain. She began each day with morning Mass, celebrating the Eucharist, which remained for her the center of existence. Then she went home, and with whatever energy she had left, she wrote.

A BOOK OF this sort ought to contain a great conversion scene, the moment when the scales fall from the eyes and all becomes clear. The reality is far more complicated. I don't believe I will ever see things clearly, not in this mortal life. Here we see through a glass darkly. The best we can hope for is to be looking in the right direction, facing the right way.

The turning began for me when I met A——, but I finally felt like I was properly oriented on the day I made my confession and received the Eucharist. I cannot do any better than O'Connor in describing the significance of this act. I can only say that since then, I too have tried to make it the center of my existence.

No one should be satisfied being a Christian who has not attempted the alternative, Nietzsche said. But I had attempted it. I had attempted it honestly, with every hope and expectation that it would work, and it had not. I don't want to suggest that I simply gave up trying and decided to believe again. I don't think it's possible to choose belief in this way. If it were, I probably would have chosen it sooner. Perhaps I never would have stopped choosing it in the first place. What I can say is that the path I'd been on all this time had brought me to the place where I was both intellectually and emotionally prepared to listen to the voice within, a voice that I know had been there all along, a voice I had been taking great pains to keep quiet.

If you have been expecting me to conclude with a rational proof for faith, I have to disappoint you, because I don't think that such a proof exists. But I do believe it is possible to make a rational case for listening to the whispering voice within our souls. While I don't think for a moment that every voice will sound like my own or say what my own does, I do think that every one of us has such a soul voice, even those of us who do not believe we have souls.

Belief can be rationally *justified*—that is, taking the step into belief can be rationally defended. Belief can be made consistent with reason. But belief itself cannot be made rational, for belief is a step beyond reason. To borrow Kant's metaphor, it amounts to leaving the island of knowledge, setting out onto the dangerous sea. It is a treacherous venture, but for some of us it is a necessary one, because we have needs that the island can't meet. And the only way to get started is simply to set out.

"Believing begins with belief," Wittgenstein wrote in one of his journals. "From words no belief follows." What did he mean by this? As he told Russell after the war, he had carried Tolstoy's redaction of the Gospels with him at all times in the trenches. He loved the accounts of Jesus on earth, because in them the meaning of Christianity is shown through a form of life rather than being explained. The meaning of Christianity, in Wittgenstein's view, was—live like this:

> Christianity is not based on a historical truth; rather it offers us a (historical) narrative and says: now believe! But not, be-

> lieve this narrative with the belief appropriate to a historical narrative, rather: believe, through thick and thin, which you can do only as a result of a life. *Here you have a narrative, don't take the same attitude to it as you take to other historical narratives!* Make a *quite different* place in your life for it.—There is nothing *paradoxical* about that!

Imagine a person utterly committed to transforming his life through love. He decides to follow the example of Christ in the belief that the historical Jesus was the most exemplary case of a loving human who ever lived. Now imagine another person who follows the example of Christ in the belief that the historical Jesus was something far greater than that, God come to earth to save us through his love. In each case, following the example would amount to the same thing, yet these are obviously different beliefs. How would this difference show itself? Presumably the second person would follow the example with even more urgency, even more dedication. He would, as it were, be more faithful to it.

Now suppose that the first person became so committed to the example that he hoped to act in such a way that anybody examining his behavior could only conclude that he believed Jesus to be God come to earth to save us through his love. This person became so committed to this example that if given the choice between betraying the example and suffering death, he would freely choose death. Now suppose this person decided that as part of the effort to live a life indistinguishable from the life of a true believer, he would follow all the believer's actions, up to and including professing belief in the divinity of Jesus Christ. Would we say that this person is a liar? A hypocrite? If his actions are consistent with what he claims to believe, where are the lie and the hypocrisy? And if his actions are not consistent with his claims, if he falters in his commitment, is this a failure of belief or a failure of will?

Here it might be relevant to note that the Latin *credo* ("I believe"), the word from which *creed* is derived, has its own roots in the Proto-Indo-European word *kerd* or heart. To believe something in this sense is to "take it to heart." Surely the person we're considering here has taken the divinity of Jesus to heart?

This raises another obvious and common question: If I'm right that the meaning of God is love, why not leave Jesus out of it? Why profess any beliefs on the man at all? Why not just stick with love? The church's answer would be that humanity tried that already, and that it didn't work. All I can say for myself is that *I* tried it, and it didn't work for me. "The Christian religion," Wittgenstein wrote, "is only for the man who needs infinite help." Over many years I have come to discover that I am that man.

MEANWHILE, A—— remained an atheist, and somewhat perplexed to find herself married to a practicing Catholic. She was particularly perplexed when she heard me telling other people that she was the reason I believed in God. She was completely supportive and mostly good-natured about it, despite her reservations. She recognized that belief was good for me. She thought of my weekly trip to church as a meditative practice, or even a form of therapy, a way to take time out of life for quiet reflection.

But she would sometimes be struck by the full range of the claims to which I seemed to assent, and then she would be moved to ask: "A teenaged virgin gives birth to a baby that is also God. He walks on water, gives sight to the blind, raises the dead. He's executed and comes back to life and ascends into heaven. Now the priest says certain words in a certain order, and it turns bread and wine into the God-man's body and blood, which you eat and drink. Do you believe all that? I mean, do you *really* believe it?"

Perhaps you're inclined to ask the same questions. (After all, you both take after her.) I will give you the honest answer: Sometimes I do. Sometimes I don't just believe it but know it, with the clear and certain knowledge of intuitive truth. Sometimes I feel it as the sun on my face, and to deny its reality seems just as willful and obtuse as denying that something out there causes that warmth. At other times the cloud of unknowing that separates me from this truth feels too thick to be pierced by love. In these moments I still have an intellectual sense of what is up there somewhere, but I don't feel it as a reality. There are even times when it feels as ridiculous to me as it might sound to you. At such times, I doubt that I ever really did believe. Perhaps it was all wishful thinking.

But even then I try to act as though it were true, which I take to be a form of belief. I have learned that if I keep faith, the clouds will part and the sunlight will return. In that moment I will not only feel the sun again but also understand that it was there all along. Even on the cloudiest day, whatever light we have here on earth, whatever warmth we feel, whatever energy and life exist, still comes from the sun. Belief is not, after all, something that is done once and for all so that you can be finished with it. If the way to believe is to live, then you must keep on doing it, and you can falter at any time.

The author of the *Cloud* speaks of coming down from the heights of contemplation, saying that "it is beneficial and necessary to do on occasion." The passages on the subject call to mind Nietzsche's writing about Zarathustra coming down from the mountain or Socrates on coming back into the cave, blindly stumbling around after your eyes have adjusted to the world above. One reason to do this is to tell the others what they're missing: There is a whole world up above their heads! But these writers all agree that the sunlit world can't be made real to another person in this way. The more pressing reason to come down from the heights is that we have a life to live down here.

There are many stories of would-be saints going in search of martyrdom so that they might end their earthly existence while assuring their place with God in eternity. These efforts always end badly. God wants us to live out our full allotted time here. And most of us are not called to spend all of that time in the heights. We are simply called to remember what's up there.

In the years since returning to the church, I have often contemplated the scene from Matthew's Gospel in the garden of Gethsemane. On the night before his crucifixion, Jesus goes up to the garden to commune with his father about his fate. He brings his three favored apostles along and asks them all to "stay awake and pray" so that they don't fall into temptation. He adds a famous warning: "The spirit is willing, but the flesh is weak." Three times he goes away into solitude, and each time he returns to find them sleeping.

Why is it so easy to fall asleep? Why is it that even those who knew Jesus personally and loved him best could not stay awake for him? "The very reason I write," Zadie Smith once remarked, "is so that I might not sleepwalk through my entire life." I keep those words written on an index card in my desk drawer, because they are how I have come to understand my own vocation. I am no longer trying to create a great monument that will outlast me, for I have come to believe that it is precisely our loving selves that will last when all of the monuments of this world have turned to dust. In the meantime, I am only trying to stay awake, to pay attention, to listen more closely.

So this book ends where my real journey began. As it turns out, the decade that has followed the turn I'm describing has been the most difficult of my life, if measured simply by the amount of physical and emotional effort it takes to get through each day. It has also been by far the happiest. This difficulty and this happiness have the same source: the two of you, who have taught me, more than anything else could have, the meaning of creation through love.

Although you're both baptized in my faith, you know that your mother and I have different beliefs about these things. But we share the hope that you will live lives full of meaning and love. We cannot possibly tell you what to believe, because belief is a form of life, and we cannot live your lives for you, as much as we might sometimes wish otherwise. You may not find yourselves among those who need infinite help. But if you do, I want you to know that such help exists.

Perhaps as you go along your journey, you'll want to know exactly what your father believed, and why he believed it. That is not a simple matter. To explain what I believe means first explaining what I think it means to believe. It means explaining how it could possibly be rational to listen to the whispering voice within, even when that voice itself seems to defy reason. It means explaining how one could look the world frankly in the face and see there a reality ordered by something larger than us, something that created us and loves us and wants us to love each other. It means explaining how it might be possible to be a skeptic and a believer both. Telling the story of my belief would mean telling the story of my life. That's what I have tried to do.

IF YOU'VE GOTTEN this far, you might have one more question: What about that angel? Was it a miracle, or a perfectly explicable physical event? My rather frustrating answer is that I think it was both. I know what "caused" these visitations, from a strictly material standpoint, but I also know what they in turn caused—a lifelong journey that I am still on. And I know that one must consider their final cause as much as their efficient cause when trying to grasp their meaning. I also know that their physical cause cannot explain the mental form they took, because physical causes can't explain mental realities. And if we take the word *miracle* to describe an event that can't be reconciled to the natural physical order, then every thought is a miracle, and every thought put into action is a miracle indeed.

ACKNOWLEDGMENTS

This book tells the story of a man who needs infinite help—and has been lucky enough to get it. Acknowledging so much help in this space would not be possible, so please take what follows as a radically incomplete list.

By far the greatest help of my professional life has been Sarah Burnes. Every book I've published since she took me on as a client fifteen years ago owes something to her, but this one owes her a particular debt. Long before I considered writing any of this down, we had many long conversations about the topics covered in these pages, and she was the first person to suggest that this story was worth telling in this form. Having encouraged the project into existence, she remained intimately involved throughout its gestation. I've never felt more acutely my good fortune at having her in my corner.

Among Sarah's gifts to this project was getting it into the hands of Virginia Smith Younce, who has been the ideal editor at every step along the way. Working with someone on a book at once so philosophically abstract and so deeply personal requires enormous trust, and Ginny has consistently rewarded that trust with her rare combination of intellect and sensitivity. She also trusted me, even when I delivered a manuscript two years overdue and a hundred thousand words overlong. (I wish these were exaggerations.) Her steadfast belief that I could do what I'd set out to do and that it was worth doing kept me going when I had doubts on both fronts.

I'm incredibly grateful to Ann Godoff for her commitment to this idea. Everything about Penguin Press has exceeded my (very high) expectations. Caroline Sydney played an essential role in the editorial process. While I'm glad this book is finally done, I'll miss the excuse for long conversations with Sarah, Ginny, and Caroline. Thanks to Iris Chen for seeing things across the finish line, and to everyone at Penguin who has played a part in getting this book out into the world.

During my second stint at *Harper's Magazine*, long conversations with smart people about life's urgent questions were a near-daily experience. Most of my colleagues did not share my particular answers to those questions, but I was always grateful for the eagerness, thoughtfulness, and openness with which they took them up. I especially want to acknowledge Joe Kloc, Charlie Lee, Stephanie McFeeters, Virginia Navarro, Rachel Poser, Katie Ryder, Matthew Sherrill, and Will Stephenson.

I was also lucky during that time to work with many brilliant writers whose thinking informed this work. I am grateful to all of them, particularly Ayad Akhtar, John Crowley, Mark Edmundson, Jennifer Frey, Greg Jackson, Rafil Kroll-Zaidi, Hari Kunzru, Rachel Kushner, Jackson Lears, Nancy Lemann, Ben Lerner, Thomas Meaney, and Thomas Chatterton Williams.

Thank you to John Carr, Bret Asbury, and Brian Deleeuw, my stalwart early readers, who tackled this manuscript when it was twice its current length. Justin Smith-Ruiu gave a particularly sensitive read. At a moment of real insecurity, I was incredibly reassured to be told by one of the most brilliant philosophers alive that I might be on the right track. Thanks to the priests and parishioners of the Brooklyn Oratory parishes, especially

Father Anthony Andreassi. I am eternally grateful for support of every imaginable kind from Lynn Ducommun, and for so much stimulating talk (and so many laughs) with Bob, Palmer, Lindsey, and Charlie. Jax Preyer took incredible care of our children while Ally and I toiled away at our respective books; one day you'll all be reading her work.

Among many other gifts, my parents provided a constant model of living faith. They taught me to put the question of the good at the center of life, and they supported me absolutely when my efforts to answer the question in my own way sent me off in wild directions—and even when I lost sight of it entirely. Words cannot express my debt to them. My father also gave the manuscript several valuable reads and composed a publication-worthy essay in response. I was glad for the help, but more than that I was glad for the long and meaningful conversations that resulted from it.

Alice Teti is the greatest example I have of a life lived according to one's beliefs, with all the sacrifice, hardship, joy, and surprise that entails. If she does not loom large in my personal writing, that is only because my relation to her is one of uncomplicated love and admiration, which is not the stuff of thrilling literature. Her impact on me has been enormous. My awe for her, Len, and their family increases with every passing year.

My unique attachment to my brother, Jim, sent this journey into motion, and it has been a touchstone throughout my life. Our conversations remain one of the great pleasures of my life, as they have been since I learned to talk. One of the many things for which I love and admire his wife, Alyson, is the grace with which she has accompanied him on his own spiritual journey.

In so many ways, I owe my belief to Ally's arrival in my life. I hope this book has already gone some way to expressing my love and gratitude for her, but I want to acknowledge in particular her support during the long composition of this book. She made many sacrifices to allow me the time to get it done, she was an incredible listener as I sounded off on my latest philosophical obsession, and she reminded me by her daily presence what the whole thing was about.

This book began as an effort to answer her honest question: *But what do you actually believe?* It eventually became an effort to express that belief in a way that our children might understand when it comes time for them to answer these questions for themselves. I could not imagine a better partner with whom to be raising these kids—or better kids to be raising. Olive and Henry: I hope one day this book might mean to you a fraction of what you've meant to this book. Your kindness, curiosity, and wonder are an endless inspiration. I love you so much.

NOTES

Prelude: Looking the World Frankly in the Face

9 **In 1940, the City College:** Bertrand Russell, *Why I Am Not a Christian* (Simon & Schuster, 1963). An editorial appendix by Paul Edwards explains this publication background. The quotes that follow are from the title essay.

17 **Every important advance:** Richard Dawkins, *The God Delusion* (Houghton Mifflin, 2006), 126.

17 **with the image:** Sam Harris, *The End of Faith* (W. W. Norton, 2004), 11.

17 **On the first page:** Dawkins, *God Delusion,* 1.

17 **gets all the way:** Christopher Hitchens, *God Is Not Great* (Twelve Books, 2009), 28.

18 **"toxic religious mania":** Daniel Dennett, *Breaking the Spell* (Penguin, 2007), 72.

18 **unenclosed swimming pools:** Dennett, *Breaking the Spell,* 299.

18 **good deal further:** Harris, *End of Faith,* 14.

21 **So a voice:** Augustine, *Confessions,* trans. E. B. Pusey (Project Gutenberg).

22 **somewhat portentous word:** William James, *Pragmatism and Other Writings* (Penguin Classics, 2000), 7.

23 **species of what:** Charles Taylor, *A Secular Age* (Harvard University Press, 2007). I have relied on Taylor's work throughout.

32 **In response to this accusation:** John Henry Newman, *Apologia Pro Vita Sua* (Penguin Classics, 1994), xxix.

Chapter One: Strange Prisoners

40 **most famous metaphor:** Plato, *Complete Works,* ed. John M. Cooper, trans. G. M. A. Grube et al. (Hackett, 1997), 1132–35.

Chapter Two: From Generalities to Particulars

48 **study of nature:** Aristotle, *Physics,* ed. David Bostock, trans. Robin Waterfield (Oxford University Press, 2008). My reading of Aristotle and in particular of his views on causality is indebted to Jonathan Lear, *Aristotle: The Desire to Know* (Cambridge University Press, 1988).

52 earliest and clearest: Michel de Montaigne, *The Complete Essays*, trans. Donald M. Frame (Stanford University Press, 1965). Quotes from Montaigne throughout the chapter are drawn from this collection.

Chapter Three: The Bounds of Human Empire

56 statesman and philosopher: Francis Bacon, *The Major Works*, ed. Brian Vickers (Oxford University Press, 2008). Quotes from Bacon throughout the chapter are drawn from this collection, and my biographical narrative relies on the notes and introduction by the collection's editor, Brian Vickers.

59 Born into a Catholic family: René Descartes, trans. Donald A. Cress, *Discourse on Method and Meditations on First Philosophy*, 4th ed. (Hackett, 1998). Quoted throughout the remainder of the chapter. I also relied on an editorial introduction by Tom Sorrell in the Everyman Library edition of these same two texts (2003).

Chapter Four: The Restless Desire of Power

67 secular social theorist: Thomas Hobbes, *Leviathan*, ed. Ian Shapiro (Yale University Press, 2010). Quoted throughout the chapter. This edition includes essays by Ian Shapiro, John Dunn, David Dyzenhaus, Elisabeth Ellis, and Bryan Garsten, all of which were consulted during the writing of this chapter.

Chapter Five: The Empty Cabinet

79 Because nature consists: Thomas Hobbes, *Leviathan*, ed. Ian Shapiro (Yale University Press, 2010), 400.

79 As he describes: John Locke, *Essay Concerning Human Understanding* (Penguin Classics, 1997). Quoted throughout.

82 Not every empiricist: George Berkeley, *A Treatise Concerning the Principles of Human Knowledge* (Hackett, 1995).

87 posthumously published *Pensées*: Blaise Pascal, *Pensées* (Penguin Classics, 1995), 123–24.

87 "Believing in God is not": Richard Dawkins, *The God Delusion* (Houghton Mifflin, 2006), 104.

88 arguments for liberalism: John Locke, *Two Treatises of Government and A Letter Concerning Toleration*, ed. Ian Shapiro (Yale University Press, 2003).

Chapter Six: Passion's Slave

91 about his achievements: John Locke, *Essay Concerning Human Understanding* (Penguin Classics, 1997), 11.

92 "Reason," he wrote: David Hume, *A Treatise of Human Nature* (Digireads, 2019), 296.

92 this category included: Hume, *Treatise of Human Nature*, 8.

92 "fell *dead-born*": David Hume, *An Enquiry Concerning Human Understanding*, ed.

Eric Steinberg (Hackett, 1993), ix. This line from Hume's autobiography, *My Own Life*, is quoted in Steinberg's introduction.

93 **his terminology differs:** Hume, *An Enquiry Concerning Human Understanding*. Quoted throughout the remainder of this chapter.

97 **examine any action:** Hume, *Treatise of Human Nature*, 333.

97 **Chief among these:** David Hume, *An Enquiry Concerning the Principles of Morals*, ed. J. B. Schneewind (Hackett, 1983), 17.

99 **favorite atheist genre:** David Hume, *Dialogues and Natural History of Religion*, ed. J. C. A. Gaskin (Oxford University Press, 2009).

Chapter Seven: Experiments of Living

103 **The proper construction:** Jeremy Bentham, *Introduction to the Principles of Morals and Legislation* (Clarendon Press, 1823). Quoted throughout this chapter.

107 **the French theorist:** Michel Foucault, *Discipline and Punish*, trans. Alan Sheridan (Vintage Books, 1995).

108 **As described in:** John Stuart Mill, *Autobiography*, ed. Mark Philp (Oxford University Press, 2018). Quoted throughout this chapter. I'm indebted to this edition's introductory essay by Mark Philp.

110 **Comte believed himself:** August Comte, *Introduction to Positive Philosophy*, trans. Frederick Ferré (Hackett, 1988).

112 **"What Bacon did":** John Stuart Mill, *On Liberty, Utilitarianism, and Other Essays*, ed. Mark Philp and Frederick Rosen (Oxford University Press, 2015). Quoted throughout the remainder of this chapter.

Chapter Eight: Embryo Englands

122 **a better explanation:** Charles Darwin, *The Origin of Species* (Signet Classics, 2003). Quoted throughout this chapter.

127 **"Wherever the European has trod":** Charles Darwin, *Voyage of the Beagle* (Penguin Classics, 1989), 322.

127 **he finally states:** Charles Darwin, *The Descent of Man* (Penguin Classics, 2004). Quoted throughout this section.

129 **his irreligious upbringing:** John Stuart Mill, *Autobiography*, ed. Mark Philp (Oxford University Press, 2018), 25.

Chapter Nine: Robbing the Gods

131 **these cultural developments:** Ray Monk, *Bertrand Russell: The Spirit of Solitude* (Free Press, 1996). This is the first volume of Monk's monumental two-volume life of Russell. The second is *Bertrand Russell: The Ghost of Madness* (Free Press, 2000). He also wrote the definitive biography of Wittgenstein: *Ludwig Wittgenstein: The Duty of Genius* (Penguin, 1990). I have relied heavily on all three for my accounts of the two men's lives and their fraught relationship.

131 **"inflicted upon me":** Quoted in Monk, *The Spirit of Solitude*, 8.

132 "surrounded Queen Victoria": Monk, *The Spirit of Solitude*, 15.
132 Bertrand was eleven: Monk, *The Spirit of Solitude*, 26.
132 "formula in algebra": Monk, *The Spirit of Solitude*, 30.
133 "I had not read Hume": Bertrand Russell, *The Philosophy of Logical Atomism* (Routledge, 2009), 127.
133 Almost sixty years later: Bertrand Russell, *Why I Am Not a Christian* (Simon & Schuster, 1963). Quoted throughout this section.
135 complex mathematical operations: Bertrand Russell, *The Principles of Mathematics* (Routledge, 1992).
138 The logical positivist Rudolf Carnap: Rudolf Carnap, *The Logical Structure of the World and Pseudoproblems in Philosophy*, trans. Rolf A. George (Open Court Classics, 2005), 333.
139 an equivalent elucidation: Daniel C. Dennett, *Consciousness Explained* (Back Bay Books, 1991), 21.
141 a simple point: Richard Dawkins, *The Selfish Gene*, 40th anniversary ed. (Oxford University Press, 2016). Quoted throughout this section.
141 a "universal acid": Daniel Dennett, *Darwin's Dangerous Idea* (Simon & Schuster, 1995), 61.

Chapter Ten: Some Hard Problems

144 his own critique: Bertrand Russell, *Why I Am Not a Christian* (Simon & Schuster, 1963), 6.
144 Soon after publishing: Carlo Rovelli, *Reality Is Not What It Seems* (Riverhead, 2017), 201.
146 our various theories: Sabine Hossenfelder, *Existential Physics* (Basic Books, 2022), 37. I've relied on Hossenfelder throughout this section.
146 "First Cause" arguments: Russell, *Why I Am Not a Christian*, 7.
148 "constitute their way": Rovelli, *Reality Is Not What It Seems*, 120. I rely on Rovelli's work in general throughout what follows.
150 a multidisciplinary approach: Steven Pinker, *How the Mind Works* (W. W. Norton, 2009). Quoted throughout the chapter.
151 a now famous distinction: David Chalmers, *The Conscious Mind* (Oxford University Press, 1997). Quoted throughout this section.
152 the phenomenal quality: Thomas Nagel, *Mortal Questions* (Cambridge University Press, 1979), 166. I have relied on various essays in this collection apart from "What Is It Like to Be a Bat?" Other works by Nagel have also influenced my thinking, especially *The View from Nowhere* (Oxford University Press, 1986) and *Mind and Cosmos* (Oxford University Press, 2012).
154 calls the "intentional stance": Daniel C. Dennett, *The Intentional Stance* (MIT Press, 1989), 17.
155 "Some people are tempted": Daniel C. Dennett, *Consciousness Explained* (Back Bay Books, 1991). Quoted throughout the remainder of the chapter.
162 an atheist committed: John Searle, *The Rediscovery of the Mind* (MIT Press, 1992), 3.

Chapter Eleven: A Satisfied Pig

165 fine analytic tradition: Daniel Dennett, *Elbow Room: The Varieties of Free Will Worth Wanting* (MIT Press, 2015). Quoted throughout this section.

174 "backward states of": John Stuart Mill, *On Liberty, Utilitarianism, and Other Essays*, ed. Mark Philp and Frederick Rosen (Oxford University Press, 2015), 13.

175 "human being dissatisfied": Stuart Mill, *On Liberty, Utilitarianism, and Other Essays*, 124–25.

177 "products of evolution": Richard Dawkins, *The God Delusion* (Houghton Mifflin, 2006), 100.

Chapter Twelve: How Little Has Been Done

180 In the spring: Ray Monk, *Bertrand Russell: The Spirit of Solitude* (Free Press, 1996). See also Ray Monk, *Ludwig Wittgenstein: The Duty of Genius* (Penguin, 1990), which is relied upon throughout.

182 arguably the greatest: Ludwig Wittgenstein, *Major Works*, trans. C. K. Ogden (Harper Perennial, 2009). Quoted throughout this chapter.

Interlude: The Refuge of Art

199 a dozen pages: Bertrand Russell, *A History of Western Philosophy* (Simon & Schuster, 1972).

199 anthology of atheist: Christopher Hitchens, ed., *The Portable Atheist* (Twelve Books, 2007).

Chapter Thirteen: The Intellectual Love of God

205 to follow Descartes: Steven Nadler, *Spinoza: A Life* (Cambridge University Press, 2022). Relied upon throughout this chapter. In addition to this fairly academic biography, Nadler has written several books on Spinoza for general readers, which also informed this chapter.

206 Following his excommunication: Baruch de Spinoza, *The Collected Works of Spinoza*, vol. 1, ed. and trans. Edwin Curley (Princeton University Press, 1985). All quotes from the *Emendation* and the *Ethics* are from Curley's translations.

209 other major work: Baruch de Spinoza, *Theological-Political Treatise*, trans. Samuel Shirley (Hackett, 2001). Quoted throughout the remainder of this chapter.

Chapter Fourteen: Consult the Inner Light

223 In 1749, the Academy of Dijon: Jean-Jacques Rousseau, *The Major Political Writings*, trans. John T. Scott (University of Chicago Press, 2014). Quotes from both the *Discourses* and *On the Social Contract* use the Scott translations collected here. I am also indebted to Scott's introduction to the collection for biographical information.

233 *Social Contract* appeared: Jean-Jacques Rousseau, *Emile, or On Education*, trans. Allan Bloom (Penguin Classics, 1991). Quoted throughout this section.

237 last major work: Jean-Jacques Rousseau, *Confessions*, trans. J. M. Cohen (Penguin Classics, 1953), 328.

Chapter Fifteen: Denying Knowledge to Make Room for Faith

239 decade before producing: Immanuel Kant, *Critique of Pure Reason*, trans. Werner S. Pluhar (Hackett, 1996). Quoted throughout this chapter. I'm also indebted to Paul Guyer, ed., *The Cambridge Companion to Kant's "Critique of Pure Reason"* (Cambridge University Press, 2010).

246 He takes up the possibility: Immanuel Kant, *Critique of Practical Reason*, trans. Werner S. Pluhar (Hackett, 2002).

Chapter Sixteen: The Artist Forming the Work

253 "the very sanctuary": Heinrich von Kleist, *The Marquise of O— and Other Stories*, trans. David Luke and Nigel Reeves (Penguin Classics, 2004), 11. The story of Kleist's post-Kantian collapse is told in Luke and Reeves's introduction.

254 Born into a wealthy family: Bryan Magee, *The Philosophy of Schopenhauer* (Clarendon Press, 1997). Relied on for biographical points throughout this chapter.

255 elaboration or extension: Arthur Schopenhauer, *On the Fourfold Root of the Principle of Sufficient Reason*, trans. E. F. J. Payne (Open Court Classics, 1997).

260 as a "preface": Arthur Schopenhauer, *The World as Will and Representation*, trans. E. F. J. Payne (Dover, 2023). Quoted throughout the remainder of the chapter.

Chapter Seventeen: Man Is Something That Should Be Overcome

275 Wagner spent much: Friedrich Nietzsche, *Untimely Meditations*, ed. Daniel Breazeale, trans. R. J. Hollingdale (Cambridge University Press, 2005). The story of Nietzsche's relationship with Wagner is told in many places, but Daniel Breazeale's editorial introduction to this volume is a good start.

276 his first book: Friedrich Nietzsche, *The Basic Writings of Nietzsche*, ed. and trans. Walter Kaufmann (Modern Library, 1992). This collection includes Kaufmann's translations of *The Birth of Tragedy*, *Beyond Good and Evil*, *On the Genealogy of Morals*, and *Ecce Home*, all of which are quoted in the pages that follow. Kaufmann's introduction and his *Nietzsche: Philosopher, Psychologist, Antichrist* (Princeton University Press, 2013) are definitive resources on Nietzsche's life and work.

279 Many Germans saw: Nietzsche, *Untimely Meditations*. I also quote Hollingdale's translations of Nietzsche's *Daybreak* (Cambridge University Press, 2007), *Human, All Too Human* (Cambridge University Press, 2010), *Twilight of the Idols* (Penguin Classics, 1990), and *Thus Spoke Zarathustra* (Penguin Classics, 2003).

281 Nietzsche's classic parable: Friedrich Nietzsche, *The Gay Science*, trans. Walter Kaufmann (Vintage Books, 1974), 181. Also quoted throughout.

283 "moral dissecting table": Nietzsche, *Human, All Too Human*, 32.

283 "power to requite": Nietzsche, *Human, All Too Human*, 37.

284 "Only the Englishman": Nietzsche, *Twilight of the Idols*, 33.

285 "Man may bleed": Nietzsche, *Human, All Too Human*, 60.

285 "nothing but errors": Nietzsche, *The Gay Science*, 169.
287 "honest, fervent zeal": Nietzsche, *Daybreak*, 62.
294 "versus the Crucified": Nietzsche, *The Basic Writings of Nietzsche*, 791.
294 "lighten the heart": Nietzsche, *Human, All Too Human*, 67.

Chapter Eighteen: In the Face of Nothing

298 While still a teenager: Martin Heidegger, *On Time and Being*, trans. Joan Stambaugh (University of Chicago Press, 2002). Heidegger recounts his early experience with Brentano's work in the essay "My Way of Phenomenology."

298 Brentano had been responsible: Franz Brentano, *Psychology from an Empirical Standpoint*, trans. Linda McAlister (Routledge, 2015). For Brentano's relationship to positivism and Aristotle and his hopes for psychology as a science, see book 1, "Psychology as a Science." For his description of intentionality, see book 2, "Mental Phenomena in General."

299 transcend the empirical: Edmund Husserl, *Ideas: General Introduction to Pure Phenomenology*, trans. Boyce Gibson (Martino Fine Books, 2017). Quoted throughout this section.

301 Heidegger wrote to the priest: Mark A. Wrathall, ed., *The Cambridge Companion to Heidegger's "Being and Time"* (Cambridge University Press, 2013), 60. I've relied on this book for a lot of background on Heidegger and *Being and Time*, including its rush to publication following the announcement of Husserl's retirement. The particular anecdote about his son's baptism comes from the chapter "Martin Heidegger's *Being and Time*: A Carefully Planned Accident?" by Alfred Denker.

302 nearly six hundred pages: Martin Heidegger, *Being and Time*, trans. John Macquarrie and Edward Robinson (Harper Perennial, 2008). Quoted throughout the remainder of this chapter. Taylor Carman's foreword to this edition was also a help.

Chapter Nineteen: A Total Absence of Hope

316 In a famous 1946 essay: Jean-Paul Sartre, *Existentialism Is a Humanism*, trans. Philip Mairet (World Publishing, 1956), 15.

316 "Letter on Humanism": Martin Heidegger, *Basic Writings*, ed. David Farrell Krell (Harper Perennial, 2008), 219. The "Letter on Humanism" is here translated by Frank A. Capuzzi and J. Glenn Gray.

317 Born in 1883: Karl Jaspers, *Philosophy of Existence*, trans. Richard F. Grabay (University of Pennsylvania Press, 1971). Quoted throughout this chapter. Grabay's introduction to this volume contains various details about Jaspers's life and the circumstances surrounding these lectures.

320 the German occupation: Albert Camus, *The Myth of Sisyphus*, trans. Justin O'Brien (Vintage International, 2018). Quoted throughout this section.

324 Throughout the occupation: Albert Camus, *Resistance, Rebellion, and Death: Essays*, trans. Justin O'Brien (Vintage International, 1995).

Chapter Twenty: Among the Ironists

327 **a classic study:** Thomas Kuhn, *The Structure of Scientific Revolutions*, 50th anniversary ed. (University of Chicago Press, 2012). Quoted throughout this section.

330 **the long-standing search:** Richard Rorty, *Philosophy and Mirror of Nature* (Princeton University Press, 1981). Quoted throughout this section.

331 **in the position:** Richard Rorty, *Contingency, Irony, and Solidarity* (Cambridge University Press, 1989), 75.

339 **Daniel Dennett decried:** Daniel C. Dennett, "Why Getting It Right Matters," *Free Inquiry*, Winter 1999/2000, secularhumanism.org/wp-content/uploads/sites/26/2018/08/FI-Winter-99-00-Pages.pdf.

339 **Steven Pinker complained:** Steven Pinker, *The Blank Slate* (Penguin, 2003), 416.

339 **"being held responsible":** E. O. Wilson, "Back from Chaos," *Atlantic*, March 1998, theatlantic.com/magazine/archive/1998/03/back-from-chaos/308700/.

340 **This was the age:** Francis Fukuyama, *The End of History and the Last Man* (Free Press, 2006), xi. In the book's introduction, Fukuyama quotes an earlier essay, "The End of History?," published in *The National Interest* in 1989, in which he first advanced this thesis.

341 **American college students:** Natalie Daher, "41% of Young Voters Say United-Healthcare CEO Killing 'Acceptable,'" *Axios*, December 17, 2024, axios.com/2024/12/17/united-healthcare-ceo-killing-poll.

341 **he declares "woke":** "Does Woke Count as a Religion?" posted October 10, 2023, by The Poetry of Reality with Richard Dawkins, YouTube, youtube.com/watch?v=cubkdBuvJAQ.

343 **despite his belief:** Rorty, *Contingency, Irony, and Solidarity*, 85.

Chapter Twenty-One: The Way Out of the Bottle

345 **didn't stay long:** Ray Monk, *Ludwig Wittgenstein: The Duty of Genius* (Penguin, 1990).

345 **"well-meaning commentators":** Ludwig Wittgenstein, *Movements of Thought*, trans. Alfred Nordmann (Rowman & Littlefield, 2022), 11. Quoted in an introduction to this volume written by the ubiquitous Ray Monk.

346 **The later Wittgenstein did:** Ludwig Wittgenstein, *Philosophical Investigations*, trans. G.E.M. Anscombe, P.M.S. Hacker, and Joachim Schulte (Wiley-Blackwell, 2009). Quoted throughout the remainder of the chapter.

350 **in a notebook:** Ludwig Wittgenstein, *Culture and Value*, trans. Peter Winch (University of Chicago Press, 1984), 18.

350 **"human beings *say*":** Wittgenstein, *Philosophical Investigations*, 94.

350 **"*goes on holiday*":** Wittgenstein, *Philosophical Investigations*, 23.

351 **"A confession," he noted:** Wittgenstein, *Culture and Value*, 18.

351 **returning to Otterhal:** Monk, *Wittgenstein.*

352 **"resources of language":** Wittgenstein, *Philosophical Investigations*, 52.

352 **"soothe the mind":** Wittgenstein, *Movements of Thought*, 41.

352 **"show the fly":** Wittgenstein, *Philosophical Investigations*, 110.

Postlude: The Man Who Needs Infinite Help

371 The fourteenth-century English: Anonymous, *The Cloud of Unknowing and Other Works*, trans. A. C. Spearing (Penguin Classics, 2002), 23.

371 "There are three things": Meister Eckhart, *Selected Writings*, trans. Oliver Davies (Penguin Classics, 1995), 175.

371 anchoress named Julian: Julian of Norwich, *Revelations of Divine Love*, trans. Barry Windeatt (Oxford University Press, 2015), 7.

372 which she described: Saint Teresa of Ávila, *The Collected Works*, vol. 1, trans. Kieran Kavanaugh and Otilio Rodriguez (ICS, 1987), 175.

374 Teresa insisted that: Saint Teresa of Ávila, *Collected Works*, 68.

375 great twentieth-century rabbi: Abraham Joshua Heschel, *Man Is Not Alone* (Farrar, Straus and Giroux, 1976), 8.

376 Another twentieth-century scholar: Gershom Scholem, *On the Kabbalah and Its Symbolism*, trans. Ralph Manheim (Schocken, 1996). See especially the essay "Religious Authority and Mysticism."

380 the official one: *Catechism of the Catholic Church*, vatican.va/archive/ENG0015/__P2.HTM.

383 the late 1940s: Flannery O'Connor, *The Habit of Being: The Letters of Flannery O'Connor* (Farrar, Straus and Giroux, 1988), 125.

384 She had come to find: Flannery O'Connor, *Prayer Journal* (Farrar, Straus and Giroux, 2013).

386 "Believing begins with belief": Ludwig Wittgenstein, *Movements of Thought*, trans. Alfred Nordmann (Rowman & Littlefield, 2022), 73.

386 through a form: Ludwig Wittgenstein, *Culture and Value*, trans. Peter Winch (University of Chicago Press, 1984), 32.

388 "The Christian religion": Wittgenstein, *Culture and Value*, 46.

390 "The very reason I write": Zadie Smith, "Fail Better," *Guardian*, January 13, 2007.

INDEX

INDEX

INDEX

INDEX

INDEX

INDEX

INDEX

INDEX

INDEX